CHAD

KANO • AZARE

N.

EGIO

NASERU
NINGI

GOMBE

ADUNA

BAUCHI

JOS

PANKSHIN
LANGTANG

KWOI
KAGORO

GBU

LAFIA

R.

BENUE

MAKURDI
GBOKO

ENUGU

E.

EGIO

N

MAMFE

CALABAR

KUMBA

MT.
CAMEROON

C
A
M
E
R
O
O
N
S

CROSS R.

VICTORIA

AN O' WAR BAY

FERNANDO PO

AFRICA

New
Nigerians

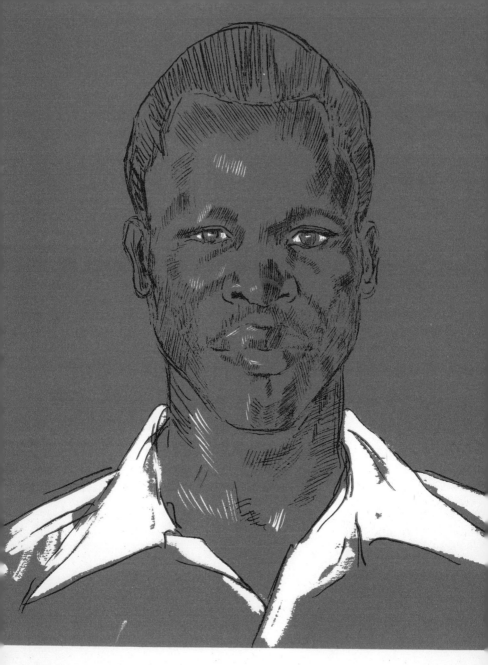

Frontispiece

Young Nigerian

NEW NIGERIANS

by Mora Dickson

WITH ILLUSTRATIONS
BY THE AUTHOR

DENNIS DOBSON · *LONDON*

for
ALEC

'He has the right to criticise
who has the heart to help.'

ABRAHAM LINCOLN

Designed by John Mitchell

Set in eleven point Monotype Imprint one point leaded
Printed by the Anchor Press Ltd., Tiptree, Essex, for
DOBSON BOOKS LTD.
80 Kensington Church Street, London, W.8

First published 1960

Contents

Illustrations

ILLUSTRATIONS

SAPELE

PART ONE

MAN O' WAR BAY

STEPHEN ADEGBEMI
NIGERIAN RAILWAYS

MAN O' WAR BAY, THE BIG HOUSE

CHAPTER I

Making the Impossible Possible

'THERE they are!' we said, straining our hearing to the limit and catching, so it seemed, a faint rumble through the darkness. Suddenly we felt very nervous. Any moment now two lorries would rattle and groan through the banana trees that enclosed the compound, laden with tired, amazed, disgruntled young men, some of whom had travelled over one thousand miles to get here, and the experiment would be no more a fine theory but a reality.

The rumble had taken on a distinctive character now, the crashing grinding of heavy-laden vehicles in low gear on an atrocious road. A faint glow flickered up and down among the banana fronds as headlights rose and fell over the bumps. Up at the big house they had heard it too and lamps were brought out on to the steps; voices began to call out from the kitchen and staff quarters; behind us Ali, our second steward boy, materialized silently out of the night and observed:

'Studie done come.'

As we made our way across the field towards the reception point the lorries staggered round the final corner in a blaze of headlights and collapsed. Very slowly, with limbs stiffened by long confinement, figures began to climb out and peer about them in bewilderment. A rich, strong, confident African voice shouted orders:

'Each man find his load and come up here. Come on now, come on. Chop ready.'

Two friends greeted each other enthusiastically:

'How you are, ma friend? How this road?'

'*Hai*, bad. Very bad.'

The pale ghosts of white men met in the darkness with more stolid salutations. Great basins of steaming food were carried over the grass to the dining hall by aproned cooks and, galvanized perhaps by this sight, the clumps of humanity began to sort themselves out, to take on recognizable identity, and to trickle up the stairs to the dormitories with their loads.

The students had arrived. The course had begun.

These young men came from every part of Nigeria, East, West and North; and from the Cameroons. They had, for the most part, been two days on the lorries from the railhead four hundred miles away, and some of them perhaps two weeks before that on foot, in canoes, on horseback, or on wheels. They were coming to take a course, a new kind of course for Africa, and most of them had no idea what lay before them, while all were a little afraid. Some, indeed, had not arrived at all but, overcome by this fear of the unknown, had quietly turned and gone home somewhere along the way. Even the name of the place at which they had now arrived played a part in their doubts and questionings. Man O' War Bay. What did this mean? Was it some secret way of turning them into soldiers: was it a kind of prison: was it hard labour? Now, however, the die was cast and, enveloped in red dust, stunned by constant jogging on a hard wooden seat, even the most timid were past caring about the future, and the offer of food and sleep seemed to indicate that, for tonight at least, the worst fears were unfounded.

We had fears too—about them. We had asked that these young men be sent to us by their employers. There were clerks employed by Government or by Companies; teachers employed by missions or by native authorities; policemen; coalminers; forestry assistants; nurses and dispensers; councillors and Members of the House of Assembly; and many other professions represented. We hoped that each man had been chosen because he showed signs of leadership and responsibility, and, given this qualification, our job was to try in one month, which was the maximum time that they could be spared by their employers, to show each man what powers lay within himself, how he could train them, and some ways in which he could use these powers to help other people. At this moment, tense with excitement, tired already with hard preparation, confronted by an amorphous mass of bedraggled, unresponsive humanity, we anticipated for a fleeting second the bitter taste of failure. Then, out of the darkness, the flash of brilliant teeth in a friendly smile would bridge in an instant the gulf of doubts and fears, establishing a warmth of personal contact, reminding us that these were alive, individual, young men with a spark within them needing only the right approach to fan it ablaze.

It was nearing midnight before all the new arrivals had been fed and had fallen asleep on their wooden board beds, while weary staff scattered to their quarters to make the most of the short night.

The course had begun. From now until the end of the month every moment was valuable; the next day (and all the days following it) began publicly at 6.30 a.m. and went on till 10 p.m., with little or no respite. There were those, both black and white, who grumbled at such intensive dedication to the job in hand, but none, I think, would now deny, looking back from a more leisured existence, that it was this very application, the compressing of a spring to its uttermost limit, which helped to produce an atmosphere of urgency and adventure resulting very often in a creative rebound when pressure was withdrawn and the course ended. Meantime, crawling under my mosquito net in the hot, shrilling night I felt overwhelmed by the plans and hopes of tomorrow, and as I started to think about them fell instantly asleep.

It was Ebenezer who woke us in the darkness at 6 a.m. Gnarled old black hands untucked the mosquito net and threw it back, a tray of tea was placed beside us and Ebenezer stood back to break the morning's news. He very much liked to be able to tell us the local scandal at this moment when we were at his mercy, and if it were bad news an undeniable spice was added to the telling.

'Lorry done break,' said Ebenezer, watching closely for the effect of his words even while he appeared to be engaged in fiddling with the window curtains. Disasters are so common in

EBENEZER ON TREK

'I SAW THE SEA'

Africa and mechanical transport such a constant headache that this was scarcely news at all and we remained unmoved.

'Which lorry?' said my husband, already out of bed and half dressed.

Ebenezer, aware that his bombshell had only proved a squib, became rather huffy and muttered to no one in particular as he left the room:

'Dominic's boy say lorry done break.'

The day was upon us. It was my job to see that everything domestic was subordinated to the running of the course. Meals had to appear at that critical moment when there was time to eat them; visitors must be fed and entertained in whatever numbers and at whatever time they chose to arrive; hot baths and lights, both requiring careful management to produce at all, had to be ready for an indefinite number of people at the precise moment when they rushed panting over the grass from the Centre and shouted for them. Lucas, our cook, Ebenezer and Ali recognized (as no European servant would ever have done) that our domestic life was orientated in this difficult and demanding fashion, and they accepted it faithfully. But the timing, the imagination and the administration fell

14

on me, as did also, very often, the anguished recriminations when something went wrong. For a new wife, living for the first time in a tropical country, it was a heavy responsibility.

Meanwhile, on this first morning, coming out of our house to watch the parade of our new students I saw, standing alone on the cliff edge gazing out to sea, a solitary young man in the long white gown of the Northerner. It was our policy and practice to set our-selves a time limit within which we must know the names of all these sixty-odd young men, about five days, certainly no longer than a week, so I began at once with this one.

'Good morning. What is your name?'

'Good morning, Madam. I am Ibrahim.'

A charming young face turned towards me with a gentle smile.

'What is that, Madam?' he said, looking back and raising his chin towards the water.

'That is the sea.'

'The sea,' he repeated. 'The sea. Last night, in my sleep, I hear always a strange noise. This makes me afraid and when it is light I get up to look. All this water! Now I will surprise my children when I go home!'

We had many young men for whom this was an unforgettable experience; one, a councillor, when asked at the end of his course what he would tell his people, said simply: 'I shall say to them, "I have seen the sea." '

At the very instant we began to speak the prow of a boat obtruded round the left-hand horn of the bay to be followed rapidly by the rest of the vessel: an Elders & Fyffes banana boat en route for Liverpool, thirteen days away.

'Look, that boat's going to England,' I said. 'It will be thirteen days on the journey and all that time it will only see the land once again until it sees the shores of Britain. Every day nothing but sea!'

'*Kai!*' said Ibrahim, immersed in the imaginative effort of visualiz-ing so much water. I remembered how astonished I, too, had felt on the journey out to the Cameroons, my first long sea voyage, as day followed day and we ploughed on surrounded always by water and sky; and how miraculous and exciting it was, in the very early grey-blue dawn of the last day, to come up on deck and see the Little Cameroon mountain looming out of the mist. To have hit the exact spot on the whole coast of Africa, to have found any land at all in that immensity of ocean, seemed a miracle which the ingenuity of science neither detracted from nor explained. So we watched the banana boat steam proudly out of sight round the right-hand horn of the bay, both of us with feelings of awed surprise.

But Ibrahim was going to find many things to surprise him very much in the next few days. Already he was being summoned to come and be issued with working clothes. Each man put his own garments in his tin box under his bed and received instead cotton shorts and singlets, the latter in different colours marking a division into teams. It is astonishing how much of his manner a man puts on or off with his clothes. For the Southerner, accustomed already to wearing shorts, there was no fundamental change; but stripped, in some instances, of dark glasses and a flashy American tie he appeared less sure of himself, more aware that he was about to meet tests which would penetrate beyond his self-erected façades; but for the Moslem Northerner, accustomed since birth to the view that it was sinful to expose any save very small portions of the body to sight, the discarding of his long outer garment and the exposing of his limbs was a real ordeal. Many would have found it impossible had they been still in their own country and among their own people: public opinion would have been too strong, the loss of prestige too vital. But here, in a strange land, on a course already accepted as a necessary ordeal to be faced, with public opinion definitely for the change of garments, they flinched but complied with instructions. And with acceptance the first battle was won for, emerging out of their cocoon of cotton, they emerged a little also out of their traditions and prejudices, prepared to consider new ideas and to accept their common humanity with others not of their religion, race or background.

At this point my husband interviewed all new students in the company of two of his staff, and tried to make a rapid assessment of each man's potentialities, character and general background in order to divide the course up into four reasonably balanced teams and choose the first four leaders. This interviewing took place in our tiny house because, at that stage of development, there was nowhere else reasonably private. It may have had disadvantages, and some of our correct young civil service staff plainly felt that it had, but for me it was wonderful. I could watch the young men as they sat waiting on our verandah, by now each with his name on a ticket pinned to his chest, and eavesdrop as I beat up ice cream and arranged the meals. Now, for the first time, I could start to store up in my memory the physical characteristics combined with a name which would enable me to say next morning:

'Good morning, Dauda. Good morning, William,' giving two strangers the gratified feeling of regained identity and the first stirrings of 'belonging'. Some it was easy to remember after only a glance, the very handsome or the very plain; the eccentric who retained his quirks even under stress; the unco-operative who made himself difficult. It was the middle ranks who were hard to fix in the mind, the ordinary, decent, polite citizens, indeed the very backbone, often, of the course; the ones who, once stirred, possessed the stamina and earnestness to continue doing their best however unrewarding the circumstances.

It was curious to realize as they passed before me, some with a little bow, some saying, 'Good morning, Madam', some with a smile, some too preoccupied to notice me at all, that in a few days' time these strangers would have become intimately known to me. Their hopes and fears, courage and failure, laughter or anger would matter deeply to me and all my own efforts be bent on helping them to do the best they could; that many would come to me with intimate family problems and a touching faith in my ability to solve them; and that, though our lives would touch for one month only, nevertheless with some bonds would be forged which would last through years.

Already a feeling of being one of a group was emerging. Shirts of one colour began to drift together; a slight tension was growing in the atmosphere with the knowledge that the preliminaries must be nearly over and that the tales told of adventure and sweat could not be wholly false. Quite soon now this bubble of security must burst and the real work begin. But there was a feeling now which was not entirely apprehension: the staff were not after all ogres, they were human and had proved kindly, perhaps the course would even be enjoyable. A slender tingling of anticipation was detectable.

For some this was horribly dispelled when the afternoon's programme was announced. Everyone must go down to the sea to have their swimming tested. For the men from the creeks and rivers of the coast, accustomed all their lives to boats, living as much in the water as out of it, this was no ordeal; for others, used to the sight of water though never in it, it was unpleasant but not terrifying; but for those from the far interior, to whom this was a new element, the prospect was horrifying. To walk gently into the sea letting it deepen round their legs and thighs required an effort of will and courage that was very genuine. Some there were who found it almost beyond them and who needed many hours of individual encouraging and coaching before they were strong-hearted enough to venture into deep water. For all, even for the very good swimmers who learnt to dive and to use their skill to help and save others, the sea was the first introduction to their own undiscovered capabilities, an impartial, demanding teacher for black and white alike. It is to the credit of the young Nigerian that out of the many whom we eventually had on courses the numbers who failed to learn to swim could be counted on one hand, and many mastered it with surprising speed.

It gave us all a feeling of exhilaration to come up from the beach, if the stony little slipway could be called a beach, to tea. The first ordeal had been met and mastered. As they straggled in single file up the steep path to the house the students began to sing. Glistening and grinning, their heads up, they were prepared to meet now whatever would come, some because they felt they had faced the ultimate and were still alive, some because they knew themselves to be more than equal to the sea and thought, mistakenly, that this made them equal to any other element, some simply because they had done their best and it had been considered adequate. And then, at the end, the two or three for whom the experience had been a nightmare and who felt that hell now lay before them. To these, especially, we tried to say a personal word, to give them the feeling that someone minded about their failure and believed in their future success. This was sometimes so well expressed in my smile that I had a visitor as soon as dusk fell beseeching me to have pity on him and explain to the Principal why it was impossible that he should ever go into the sea again!

But the day was not over, the real adventure of it lay directly ahead.

The word 'adventure' had been much used in talking about this course but very few of the students were quite sure what adventure meant. There is no word equivalent to it in any Nigerian language and when asked each man found difficulty in translating it: 'something of danger and magic', 'something of surprise', 'a difficult journey', 'to be in a strange place', they would say and, indeed, it is something of all these things. So now, with them all assembled in the dining hall of the big house, my husband would speak to them of this word— adventure. What did they think it meant? Who could tell in words? Well, words were not enough, they were going to find out—NOW.

In ninety seconds every man must have changed into his bathing pants and be back in the dining room ready for adventure.

He clapped his hands and pandemonium broke out. In an instant the room was clear and the ceiling thundering under the heavy steps of racing young men. Cries and laughter floated down the stairs as clothes were ripped off and bathing trunks pulled on. Before the staff had time to appear in their own bathing attire (worn discreetly under shorts as a result of forewarning) and collect life-jackets for each man of their section, the students were ready and smartly lined up for action. Each man was issued with a life-jacket and then, with all the staff both black and white divided out amongst them, they followed-my-leader down the cliff path behind the house to the sea shore.

It was late afternoon and the sky held the clear translucent light that precedes sunset and dark. The sea rolled into the bay and beat on the cliffs in the endless swell that even the calmest days never stilled. The cliffs, the only cliffs on the West African coast for hundreds of miles, rose out of the sea, pink and mauve and lava black in the late light, crowned by a profusion of trees, all the richness of true tropical jungle, and shrill with birds and monkeys. At intervals, secret and accessible only by water, the rock was pierced by holes and caves into which the swell sucked and thundered while small black crabs scuttled over walls and roof and clusters of bats squeaked and stirred. One such hole opened into what must have been once a small volcanic crater; a dark circular pool, overhung by ferns and tropical foliage, the home, so rumour had it, of unmentionable creatures which rose from the waters to cast their spells. It was, indeed, perfectly possible to believe this when at the foot of the grotto in the green twilight shade of the towering rim, black stones underfoot, black, slowly-sucking water swirling through the hole in the outer bastion and retreating with a faint echoing boom. All normal sounds cut off and muffled by the forest, the abnormal that remained might have belonged to any half-world, to any legendary creature out of the waters. The sudden piercing scream of an angry monkey sounded in that place like a soul in hell; the scuttle of crabs or the rushing wings of toucan or fish eagle was the stealthy approach of some sinister spirit.

It was round the foot of these cliffs and through this grotto that the students were now going on a journey of exploration that held for many of them all the elements of true adventure: danger, strangeness, a difficult journey, magic and a strange place. To travel along the base of the cliffs clinging with hands and feet to whatever small protuberance of rock could be found while the ocean sucked and pulled at uncertain legs; to feel panic rising in the throat and know that there lay no way out but forward (for to return now held as many hazards); to hear a cheerful voice encouraging and find a helping hand held out, maybe the voice and hand of a man from another tribe; to find physical exhaustion gaining ground and spiritual terror growing rapidly; to imagine that the crossing of the mouth of the grotto on a rope was an impossibility, and then to find, with no knowledge of how it had happened, that the terrible place had been crossed after all and life still beat strongly through the blood; to feel, slowly, unbelievably, that it was going to be possible to triumph; to see the end approaching and know that there was strength enough to get there after all; to arrive, the sea overcome, the spirits vanquished, fear, terror, the desire to give up all mastered, all this, and much more according to the temperament of each individual, brought them up the steep path again, to the top of the cliffs where I stood waiting for them, shouting with the glory of it, sure now that life held nothing more to fear. Manhood had triumphed, some undreamt spiritual stiffening come to the rescue.

'Now I know what Mungo Park felt like!' said one young Ibo, exuding pride in achievement.

'When I saw the sea I thought I had come to my death,' exclaimed another young man, 'I could not understand how I was to come through alive.'

One teacher, from the Middle Belt of Nigeria, came up limping slightly. He said nothing of what was wrong until I asked, casually, as he was turning away, whether he would like some Elastoplast. Then he squatted down on the ground and turning up his foot showed me, to my alarm, that his small toe was hanging on only by a narrow piece of skin. He had caught it on a sharp edge of rock. It was a minor irritation to him; we did it up with plaster and in a few days it reknit and was as good as new. Physical hurt was of small account for him, it was the spiritual pains and terrors that were to be feared.

Though this was only the evening of the first day it had been so supercharged for us all with new experiences and activities that I was already beginning to feel that I knew some of these young men very well. The same loosening of reserve, an outgoing of friendship,

THE GROTTO

was apparent in them too. We smiled at each other now not as hesitant strangers unsure of the reaction but as friends with the intimacy of a shared experience. I had stood at a vantage point on the edge of a promontory opposite their perilous traverse and watched them crawl, unsure two-legged crabs, along the cliff face and out of sight round the corner to the grotto mouth. I knew exactly how many of them felt for I, too, would have feared this exercise and I waited, keyed up with nervous tension, for their reappearance at the top of the cliff. Would anything go wrong? It was always possible that panic might utterly overwhelm one of the more fearful, and, because in the last resort humanity is not predictable and there are resources for evil as well as for good in the spirit of man, this panic might destroy him. Once a young Southerner became paralysed halfway up the cliff on the climb which ended the course and it took many moments of patient coaxing to persuade him that he could go on; for me any such incident was double edged, involving not only defeat for the young man who was in our care but also possible disaster of a different kind for my husband whose responsibility it was. So that when the students panted up the last few yards of path, answered to their names and grinned at me in the triumph of the impossible made possible (this phrase invented by one of their number in the early days) my answering smile was composed of the same elements. We had both escaped from the shadow of accident; we had both nerved ourselves for mischance and, astoundingly, it had not happened; we had both overcome, they their nature and their fears and I, in my imagination, our critics.

That night, when the Principal spoke to them of their responsibilities in their communities and the things that we hoped to teach them about themselves and the things they could do to help others, many were sitting in a drowsy coma exhausted by the strangeness of the day. But for most, I think, there began to be some stirring of understanding of what was expected from them and, if not understanding, a response to the challenge which they recognized they were facing.

The next day brought the first introduction to pick and shovel work. Later on in the course we would go into the 'bush' to assist some village to help itself with the physical construction of a road, a bridge, a dispensary, or some similar public work, but young men of the position and education of ours did not always take kindly to the idea of manual labour and the belief that they could, and should, take a lead in helping their communities in this way needed to be carefully presented to them.

On this second morning at Man O' War Bay, when headpans and picks were handed out and it was taken for granted that every man would use one or the other, there were some who looked mutinous. But public opinion and a framework of discipline gave the rebellious no opportunity to spread disaffection. No one was asked what he wished to do; this was the programme and every man was expected to adhere to it. So the group was equipped and out on the road before the more unco-operative members had had time to formulate their arguments against the physical employment of educated men.

Though a most careful programme was made out before each course began, a process requiring much hard work and a mind good at crossword and jigsaw puzzles, we did not show it to the students. They knew only in the morning what lay ahead for that day. Although the staff were not unanimous in agreeing on this policy we felt there were sufficiently powerful reasons for it. Many of the exercises which we undertook and the skills which we required our young men to learn were not only strange to them but also abhorrent. The whole nature of the course was outside their experience and tradition and many had come reluctantly because their employers had said they must. The balance, at the start of every course, between success and failure was very delicate; one voluble dissenter could upset it irrevocably. We knew, on the other hand, first from a recognition of the factors that affect human nature and later from experience, that most of these young men would end up enjoying every moment of their time with us and that for many of them it would constitute a landmark in their lives, but this depended on our being able to convince them at the beginning that the things we asked them to do were worthwhile and this conviction could only come with the doing of the things themselves. If they had time to brood ahead over what was to come and, being articulate young men, to debate

OFF TO WORK

23

imagined future indignities, all might be lost. Not knowing the programme, each day was started in a quiver of anticipation and as the days went on, and more and more surprising things happened, their minds grew into a pattern of mental alertness as their bodies hardened into physical fitness so that they felt prepared for anything and, at last, ready to overcome any difficulty.

This was the theory: to a great extent it was also the practice, but there were always the failures.

One young man, from Sokoto in the remote Northern provinces, having travelled well over one thousand miles to reach Man O' War Bay, refused when he arrived to do anything at all. He would not discard his *riga*, his Northern dress, and sat miserably in his dormitory or wandered disconsolate on the flagstaff promontory moaning to himself. No argument, no talk in English or in Hausa, could convince him that it was foolish and indeed shameful to come so many miles and then to take no part in the course he had come for. He began to affect his companions who felt that as long as he retained his dress and refused to work they were in some way betraying their faith. It was pointed out to him that he had travelled down on special transport and that the return, alone and in disgrace, would by no means be so easy. But his mind was closed to all arguments and at last he was given some money and sent away. At once the morale of all his fellow-countrymen improved. The accusing eye of their unregenerate brother removed, they were free to form their own judgments about the things they were asked to do.

It is interesting to note that had this incident happened at a later stage of the course both the reaction and the result might have been very different. On one or two occasions when the time came for some of the more arduous exercises a man weakened and fell out. Then, in the case of a Northerner, the group of his fellows would coalesce round him. Deputations sometimes came to my husband to plead for an unco-operative comrade. 'It will shame us all if he is sent away,' they would say. 'Let him stay and we will see that he behaves.'

Once we had a strike when a course was asked to repeat again an exercise of which they had been afraid. Between the first undertaking and the repetition lay three weeks of hard work and rigorous training and we hoped to gain some idea of what this meant in their performance. They refused. A spokesman informed the chief instructor that no student would do this exercise again.

There could be no compromise on this issue; either they must do the exercise or the ringleaders, whom we knew, must be dismissed. My husband sent for the whole course; section by section they came down, awed and a little shamefaced, but persistent in their refusal, and sat on our verandah. One by one he summoned them into the sitting room and, after talking for a little while, said: 'Ali (or John) do you still refuse to do this exercise?' And Ali (or John), deprived of the support of his fellows and placed on his own to make a decision, said: 'I will do it, Sir.' He was then sent out to sit on our back verandah where he had no contact with his dissident comrades. After the first half-dozen it was possible to say to each individual: 'All the others have agreed to do so,' and, such is the power of the mass, he would agree without more ado. In the end the whole course had consented to go through with the exercise and had made themselves responsible for seeing that the ringleaders did so too.

I went up to watch them do it. I was nervous in case of any accident and because I felt the situation to be still very precarious. To my astonishment the whole thing went off splendidly. They not only did the exercise superbly but did it in the fastest time ever recorded and afterwards sang better and joked more wholeheartedly than had been the case for some days before. This inability to bear a grudge for long and the capacity to laugh at a joke against themselves were endearing characteristics in our students.

The European staff found it less easy to meet adverse circumstances in the same cheerful spirit. There may have been reasons for this. Man O' War Bay was remote, with no easy access to a European community or the sports and club that make up a large part of life for so many Englishmen abroad. The climate, especially when the rains began, was humid and enervating, and we worked extremely hard. Also it seemed that the nature of the courses, adventurous, experimental, unknown in this part of the world, attracted men whose characters were out of the ordinary—both very good and otherwise. Whatever the reason, and maybe the differences in national character were the most important, European rows (in contrast to African ones) seemed to be bitter and unforgiving.

Major X came to us fresh from the Army. On arrival in Lagos he had been offered the choice of working in the Secretariat on the Scholarship Board or coming to Man O' War Bay—'some kind of civilian commando training'. Understandably he chose the latter; for both us and him it was a disastrous choice.

From the beginning he had no clear understanding of what we were trying to do. There was enough similarity between our discipline and methods and those of the Army in which he had spent his life for him to think that he knew all about it: but when told that he had to convert young men to his point of view by conviction and example rather than by orders blindly obeyed he was bewildered. At the first sign of defiance he wanted the offender put on a charge and punished, but a cheerful insolence is one of the hallmarks of the Southern Nigerian, the outward sign, often, of the inward dynamic and ebullience which we hoped to channel into constructive service.

Major X ate with us. There was a small mess in which all the other young European officers fed together, but this he regarded as the non-commissioned officers' mess and not for him. I do not think, in fact, that he rated us much higher, but by virtue of my husband's position as Principal we came into the commissioned ranks. One day he took my husband aside and told him that life was quite intolerable unless we promised not to talk shop at meals.

We were appalled. In a long and exciting day mealtimes were often the only chance we had in which to meet each other and discuss the job. We both loved our work and our students and found them the most interesting subjects in the world—particularly as this world held no daily papers, no daily letters, no wireless (the proximity of the mountain making this very difficult), and very little contact with outside.

However, we recognized that it was important that our staff should be humoured and so we agreed to try. Some weeks of misery followed. We met for lunch after a morning filled (for me) with many excitements. Jonathan had at last learned to swim; Saidu had come to ask if I could give advice on some ailment of his sister's; Dauda had lost his spectacles and so found weaving very difficult; was it all right for me to change the First Aid lesson and borrow one of the African staff to help? My husband rushed in just as Ebenezer was about to serve the meal. I could see that he was worried and upset and longed to ask him how his morning had gone. Instead we sat down in silence which was presently broken by Major X making some remark about the war in Korea. Neither my husband nor I had much idea what was going on in Korea and neither of us cared very much. We tried to show an intelligent interest, but our ignorance and abstraction were so apparent that the conversation soon lapsed. It was started again by Major X giving an informed résumé of the

Grand National. He knew the form and could instruct us on likely winners. We had never raced and so found it difficult to contribute anything at all. Coffee was drunk in silence, a silence painful to us but apparently the lesser of two evils to Major X.

This self-control had the same effect on all of us. He drove us nearly mad, but we did the same for him and one day, in an outburst which brought him close to tears, he implored us to get him a posting elsewhere. This we were only too glad to recommend and in due time he left us for a more routine job with fixed hours and all interest in work cut off as soon as the office was left behind.

Before he went, however, he offered to give a lecture to the students on the Korean War. He felt, quite rightly, that we were all singularly uninformed about this extremely important event from which he had but recently come. This was true and we welcomed the idea, only warning him that his talk must be couched in very simple terms. While it might be regrettable that we should know so little about such a major issue, nevertheless geographical position, climate and the natural preoccupation of human beings with their own business and the affairs of their nearer neighbours made our ignorance pardonable, and if the talk was to be of any benefit to us it must be in language we could comprehend.

Major X agreed. Perhaps he did think that what he said was simple but for his hearers it became a nightmare of army terms, proper names, and the occasional flashing idiom whose literal meaning (the meaning it held for all but a very few of his audience) was far removed from the picture he meant to paint.

'Then I said to old Bertie Wotherspoon of the 11th who lay on our right that he'd better do a sweep to the south and see if he could get a brush with the enemy. But Harding of the Gloucesters, a fine chap who'd done very well at Eton, came in and told us that guerrillas were raiding into our lines where the Turks were flung out on the wing.'

I could see by the bewildered looks on the black faces before me that the idea of Bertie Wotherspoon and the enemy taking a brush and sweeping something (but in heaven's name what) battled with a confusion about there being gorillas in Korea which had somehow got mixed up in the war. Some gazed at him fascinated, doing their very best to make sense out of the rigmarole and feeling, even, that the very incomprehensibility meant that they were being let into an important military secret. Others, the weaker vessels, and this included some of the staff, exhausted by a day of hard physical activity in a tropical climate, began to doze gently.

Suddenly the room was electrified by a shout and the clatter of a heavy object pitched hard across it. Major X had observed that one of his audience had passed out of his sphere of influence. He snatched a large bunch of keys from his pocket and flung it at the offender's face, shouting:

'You rude man!'

The silence for some seconds was absolute. These young men were all educated and responsible citizens unaccustomed to having things flung at them for trifling discourtesies. I think we all recognized in that moment that Major X lived in a different world from ours and that it was useless to attempt to open the door through. The victim picked up the bunch of keys and returned them courteously.

If Major X was still under any illusion that he had made himself understood it cannot have lasted very long. Shortly after the incident of the keys he brought his talk to a close and asked for questions. The first young man to stand up asked a very pertinent one which brought the colour flooding into the Major's already apoplectic cheeks.

'Which Army were you in, Sir?'

.   .   .   .   .

Man O' War Bay was the ideal site for the kind of adventurous training which we had devised for our young Nigerians. The bay itself was all that a bay should be. It was small enough for the whole bay to be visible from any point on the shore, yet large enough to give shelter to the men o' war in the days of the suppression of the slave trade and it was for this reason that it had come to be named Man O' War Bay.

The headlands which protected the bay from storms curved towards each other giving symmetry. The coastline, thickly wooded with true tropical forest, came to the edge of cliffs of black volcanic rock. In these cliffs caves and holes abounded. There was a ceaseless heavy swell and the tide ran in and out over inky pebbly beach. Monkeys swung themselves about among the trees and black and white fish eagles sailed majestically overhead.

Inland Mount Cameroon, 13,350 ft., dominated the landscape

'OPERATION ADVENTURE', MAN O' WAR BAY

with the triangular Little Cameroon, 5,800 ft., beside it. The fifteenth-century Portuguese explorers had called the estuary Rio dos Camaroes, Shrimp River, and this name had been retained though, for most people, its origin was forgotten. The land between the mountain and the sea, a honeycomb of little hills, each heavily forested, was divided into plantations growing millions of stems of bananas. These were exported from Tiko, the steamy creek port to the south of Man O' War Bay, on special ships which left for England every eighth or tenth day. At Tiko also is an airfield where the tiny Doves of West African airways flew in from Nigeria.

To the north of Man O' War Bay the sea takes a larger bite out of the land; this is Ambas Bay and on its shores stands the town of Victoria, named after the Queen by the Baptist missionaries who, expelled from Fernando Po in 1858, established themselves here. About this date many Englishmen extolled the beauty and the possibilities of Ambas Bay and did their best to persuade H.M. Government to annex formally the Cameroons. One spoke of making it the 'Singapore of the West', others suggested that it might become a penal settlement, and that convicts sent there might be encouraged to intermarry with the local people. Sir Richard Burton wanted to build a sanatorium for stricken West African travellers on the slopes of the mountain, and all the time letters travelled back and forward to the Consul at Calabar and to the Foreign Office in London from the missionaries and various influential travellers, even from some of the chiefs themselves, in an endeavour to stir these bodies to positive action. It is fascinating to speculate upon the history of the Cameroons had that action been taken.

But it was not. On March 19th, 1884, forestalling Consul Hewitt, who had been at last advised to take action, the German explorer Dr Nachtigal was instructed by his Government to proceed to the annexation of the territory. On July 10th the English, riled that their continued procrastination should have lost them the prize, sent a gunboat, *Goshawk*, to the Cameroon River. What happened to cause a change of mind is not clear but the next day the *Goshawk* sailed away again, leaving the Germans a clear field. Nachtigal rushed through arrangements with the chiefs and on July 14th, 1884, the Cameroons were declared a German Protectorate. The British Consul protested on July 19th (though his protests would have been better directed to London whose dilly-dallying was the cause of this state of affairs), the Germans acknowledged the protest and hoisted the flat at Bimbia. 'In this nefarious and undignified manner the German Government obtained a foothold in the Gulf of Guinea', concludes the historian with what seems at this distance in time rather a distorted view of the situation.

After the First World War the Cameroons were divided arbitrarily into two and the pieces handed over as Trust territories to France and Britain. The German plantation owners had been dispossessed and the plantations came under the Custodian of Enemy Property. No provision, however, was made for running them and, after unsuccessful attempts to interest possible British buyers, they were put up for sale by public auction in London in November 1924. With the exception of three small lots all were sold and most of the buyers were the former German owners. So the Germans, though in a territory now under British trusteeship, restored the plantations to something of their former splendour. So secure, in fact, did they feel themselves and so convinced of eventual triumph that by 1939 the Cameroons was found to have a Nazi hierarchy completely organized, and Gauleiters and other party officials were ready to take over. For a short time the issue hung in the balance but the chance was missed and once again the plantations lost their owners and returned to a state of semi-production and semi-neglect. This time, however, the lesson had been learnt and when the war ended a Corporation on the lines of nationalized industries in Britain was set up to run all the plantations as a business for the benefit of the people of the Cameroons.

Man O' War Bay was one of the earliest of these German plantations, and, because it was difficult of access, had been left derelict since the end of the war. The enormous wooden plantation house stood empty and decayed. The four miles of road out from Victoria, never very good, had become virtually impassable; the jungle had overgrown it and the rain gouged huge holes in the soft earth. Bananas still grew there, but for the most part in a natural disarray untended by man. A skeleton African staff lounged about in the sunshine rarely visited by authority and thinking with nostalgia of the good days when a white man lived in the big house. We talked with many Cameroonians about the German days and never once did we hear condemnation. Hard masters they may have been but they loved their plantations and treated their labourers justly. The impersonal administration of a Corporation was no substitute to these men for the family atmosphere of the past.

This dissolution, so sad for the plantation itself, was a lucky thing for us.

My husband had heard stories of Man O' War Bay, of its beauty and romance, and when the time came to translate into reality the idea of an adventurous training centre he determined to go there to see if it offered possibilities as a site. It was a difficult journey, made partly on foot, partly by banana tractor, but, when he burst out of the undergrowth on to the cleared land of the plantation house and its offices, he knew that he had found the answer.

Though the house and its immediate grounds were derelict, neglected and deserted the Cameroons Development Corporation were nevertheless reluctant to hand them over to the Government for a training centre. It needed the personal intervention of the Acting-Governor, Sir Hugh Foot, when he came on an official visit to the territory, to make the site ours.

My husband, Sir Hugh and the Chairman of the Corporation travelled round by launch from Victoria to inspect the land. The journey was not an easy one; the small boat contained two men whose interests were utterly opposed and a third who tried to hold the balance between them. The atmosphere was tense and strained. As the launch neared the little jetty at Man O' War Bay a small reception party was seen to assemble. It was a long time since any white man had visited the plantation, and longer still since it had been honoured by guests of such importance. But the staff had not forgotten what was due to people of consequence.

There were four or five men dressed in the best clothes they could muster; an old pair of once white flannels, khaki shorts which had seen better days, a topee, sign of authority, a battered black homburg, a panama sparkling with aluminium paint. The time-keeper was there and so was the tally clerk, aware of their background of dereliction and abandon but determined that the façade, at any rate, should be brave.

The launch was nearly alongside when the clerk gave an order; the row of men drew themselves up and the notes of 'God Save the King' floated unsteadily out over the water.

Caught in the acts of preparation for landing the Englishmen suffered acute embarrassment. The Chairman muttered and tapped his stick impatiently on the bottom of the boat, but the Acting-Governor drew himself up, took off his hat and stood stiffly at attention; my husband was very moved. There was something valiant and heartwarming in the efforts of these abandoned Cameroonians to do what they felt was the right thing to welcome the representative of the King.

My own arrival at Man O' War Bay was less spectacular but, in its own way, also a saga.

I had come off a banana boat from England, newly married and expecting to find my husband, who had flown out some weeks before, on the quayside. But he was not there: he had been called away on the Government's business to Lagos. I knew all at once what it was like to

ALI

come second to the job in hand. I went first to the resthouse in Victoria where Fineboy, who had been my husband's cook before my advent, and Ali, the steward boy, came to greet me and to commiserate with me that our master was absent. The question now arose whether I should go out to the newly-built house at Man O' War Bay to start getting it into order or remain in the resthouse until my husband returned. On the one hand I would be busily and happily occupied but in a remote site, a terrible road between me and the nearest town, and I should be the only European in an African community; on the other hand I might remain within reach of shops and other wives but living in nervous idleness with any apprehensions which I might be harbouring about the future growing rapidly. I chose to go to Man O' War Bay.

There was no time to make any proper arrangements, and in any case I had not much idea how to do this. I loaded our crates containing all our household goods on to a lorry and sent them out to the house. Here they were disposed about the three rooms in the order in which they happened to come off the vehicle. The house was finished so far as walls and roof went but had still no doors or windows and the whitewash on the walls was scarcely dry.

The next day Fineboy and Ali and I climbed into the car, which my husband had left garaged in Victoria, and set off for Man O' War Bay and my future home.

Trouble only began when we left the tarmac road and headed off along the dirt track into the jungle. It had rained quite recently and pools of water lay across the way. I was not experienced then in the ways of African earth roads and discovered, too late, that these pools could be fatal traps.

In the centre of one the Studebaker ground slowly to a halt; the back wheels continued to turn but the only result was to send up a shower of liquid mud and increase remorselessly the depth of the puddle in the unresisting earth. I could have wept. Already it was afternoon and darkness descended at 7 p.m. Out at my home there was no electricity and I had not even located the lamps in all that mound of luggage. The heat seemed stifling, the car an inert mass of metal; I knew no one at all to whom I could go for help. The heavy banana branches drooped in the sun and the jungle screeched and whooped in my alarmed ears. Fineboy and Ali leapt out and put their shoulders behind the vehicle while I revved it madly, but theirs was too small a strength to effect any change. I sat at the wheel unsure whether the drops that trickled down my face were sweat or tears or both. This was marriage—and I had not envisaged it like this.

Just as it seemed that we might have to abandon the car and walk the three miles that lay ahead we saw some men coming along the road towards us. I felt my heart go pit-a-pat. The reality of being the only white woman among strangers of a different race and colour suddenly overwhelmed me. I was afraid.

The men saw our predicament and at once threw down the things which they were carrying and began to push. There were five or six of them and the car could not resist; with a rush which covered them with mud we lurched out of the holes which we had dug for ourselves and staggered on to firm ground. With cheerful grins and shouted wishes the men picked up their headloads and went on their way. We ground into second gear and set off again for Man O' War Bay. Often in the days of the war my friends and I had sent each other postcards bearing the foolish legend: 'Having a splendid time here. The natives are friendly.' Never would I have sent it with such conviction as at that moment had there been any means of dispatching a postcard from that jungle path.

ARRIVAL AT MAN O' WAR BAY

We even had a cup of tea. When we drove carefully into the compound at Man O' War Bay, drew the car up beside the house and stepped over the threshold to view the muddle of packing cases, despair began to settle over me again. But Fineboy, from long experience, was at home in this sphere and knew the remedy.

'Madam like tea?' he enquired, and to my great astonishment produced it in a very short time.

Ali, too, was determined to care for me. He had begun busily to open every available crate, without system or reason but simply because he felt it would be helpful. Refreshed by the tea and comforted by the knowledge that both these men considered themselves responsible for my welfare and would do everything in their power to promote it, I took out the lists and began to make a plan of the essentials and which cases they were in. I must have a bed; a lamp and kerosene; some cooking pots, knife, fork and plate; food and a change of clothes. Nothing else mattered for tonight, we had time only to find these things before the sun went down. With Ali's help we managed it and, rummaging in a trunk for sheets and pillow, I found as well a whistle and a policeman's baton belonging to my husband.

These things comforted me. I had no genuine expectation that anything unpleasant would happen during the night but the prospect, if it did, of being able to make a great deal of noise and lay about me with a heavy stick was reassuring. Neither Ali nor Fineboy was very good with the pressure lamp and to me, at that time, it was a fearful machine which might at any moment explode. It flared and died on one of the packing cases making a sinister hissing noise and attracting many strange insects. The walls of the little house dissolved in this uncertain light and the vacant window spaces became not openings for me to look out of but spy holes for those outside to peer in. I was not yet used to the shrill noises of the night in the tropics and the cicadas sounded deafening in my ears, though not so deafening that they shut out other sounds, the rustles and screams and rumblings of darkness in the jungle.

Fineboy came in to see that I had everything and to bid me 'Good night'. He offered to stay with me and sleep on the floor at the foot of my bed, but this kindly gesture filled me with alarm and I could not bear to think of his old, gnarled face peering at me as I prepared for sleep. So he went away to his own house on the other side of the compound, and Ali, his head on one side giving me his singularly sweet smile, went too and I was left alone amidst the dark bulk of my possessions. I could think of only one thing to do. Somehow the hours that stretched between now and daylight must be passed. I would go to bed.

It was then I discovered that I had no notion of how to extinguish the light, and I was afraid to touch it in case the worst happened and it exploded into flames. At this moment the night watchman passed on his rounds and, fearfully, I went out on to the verandah to ask his advice. It is a strange sensation talking for the first time to a black man in the dark, with only eyes and teeth flashing like *ignis fatuus* and the bulk of the flesh absorbed into the night. But he was kind and helpful and showed me what I wished to know. He gave me the wrong answers and next morning I found my few unpacked possessions drowned in paraffin, but that was a foretaste of the uncertainties of life in Africa.

I placed the whistle beneath my pillow and the baton ready at my side. It had not been possible to find a mosquito net among the baggage so I drew the sheet over my head and clutched it in a sticky hand to prevent it slipping down. This was less a precaution against mosquitoes of which I had no experience than a shield against falling snakes or roaming scorpions, products of a vivid imagination. I prepared for a night of terror and prayed to be kept safe till dawn.

And suddenly it was dawn; Ali was standing beside me with a cup of tea, there was a ripe smell of kerosene, and I was safe and well. I must have fallen asleep immediately I had finished my preparations to withstand the night's siege and slept undisturbed by realities or dreams.

Later that day when, on a shopping expedition, I emerged from the jungle and drove along the causeway that joined the last few yards of track with the tarmac road of Victoria, I felt like a returned explorer and was astonished because the rest of the world remained indifferent to my achievements. But I also felt that I was now at home in Man O' War Bay; what had appeared an inauspicious start turned out to be quite the contrary. Stripped of all the normal barriers to life in the bush which hedge most wives about I was forced to meet people and circumstances face to face. As a result I was never again afraid as I had been afraid for a moment when the car stuck and the men came along the road; and from that first morning, when I woke up in the sunshine and recognized that the half-finished house around me was my home, I loved it.

CHAPTER II

Crises and Emergencies

IT WAS part of our intention at Man O' War Bay to try to show the young men who came to us the wider horizons of their own responsibility. With the approach of self-government it was necessary that they should realize what this implied in terms of every-day decisions and readiness to shoulder burdens. They had become accustomed in times of crisis to turn to a white adminis-trator; he said what was to be done and planned how it was to be carried out, and the weight of praise or blame was his also. Now the time was coming when he would no longer be there and a real danger existed of a hiatus ensuing in which no one would be found willing to take responsibility in time of trouble.

While these things were discussed at length in the evenings, my husband felt that to talk was not enough and some more practical way must be discovered to bring home to the students, among whom we hoped would be found future leaders, the essence of this problem.

To this end original exercises were devised which we called 'Civil Crises'. Long after they had returned home letters from old students would refer to these evenings of alarm in a way that left no doubt that the lesson had been learnt and put to good use.

Preparations for these events took place in deep secrecy. Various members of the

CLIMBING PALM TREES

establishment were carefully coached in the parts they were to play, and all watches had to be synchronized on the night itself as, to be effective, the events required split-second timing. Not all our British staff saw the value of these exercises and so did not get the fun out of them that we and the African staff did: for the students it was not fun at the time but provided afterwards unforgettable memories and a fund of stories of their own prowess (or vice versa)!

After dinner we made our way up to the big house from our bungalow. The nights could be wonderful; warm, but with a softer air than the sticky dampness of the day; the sea lapped and gurgled against the cliffs and reflected brilliantly the polished silver pathway of the moon; our pressure lamp cast long eerie shadows before us and, on the verandah, Sgt-Major Riga Addingi was tuning up the men.

Riga Addingi, our Physical Training instructor, had been lent to us by the West African Frontier Force and was one of the best instructors that we ever had. A man of simple background, he had the ability to inspire other men and he understood completely the principles and ideas which lay behind the course and could fuse this understanding into the minds of others. He had a repertoire of songs which covered America, Britain and every region of Nigeria, and the knack of charming the heart and the voice out of the most timid and unmusical. But for the most part the students sang wonderfully with full deep voices which they used with abandon; to hear them singing, led by Addingi, was an experience which moved even hard-boiled visiting officials to admiration.

The evening began as usual. One or two of the students had new songs to teach us, sometimes from their own particular part of the country, sometimes a song that they had heard on the wireless and enjoyed.

Suddenly there was an interruption. Up the steps, on to the verandah came the First Aid dispenser from the plantation labour lines quite near us. He wore his clinical white coat and his face looked grave. My husband called for silence and took him aside to hear what he had to say. The staff looked concerned and interested: I tried to put on the appropriate expression for a Principal's wife about to be confronted with a crisis. The students just sat waiting for the conference to be over so that they could begin to sing again; they little knew what was to come.

39

My husband turned to me and said in a low voice:

'He thinks that he has three cases of typhoid in the camp and he's come to us for help. The telephone line is down since last week's storm and he's worried because he feels that he ought to be taking some action tonight. What should we do?'

I said: 'Oh dear, how awful. Yes, we ought to do something.'

The Principal turned to the students.

'I'm afraid we've got some trouble here. Section 1, your help is needed. Please go to your room and one of the instructors will come and tell you what is wrong. Everybody else can carry on singing.'

Looking rather startled, Section 1 file out followed by two instructors, one black, one white; those who remain are soon in full song again and the interruption is forgotten.

In their dormitory Section 1 are learning, with a certain amount of horror, that there is a suspected outbreak of typhoid in the nearby camp, that the dispenser wants help and that it is up to them to do something about it. They believe completely that this is reality and at first confusion is absolute. Eugene, a journalist on a paper that weekly urges resistance to evil in high places, asks hesitatingly:

'Shouldn't we all go home? This is a very infectious disease and we might catch it.'

He is instantly rebuked, with a touch of smugness, by a young mission teacher: 'Certainly not! We have been sent here to be leaders, we shall be expected to do something.'

Meantime the two instructors, by a judicious mixture of prodding and retreating, are trying to get the group started on some constructive planning while keeping themselves as much as possible in the background. Their job is to watch the reactions of these young men so that in a later criticism they may be able to apportion fairly praise and blame.

A little puzzled but by no means disconcerted, the remaining sections are continuing with the concert on the verandah. It is now that a vehicle is heard coming down the road very fast with a grinding of gears and a screeching of brakes. As it stops a babble of voices breaks out down below and hurrying footsteps are heard coming up the stairs. The singing falters. An uneasiness is beginning to pervade the students; not the uneasiness of suspicion but rather a faint feeling that this is an abnormal night in some way and untoward events are in the air.

Okoro, the driver of the Centre's Land Rover, bursts through the door, waving a long official envelope at my husband. He gives the impression that he has hurried desperately from the seat of Government, twenty-one miles away, with a document of the utmost importance from the Commissioner of the Cameroons. The Principal opens the letter, breaking a large red seal to do so. He looks very grave. Then he stands up and says:

'I have some bad news here. This is a letter from the Commissioner of the Cameroons saying that there has been a serious outbreak of cattle disease in the North. This means that there will be no meat coming down here for some months and a food shortage faces the South. To overcome this the fishing industry must be expanded. The Commissioner wants to know as soon as possible how many fishermen there already are around us here at Man O' War Bay; where they get their canoes; whether more canoes can be obtained quickly; what they cost; how long it will take to train men as fishermen; whether fish can be dried in this area and how they can be sent up-country. Section 2, this is an urgent job for you.'

Section 2 retire, followed by glances compounded of envy and relief from the remaining sections. Doors are banging in the background and there are raised voices and hurrying footsteps as Section 1, having now decided what they are going to do about their typhoid, scurry about collecting the things they think that they will need. Abdussalam Song, an entertaining individualist from the far North, can be heard addressing the fishing section in his clipped English:

'We must go at once in the canoes to that fishing village. Why not? The Commissioner wants to know now.'

Somehow, although everyone is convinced of the genuineness of these events, there is now a general air of expectancy that something else may well happen. It does; soon, and with devastating effect.

From a long way away a weird wailing sound is heard coming steadily nearer. It rises and falls and there is something uncanny about it. The men begin to shift uneasily on their stools and even I, who know its origin, feel a cold shiver creep down my back as it approaches. It is a man crying out something about a fire and sobbing with a kind of madness.

When he runs wildly into the lamplight among us he looks indeed demented. Wild eyes glitter beneath the shade of an ancient felt hat; he is in rags and filthy and (one could swear it) foaming at the mouth. He cries in a high, distraught voice that his village is on fire,

his family destroyed, and, waving an arm frantically behind him, he
screams the name of a nearby hamlet and rushes wailing into the
night again.

The students are petrified. A man running amok carries special
terrors in Africa, it is closely related to possession by evil spirits.
When we look round some of the less brave are missing and they
are later discovered under their beds or in the lavatory; even the
more courageous hesitate to accost the man or try to learn before he
disappears details of the disaster. Perhaps it is as well for most of
them have seen at one time or another Lucas, my courteous and
quiet young cook!

However, when all the information is pieced together there is
enough data to tell Section 3 that a catastrophe has overtaken a
certain village and it is their job to do something about it.

Confusion now seems absolute; one public-spirited citizen
rushed out as soon as he heard the word 'fire' and rang the fire bell.
This at once produced all the other sections from wherever they were
discussing fishing or fever to rush wildly about in the night seeking
the source of disaster. They had to be rounded up again and assured
that Section 3 had the fire in hand.

I was being besieged on all sides, begged for information about
treating typhoid, for the key of the First Aid box, for large-scale
remedies for burns. On one such night Magaji Gombe, another
Northerner and a very small man, came sharply round the corner of
the house on his way to the fire, one of the Centre's extinguishers
balanced on his head. He hit me, and the extinguisher went off,
drowning me in foam. However it was a salutary lesson on the
inadvisability of carrying a mechanical appliance some miles to a
fire when adequate water and sand could be found on the spot.

Section 4 were, by now, feeling sorry for themselves. The
intelligent realized that their turn must come next and were beginning to wonder if it were not just possible that they were being
deceived. When it did come, however, they no longer thought so!
The last crisis was the *pièce de résistance*, the result of much labour
and effort. At exactly 9.07, in the midst of all this tumult, a tremendous explosion on a nearby hill shook the Centre and a huge fire
blossomed in the darkness.

My husband cried: 'That aeroplane', and pandemonium broke
loose.

Earlier in the day a careful rumour had been circulated that there was an aeroplane missing on the Douala–Paris route, and that it might be in the vicinity of the mountain. At the sound and sight of this eruption every mind flew at once to the aeroplane and it was quickly assumed that this was it.

Section 4, the only unemployed section, leaped joyfully to the rescue. At least one or two were joyful, the majority were faced with a moment of fearful decision. Should they go—or should they hide? Running round the promontory in front of the house, giving a picture of a distraught wife, I stumbled over a body concealed under a bush.

'Who's there?' I said.

A quavering voice answered: 'Oh, Madam, I cannot go up there, I cannot go up there. I am afraid of snakes.'

The whole exercise was devised to panic. In every case there was total unexpectedness; the young men were taken aback—men from the North had never been asked before to carry out a survey of fishing, least of all at night without a moment's warning; in another instance the students were unnerved because they were, in fact, familiar with the dangers presented by a villager demented by disaster. But always a majority of each section did pull themselves together and set off to deal with what they honestly felt to be disaster at dead of night. A factor which added to their uncertainty was the distraught attitude and indecision of the European staff. If the Principal and his colleagues did not know what to do then, they instinctively reasoned, the situation must be bad.

At this point, while Section 4 were trying to pinch bandages and burn-jelly off Section 3 (who had had an earlier start), my husband went round to see how the others were getting on.

The typhoid section, with commendable spirit, had made up their minds that they must go down to the labour lines and do what they could. Some kind of a plan of action had at last been drawn up and they were lined up in the light of two hurricane lamps ready to set off. They carried machetes (a kind of cutlass), mosquito nets, pails with some dark liquid (later discovered to be disinfectant), some blankets, and various other odds and ends. They were prepared to send a messenger into Victoria to the doctor when they had assessed the situation, and they set off down the road with a certain swing; having decided to act they had found courage in doing so. Nevertheless when, some three hundred yards down the road, my husband called them to a halt and explained that this was an exercise, they would now return to the Centre to bed and tomorrow morning would make a survey of the labour lines and see whether their plan could in fact have been put adequately into action, they heaved a collective sigh of relief, some of the Catholics crossing themselves and the Protestants exclaiming:

'Hallelujah, no typhoid!'

The fishing section were in the heart of a dispute. Some, led by the irrepressible Abdussalam, wanted to go straight out to sea at once, dark though it was, and start prospecting for fish; others felt that they could not begin to assess the situation properly till daylight and that they would be better employed deciding what each man would do in the morning. Meanwhile they had called in the Centre's fisherman, Blackie Nelson, to give them some briefing on technical points, and they had woken up Ebenezer who was known to have been a fisherman before he became our steward. Ebenezer was not as co-operative as Lucas over things like this and he was angry at having his night's rest disturbed. So he sulked in a corner refusing to answer questions, not very sure why he was being asked them and afraid it might have some bearing on his murky past as a smuggler.

When the news was broken that this was not a genuine emergency Abdussalam looked crestfallen, one or two looked smug and hinted that they had really known it all the time, but most just looked relieved.

The firefighters, having started later than the others, were still full of initiative and effort when the news trickled through to them that there was, after all, no fire. But they thought rather well of themselves and insisted that we inspect all their arrangements before they disband.

They had indeed formed themselves into a homogeneous group with a good leader whom they were prepared to obey, and they had attempted to apportion the jobs with some regard to the nature of their members. Two not very active older men had been told to stay behind and prepare to receive refugees, two more had been instructed that their work on the spot would not be with casualties but with the women and children who might be unhurt physically but would certainly be upset. Everybody seemed to have some idea of the general plan and to be quite clear about his own personal job inside it. A very good group and rightly pleased with themselves, they went off to bed with the satisfaction of having faced the challenge.

Only Section 4, by now halfway up the hill to the site of the explosion, were having to face the actual reality of rescue. They had set off bravely in a long single file up the narrow track led by Jonathan, a blazing Tilly lamp balanced on his head. Now we could see this light bobbing rather slowly and painfully about on the steep slope of the little hill. Above it the fire had begun to die down though it still gave an occasional ghastly flicker. We set out after them up the path to await them on their journey back. The night was full of noises, the constant high-pitched scream of the cicadas, the soft rubbing and creaking of the big banana leaves, a sudden squeal from a monkey. I could perfectly understand why they feared to be alone in the jungle: it was too much inhabited. We watched the light creep painfully upward and at last vanish over the rim of the top. Now they would be finding the casualties; one white and three black, stretched out groaning by the burnt-out ashes and requiring immediate treatment.

Presently the light appeared again and began to descend. Its progress now seemed to be very erratic; for long intervals it would remain static then, in a rush, it would start to come down again. We sat on a log beside the path and waited. After a time heavy breathing began to reach us out of the darkness; someone stumbled and a voice said in annoyed tones: 'My friend, you vex me!' 'Ha, this is a heavy body,' said another voice and a groan followed. Then someone made a joke which we could not hear and there was a great burst of laughter.

We stepped quietly out on to the path. With a cry the first man nearly dropped the improvised stretcher he was carrying, but another voice cried out:

'Sir, we found them. All very badly burned, Sir, but we've tied them up very well!' and they swung past us down the path with a

BRINGING UP THE RUBBER BOAT

swagger in their gait indicating that they were pleased with themselves. As the stretcher passed me I saw lying on it, his eyes tight shut and with an air of conscious unconsciousness, Ali.

Now the light was coming down the path towards us followed by a bunch of people. The next group, too, carried a stretcher but it was empty. Its occupant strode along behind in interested conversation with his rescuers, a scrappy bandage balanced rakishly over one eye. We learnt very much later, from the student concerned, that he had handsomely bribed John Lukom (the Centre's mountain guide) to abandon the doubtful comfort of the stretcher and walk. Stoically behind them the white victim, captain of this mythical aircraft, was enduring the agonies of an inept fireman's lift. We were assured blithely that he was dead and long past feeling anything, indeed that it was they, the bearers of the burden, who were suffering too much under his weight. To his credit he accepted this interpretation of events without any sign of life.

Everyone else was in bed when we got back to the Centre, but Section 4, by now fully worked up to the part they were playing, were reluctant to let their patients go. Ali was laid out on one of the tables and I was shown with pride the improvised and rickety splints which held a broken leg in place. We were told, in a highly dramatic form, what they had all thought and felt on the climb up the hill and when they first saw the bodies lying round the fire.

'That hill was too steep,' said Simon. 'I thought I was going to die before we got to the top. And I am afraid! Very afraid! Jonathan comes very, very slowly with the light, so we hurry on. Every time I hear a noise I think this is some wild beast. I suffer, oh, I suffer. Still I believe it is true that there is an aeroplane up there and I want to help my people so I go on. Then we came to the top. Where is the fire? We look, look. No fire. Then we see it on the left hand; very low now, nearly all finished. Then I see two men lying still beside it and I think perhaps they are dead. So I go to find out. I find one man, he is John Lukom. Ha, I think. How is John Lukom in this aeroplane? I look again and there is Mr Fuller—so I know that the Principal has made this all up! We see that John is very badly burned and he cannot walk or talk, and we start to make a stretcher to bring him back.'

'And what about you?' I asked the very intelligent senior school teacher who was standing beside me and had not joined in the recital.

'I was afraid,' he said simply. 'The Mallam [he indicated a young Emir] and I were told to watch the bodies while the others went to look for wood for stretchers. It was very dark and we sat under a cassava tree, we were very afraid.'

'What were you afraid of?' I asked.

'Of leopards,' he replied.

They went off to bed with permission to sleep late in the morning when the other sections were up and about putting into practice their plans for dealing with disease, starvation and the rehousing of populations rendered homeless by fire. I did not envy them their plank beds but I do not doubt that they slept happily on them cushioned by a glow of self-satisfaction.

.   .   .   .   .

It was not until the twelfth course that we introduced the Smuggler's Evening. This was the first course that we had had for schoolboys and my husband and I were doubtful of their ability to respond to the many demands we made on them, demands which had been pioneered among men with some maturity and experience of life. In this we were proved wrong; the schoolboys not only responded magnificently but many of them have kept up a correspondence since which lets us know that they profited from the experience.

It was policy to keep the students very fully occupied. Their time at Man O' War Bay was so short, one month out of a lifetime, that every moment was valuable. We had discovered that to create and maintain a certain tempo spare time must be cut to a minimum. In the early days, when they would have an afternoon off to lie about or to go into Victoria, the atmosphere next morning would be sluggish and unwilling and it would take the whole day to reintroduce the alert, questing state in which new ideas and experiences were most readily assimilated. So we cut down the unoccupied time— and we had no complaints at all. It is the rule rather than the exception in Nigeria for a man to have a considerable amount of unoccupied leisure: to have every moment purposefully directed was a new and stimulating experience. But it was hard on the staff who had also to work sixteen hours a day, although at the end of the month they, too, had a week to recover in before they began again.

We had often thought about smugglers who were a reality on this part of the coast with two international frontiers—the French

Cameroons and the Spanish island of Fernando Po. I suspected that Ebenezer knew more about them than he would tell, for he had a varied history; he had worked for the Spanish, the French, the Germans and now the British, and his wife had a home somewhere over the border in French territory. Everything seemed to be smuggled: wine and cigarettes into British territory, cloth into French territory, food both ways, cooking utensils, hardware, crockery, it all went overland on the heads of the people concerned or slid round the coast and up the creeks in silent, black canoes. Occasionally we had a visit from the *Vigilant*, a small Customs gunboat, which came and cast anchor inside our bay, and some of her crew would come ashore and tell exciting tales of chases in their cutter, with muffled oars, up tiny creeks where larger boats could not go and how, brought to bay, a gun battle sometimes took place with the baffled smugglers. It was all very rousing and romantic to us and the sight of the *Vigilant* swinging quietly at anchor in the sunset would remind us of the men o' war who also hid here waiting to sally forth and intercept the slave traders and who gave the bay its name, and we would feel caught up in history, part of a world which had not yet stepped completely out of its past.

So, on a Saturday evening on the schoolboys' course, we decided to conjure up the smugglers.

FERNANDO PO

In the afternoon the boys were told that they were all going out on an exercise. They would go to a little promontory not very far from the big house where each section would clear a piece of jungle and build itself an improvised shelter. This hut would have to be well made for the section would spend the night in it (and it was now fairly late in the season with frequent thunderstorms). They would also cook their evening meal in the open, as would the staff, and afterwards there would be a campfire with songs and sketches from each team.

The boys were prepared to find anything fun, and they set off in the early afternoon armed with machetes, and various enamel bowls filled with their staple diet.

As soon as they had disappeared among the bananas we got busy. Ekechuku, our faithful Police Instructor, Maurice, the Able Seaman, Ali and one or two others gathered at our house. L/Cpl U. Ekechuku had come to us in 1951, one of the very first African instructors to be seconded to Man O' War Bay. He came from the Nigeria Police, Eastern Region, and neither he nor we knew then what the future had in store. One evening, before the season's courses started, a message came to my husband to say that the policeman we were expecting had arrived in the Cameroons and was awaiting instructions in the Police Barracks, Victoria. It was dark by the time we reached there and along the police lines fires were twinkling as the wives prepared the evening meal. We sat in the car while a messenger searched for L/Cpl Ekechuku, and we asked ourselves what he would be like. Much depended on him and on his ability to grasp the ideas behind the course.

Suddenly, out of the night, a figure materialized beside the car and, drawing itself up smartly, saluted.

'L/Cpl Ekechuku, Sir.'

He was a thickset man with an alert, responsible face, and it was obvious from his bearing that he had come prepared to begin the job straight away—whatever the hour of day or night. My husband opened the car door and asked him to get in so that we could talk for a little, then he began to tell this policeman, in some detail, what the qualities were that the work demanded of him. He must be prepared to devote all his time to the scheme; the morale of the students would be largely his responsibility and it would be his job to set the tone of the course. He would be constantly on duty and a high standard of conduct would be expected of him; he must be prepared to work with the students on tasks of manual labour, to swim with them, to climb the mountain with them. We could promise few rewards at this stage—for the scheme was still experimental— the only certainty about the future was that it contained hard work, and hard work, and more hard work.

My husband stopped and there was silence for a few seconds, then, out of the darkness, a quiet voice said:

'I am ready to work twenty-four hours a day, Sir. I won't let you down.'

He never did. After that first season Ekechuku returned to us again and again, an invaluable source of strength on the staff, steady, reliable, devoted.

Now a plan of action was made out whereby these men, led by my husband, would take a canoe, after dark, round through the bay and land just below the camping party. We collected together a lot of empty bottles with which to make a jingling noise to attract attention, and tied up one or two large and mysterious bundles. A young Education officer from England, who was to be on the cliff with the boys, guaranteed to start a rumour of smugglers and to give the alarm when he heard the canoe. I was to go out to the camp in the ordinary way for supper and fend off any enquiries as to the whereabouts of the Principal.

When the others had left to prepare themselves in suitable old clothes I got out our supply of black grease-paint and we transformed my husband into an arch villain, black from forehead to throat and with pink-palmed black hands. He wore long trousers and a battered old felt hat pulled very low over his blue eyes.

Ebenezer and Lucas when told that we were having dinner in the 'bush' did not wholly approve. Ebenezer, particularly, disapproved of changes of routine. He had the true old Nannie's spirit which felt that things should be done decently and in order and as befitted the dignity of his family. I fear we were often a sore trial to him. He clung, I think, with special persistence to the prim and rather pompous aspects of life because his own had been so very rakish and uncertain. It gave him a status and standing vis-à-vis the other employees at the Centre that were dear to him. Lucas, on the other hand, after initial disapproval, was prepared to be co-operative and he set to at once to make a lemon meringue pie, one of his specialities, to take out with us.

Ebenezer asked, rather sulkily, if he was expected to come too.

I said, 'Yes', feeling that it would be good for him to join in the fun and because I needed him to carry things out for me. It was not a success. He put on his best uniform, starched very stiffly, and refused to talk to me while we clambered over little ditches and under overhanging bushes. It was quite dark by now and our hurricane lamp kept getting caught up in the undergrowth and depriving us of light at critical moments.

When we began to get near the camp site, however, we heard a great deal of noise. Laughter and shouts, banging and crashing echoed around and the trees were lit up by a great fire which had been started in the middle of a cleared space. The boys had worked very hard. I stepped into an open piece of ground among huge trees: on either side huts of bamboo and palm thatch had miraculously appeared, stands had been built for cooking pots, each hut had its own small fire, and the sections had made efforts to outshine each other in do-it-yourself ingenuity. One had constructed a rack whereon we could hang our mackintoshes, another had specialized in a latrine carefully concealed in the bush. They greeted me with cries and laughter and vied to be the first to show me the results of their exertions.

'But where is the Principal?' they asked, obviously disappointed at his non-arrival.

'Oh, he got kept at the last moment. He'll be along presently,' I said, trying to make it sound convincing. In fact this was not very difficult as they all knew that my husband was desperately busy and was often called away by telephone calls or visitors.

Ebenezer was looking so disdainful and unhappy, afraid to sit down lest he spoil his best uniform, that I took pity on him and sent him home. I did not want my evening depressed by Ebenezer's constant glower! Then I went round and admired and criticized, sat on the benches, leant on the tables, peered through weak holes in the thatch and generally acted as the interested outsider.

While doing this I began to be aware that the camp had become uneasy. There were hisses of 'Shussssh', and one efficient (or nervous) soul began to turn out all the lamps. The sudden plunge into darkness, lit only by the flickering fires, was eerie and we were now all tense. I could see out of the corner of my eye two or three of the not-so-brave beginning to make for the shelter of the forest.

'What is it?' I asked. 'What's happening?'

White eyeballs gleamed in the firelight; a hoarse whisper said:

51

'I don't know, Ma, but they say smugglers are down below. Mr Williams has taken a party to see.'

'What do we do if they come here?'

'We are good men and they are bad men, they will not touch us,' replied a very smug youngster.

'What can we do? We have no weapons; we just give them everything,' said another. I had a feeling that everything included me as well.

However there were braver champions at the bottom of the cliff by now, for suddenly all hell broke loose. Cries and screams; the crash of breaking bottles and a voice saying ferociously: 'Why you no pay your customs? You bad man,' were followed by the sound of a heavy blow. This, I later discovered, was Amadu Ali, one of the smallest of the boys and one of the most gallant, attacking a supposed smuggler. I was beginning to wonder if all was going according to plan or if we had not under-estimated the courage of our young students. The noise was terrific.

Here on the cliffs eyes popped and I noticed that I began to collect a small crowd around me of those who wanted reassurance. Then bushes began to sway and snap and voices yelled in two or three languages. Obviously there was a proper fight going on. Presently, with a final shout, the bushes parted and a bedraggled team of boys dragged their prisoners triumphantly into the firelight. They had definitely proved themselves worthy citizens and upholders of the law for their victims had been very roughly handled. My husband's hat was pulled off and at the sight of his balding, sandy-haired head a gasp went up. Even then they could not quite believe it, but when he spoke for the first time (he had fought in silence for fear of giving himself away) a great wave of laughter broke out.

'The Principal!'

'Mr Ekechuku!'

'Able seaman!'

So they were all unmasked and we sat down round the blazing fires to eat our supper and conduct a post-mortem on the 'attack'.

Afterwards we sang. Each section put on a play, an activity at which they were very good, improvising and imitating with wit and skill. A favourite theme, which was enacted on nearly every course, was that of an Emir holding a council. Outside in the street a beggar is playing on a pipe a catchy, distracting little tune. The Emir becomes annoyed and sends out a messenger to tell the beggar to stop playing because he is disturbing the council.

The messenger comes out to the beggar and the following conversation (much adorned and elaborated) takes place:

'You there. You! What for you go vex us all with that music? You disturb the Emir too much. Go away.'

'What music, Master? What's that you say?'

'That music you go play-oh on that pipe.'

'Oh, you mean this . . .' At this point the beggar takes up his pipe and begins to play again the catchy little tune. The messenger's limbs start to twitch and wriggle, he gazes fascinated at the musician and gyrates faster and faster; caught up in it he cannot go away again.

Inside the Emir, annoyed at the non-return of his messenger and the continuance of the music, sends someone more important to get rid of the beggar. The same thing happens again. This goes on until the whole council is twitching and leaping in the road and the Emir, by now in a towering rage, is forced to come out himself to deal with this presumptuous musician. Of course he too is caught in the net and the scene ends with everyone dancing in a hypnotic trance around the beggar.

I never found out what the moral of this tale was meant to be or if, indeed, it had one. It seemed universal to Nigeria for sometimes a group of southern students would present it, in which case the Emir became a preacher in the midst of a long sermon.

Some of the boys had individual turns which they were prepared to perform. Lashat Lavan, a huge lad from the Plateau Province, was one of those. He sang an American Negro song, 'South Carolina':

> *South Carolina's sultry clime,*
> *We used to work in the summer time;*
> *Massa 'neath a tree would lay*
> *While we poor negroes toiled all day.*
>
> *So early in the morning. So early in the morning.*
> *So early in the morning before the break of day.*

He sang this with tremendous gusto and enjoyment and we all joined in the chorus. It did not occur to anyone to feel touchy or upset at singing a slave song. Indeed we used to tease the students, telling them that things had greatly changed and now it was 'massa' who worked all day while 'we poor Negroes' lay under the trees. They thought this a huge joke and agreed that there might even be a grain of truth in it. It is this strain of humorous realism and common sense that makes Nigerians such good friends and so rewarding to work with.

In the middle of all this the rain suddenly fell on us out of a clear sky. There was a wild scramble for shelter and capes and, as so many of the houses proved to have rather heavy leaks in their roofs, it was decided not to let the students spend the night out and we all filed back to the Centre, through dripping undergrowth, singing and laughing.

.   .   .   .   .

On an earlier course we had decided to enliven a not very exciting canoe trip by explaining to the students that they were pirates prospecting the creek to see if they could use it to make an attack on a village inland from it. They looked puzzled all through the explanation and at the end someone said:

'Please, Sir, what's a pirate?'

My husband tried to explain: a man who robbed on the sea; he appeared in pictures in gold earrings and a cloth round his head. Suddenly a voice said:

'Oh, a buccaneer!' There was a sigh of relief. 'Why didn't you say it was a buccaneer, Sir? We all know what buccaneers are!'

In due course they all appeared, splendidly attired with whatever piratical costume they could think up, led by Sgt Atanda in a striped pyjama jacket with an enormous cloth wound turbanwise about his handsome head. It was moments like these, found incomprehensible and childish by many of our own compatriots, which forged between us and our students a bond of affection which has stood the test of time. Shared fun makes men forget what colour or race they are and returns them to an innocence which takes no account of these things. So, Ibo and Yoruba, Efik and Pagan, European, Ijaw and Tiv, I watched them march off singing to engage in an adventure in which all of them shared a heightened sense of life.

Not all the adventures were wholly fun, some carried with them lessons learned the hard way. On one afternoon on each course the sections alternated between four different exercises, each one designed as a test in enterprise, initiative, the ability to lead and also to follow. This time they knew that the hazards and accidents they were asked to deal with were not genuine and the whole operation was timed and carefully watched by the staff who afterwards criticized the performances. Because the staff was stretched to its utmost in the arranging and supervising of all these activities and in seeing that each section was where it should be when it should be, I was brought in to help.

After lunch, in the blazing heat of midday, I took a ball of string and made my way with L/Cpl Ekechuku to the pathway that led down to the jetty. This ran through a deep gully with high banks crowned with thick bushes and overhung by heavy tangled trees. Here Ekechuku and I tied the end of the string to a sturdy bush at the top of the path where it entered the gully and led it in devious ways down one side, across the rutted way, up the steep opposite bank and into the undergrowth. Round trees and bushes we went, across the gully again and abruptly up the other side by way of a palm tree; eventually leading the string to an open space where it climbed into the branches of a small fruit tree and, coming down the other side, came to a stop round the bole of a large royal palm.

We had laid the trail and, ascertaining that it was firmly held all along its length, we went back to the beginning to wait our victims.

When they came, twelve or so to a section, Ekechuku and I blindfolded them quickly. For this we used the First Aid triangular bandages, now for practical reasons relegated to other jobs. When all were blindfolded and joined in a long line each man's left hand on the shoulder of the man in front of him, his right hand free to grasp the string, I made them a little speech:

'There are very many blind in Nigeria. Some of those need not be blind if they are given proper care and attention in time. We talk often about this problem and what an enterprising young man can do to help not only to prevent many people suffering like this but also to make life easier for those already blind. But however much we talk it is difficult to realize what life is, in fact, like for these people and so, perhaps, we don't see how necessary our help is. Now for a short time you are going to be blind; you are going to make a journey without the help of your eyes following this piece of string that I've put into your right hands. You'll find that you are very dependent on the friend in front for help and warning, and maybe when we next talk about blindness we'll all have a better idea what it means.'

Then we launched them on the trail.

Reactions varied greatly. Sometimes a team would have a first-class leader who, concerning himself for his men, would call back warnings and instructions and, on hearing a despairing cry of: 'My friend, where are you?' would stop and encourage the laggard; such a team when they came to the major obstacle of the tree would assist each other to climb through its branches, quite a frightening operation when a sense of height has been removed by lack of sight, by cries and calls. Very rarely there was a leader who, having climbed through the tree himself and found the string at the other side, came back round the foot to his followers and enabled them, by leading them directly to the outgoing string, to circumvent the tree altogether. But there were other teams where the leader, more concerned with his own prowess than that of his unit, forged ahead oblivious to the wails behind him; sometimes the cleverer members would pass the slow-coaches with a scornful word and press forward on their own. One lad, the owner of outsize feet which tripped him up on every occasion, was practically reduced to tears by the heartlessness of his fellows. On the other hand there were often surprising and touching demonstrations of helpfulness on the part of men whom one would not have credited with much kindness of heart.

It was with a pleasurable feeling of omnipotence that I handed out marks afterwards, enabled for once to see that virtue was suitably rewarded and that kindliness and a helping hand rated higher than brilliant individual deduction or a personal turn of speed!

THE BLINDFOLD TRAIL

CHAPTER III

Weaving

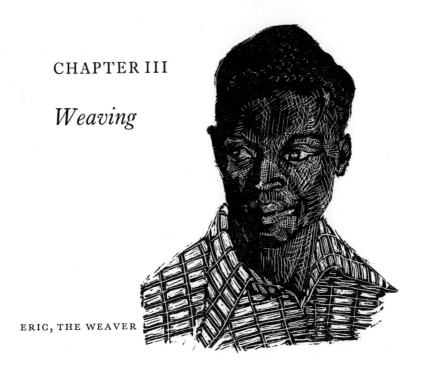

ERIC, THE WEAVER

I CAME to teach weaving almost by accident. From the beginning
it was felt that some time should be found in the programme for a
craft. Not that it would be possible to give the students any kind
of mastery in the few hours which would be all that they could
give to it, among the pressure of other activities, but there were
several reasons why we felt this kind of lesson to be valuable.

To most young Nigerians, especially the up-and-coming young
men that we hoped would be sent to us for training, the idea that a
man could produce something with his own hands was outdated and
old-fashioned. They themselves had achieved freedom from all
kinds of manual labour by virtue of being educated and they tended
to despise others who had not done likewise. To contend that a man
who worked with his hands on a skilled job might be as clever as a
man who sat on a stool in an office was ridiculous to them, and both
parents and teachers would discourage any youngster who showed
an aptitude for manual dexterity by making him feel that such
work was inferior to any white-collar job, however insignificant.
This was not an attitude confined to Nigeria, most nations have
gone through it and many still suffer from it. It can, however,

have disastrous effects; old skills die out and when a new nation comes into its own and wishes to point with pride to the things which are recognized everywhere as the outward marks of civilization, its arts and crafts, they are gone. Gone also the skilled fingers which might turn to new crafts, in industry, in printing, in architecture, and a time of hiatus and difficulty ensues before the sense of values is again adjusted to recognize that men have different gifts and that the skilled craftsman or devoted, experienced worker with his hands has as big a contribution to make to his country as the clerk or the student.

We hoped to be able to show our young men, many of whom were teachers, that a craft could be an exacting and skilled job which required intelligence and cleverness. If they already came from areas where weaving was practised we might be able to produce a forward-looking public opinion about it which would lead to new ideas being introduced instead of the gradual disappearance of the craft: for teachers we could demonstrate a new handcraft for their schools which might help to balance, in a small way, the heavily academic bias: and for the students themselves it was a good thing that in a course full of physical activity and bustle there should be moments when they sat down to a job that required peace, concentration and a delicate touch.

We acquired a large footloom and a first-class weaver, an Efik from a part of the Eastern Region which was famous for its cloths. Eric was peculiar in that he was a male weaver, for in his area of Aquete it was the women who made the cloths. He had been despised by his family for wishing to follow his mother and sisters, but he had persisted and eventually gone to the only weavers' Training Centre in the Region at that time.

He wove beautifully. Unfortunately he was not a good teacher and his own early experience as a man learning a woman's craft had made him uncertain about teaching other men, particularly men who had no special desire to learn and were boisterous and out-spoken in their objections. The first lessons were a disaster; in a class of twenty or so it was impossible to keep the attention of nineteen while the twentieth had a lesson on the loom; the fascinating intricacies of pattern-making and threading up were beyond the unskilled and uninterested without some weeks of patient prepara-tion, and Eric himself was too gentle and hesitant to be able to hold their interest.

I went to the lessons because I knew something of weaving and had experimented myself with looms and the making of cloth, but I had never taught, and compared to Eric as a weaver I was the merest amateur. When the course finished Eric himself was in despair and my husband said to me:

'Do you think you could do it? Eric can help you and he will do the demonstrating if only you could arrange the lessons and do the talking.'

I did not think I could, but I could not bear to think of failure so early, particularly in a subject with which I was familiar, so I said, 'Yes'.

Now I had to begin to think how to do it. It was obvious that we were aiming far too high. We had said that we were not trying to turn out weavers but what we had been trying to teach was what we would, in fact, have taught professionals. It was essential that every man be occupied all the time and this was impossible on one big loom which they could never master in the four or five lessons at our disposal. I remembered my own beginnings on a small wooden frame on which I had quickly been able to turn out mats, bags and other little articles and where the basic principles resembled exactly those of the larger, more complicated looms. If each man had one of those then he would have something on which he could test his own skill and if he liked to take it away with him afterwards, that too was possible. I thought of constructing sixty such frames before the next course and quailed. Then my husband said:

'But, of course, they will make their own. What's the good of being surrounded by bamboo and all kinds of wood if they don't use them?'

So, in the first period devoted to weaving in the next course, I faced my pupils. My throat was dry and I was very nervous. I had asked for L/Cpl Ekechuku to be present feeling that I might need more robust physical support than Eric could give me. I had no idea what lay before me—beyond thirty varying black faces round the tables—but I had learnt a little of shock tactics and how to create an atmosphere of expectancy from watching my husband and his colleagues and I had one great advantage denied to them. I was a woman. So my students, for one or two of whom I was the first white woman with whom they had come into close contact, were prepared to find me interesting, and their innate courtesy gave me plenty of time to get my arguments in first.

In the event the new methods proved a success, but perhaps for all of us, for me as well as for them, the real value of those periods spent quietly wrestling with the intricacies of fine cotton thread was that they enabled us to become acquainted, and many problems and personal difficulties were put before me while I corrected the tangles in a warp which I might otherwise never have known anything about.

Meantime my opening gambit was to ask those who came from an area in which weaving was done to put up their hands. There were always some, for it is a fairly widespread craft in Nigeria. Then I found out who the weavers were in different districts; from Southern Nigeria it was mostly women, but in the North it could be men, or in some cases men and women sharing the work equally. This at once silenced the grumblers who found that they had not merely to contend with me, introducing a foreign idea, but with some of their own countrymen for whom the idea was age-old. I would talk a little about the craft of weaving, not just on hand looms but also on power looms in modern factories.

At this point, when they were beginning to nod a little, I said:

'All right, now *you* are going to weave. But you're going to make your own looms first. Has everybody got his machete? All right, away we go!'

And away we went, along the path at the top of the cliffs to a spot where there were plenty of suitable trees. Here we dispersed and the promontory began to ring to the snapping of branches and the crashing of trees where some enterprising young man, seeing a suitable length at the very top, felled the whole tree to get at it.

Some of them made very bad looms; but some made very good ones. It is astonishing what a strong pull there is on the smallest warp and some superficially good constructions were shown up after a few days as a seemingly sturdy rectangle gradually became rhomboid. Some who excelled at more strenuous activities were baffled to find that their fingers would not obey them in a delicate operation; others discovered an extension of their talents and became fascinated by their own ability to make an article where nothing had been before. One said proudly to me one afternoon:

'I'm weaving myself a football jersey, Madam!'

Once, in the middle of a class, I was asked by the spokesman of a group:

'How much did Mr Dickson pay for you, Madam?'

I was taken aback, but it was obviously a serious question and they were interested in the answer. Bride price was very topical at this moment and there had been many articles about it in the national newspapers.

'Nothing,' I said.

'Nothing!' They could not believe it. I was a very good bargain; look at all the things I could do! How had he managed it?

'Ah,' said Eugene at last. 'But Government pays him extra because you teach. This is very useful to the Principal.'

'No,' I said, 'I teach because I enjoy it, but we don't get any extra money.'

'Well, how is this?' they asked. 'Does nobody in your country pay bride price? Does a young man not give his wife's parents anything for her?'

'On the contrary,' I assured them. 'Not so very long ago it was the wife who was expected to bring some money with her to her husband.'

They let out hisses of approval at this; that was the proper way to do things. We had then a long and very interesting discussion on each other's marriage customs which was revealing for both of us. I was interested to discover that it was the women who were the strongest opponents of the abolition of bride price. They did not, as I had supposed, regard it as a shameful form of slave buying, but as a solid safeguard to the good behaviour of their future husband. Later a very intelligent woman said to me:

'If they have paid highly for us they value us accordingly and will not lightly throw us away. We must retain this until the Christian values in marriage are properly established in my country, otherwise we have no security at all.'

After a class one day Saidu followed me over to our bungalow and said that he had something to ask me.

'Can I help, Saidu?' I said, as he seemed to be finding it difficult to begin. He was a small man from a remote district of Northern Nigeria whose second language was not English (as was the case with the Southerners) but Hausa.

'Please,' he said, 'I have something to ask. This is the first time I come out of my own country and I see many wonderful things. I see that most white men are bigger than my people are. I think this is because of the food they eat and I see that they do not eat the same food as we do. Madam, I have one son. I wish him to be strong and big. Perhaps if I give him the same food as your people this will make him grow. Will you tell me what I should give him?'

I was touched by his faith in me, but also perturbed. It was quite likely that, whatever he ate, Saidu junior would be small like his father, and indeed all his people. Nevertheless I felt that possibly he could be helped to more inches with a judicious extra diet; anyway, no harm would be done and maybe a great deal of good. But it was not easy, I had to recommend foods which were available and, at the same time, have mercy on Saidu junior's stomach which was unused to the diet of the whites. Together we worked out a possible régime taking in eggs, fruit and vegetables, all of which were rarely, if ever, eaten.

Saidu thanked me very much, but he continued to stand on my verandah; obviously something still worried him.

'But, Madam, there is another thing.' He hesitated. 'It is my wife. The mother of my son. She is not educated. She does not understand these new ideas. When I go back and explain this to her she will not agree. She will do it when I am there, but when I am not there she will give him our old food. What can I do?'

This is a real problem and I found it difficult to give any helpful advice. After talking platitudes for a few moments I was stopped by Saidu. He looked at me and went straight to the heart of his difficulty.

'Should I beat her, Madam?' he asked.

The rapidity of development taking place in Nigeria, the whole-sale reversal in some cases of age-old traditions, made very personal problems for almost all of our students and this one of a man growing away from the habits and beliefs of his family was often brought to me for discussion. The Muslim students from the North, in particular, found themselves in a difficult situation. It would happen that I would get into conversation with a young Ibrahim or Mustapha and would begin to ask him about his home and his village. Very frequently I would be astounded to find that he was already the husband of two, perhaps three, wives, and the father of several children. I might be told that his first wife had been chosen for him by his family when he was very small; the second, when he came to the age of thirteen or fourteen, was to cement some intertribal relationship, 'but the third,' he would say, 'I chose for myself when I grew up'. Now, however, there were complications. He himself had gone on from school to training college, maybe to politics; he had left his village and his old ways and had discovered that other men lived differently. It was not his faith that he doubted, or the rightness of polygamy, but circumstances were making it inexpedient. Only one wife was acceptable at the functions which he now attended; one wife he could perhaps educate and take around with him as other men did, but two or three—no. He had seen on his travels marriages of a different sort, and from the questions which I was so often asked I think that many of them must have found our marriage something to wonder at; what was the answer? To cast off any of the wives was unthinkable, they would be utterly lost and destitute; this would be immoral and cruel.

'I cannot tell them to go away, Madam,' I remember one young man saying to me. 'They are my responsibility, and what could they do?'

I found no solution, but the same young man gave one of the answers himself.

'I have decided,' he said, 'that I will not arrange marriages for my sons as my father did for me. I will leave them to grow up and then I will tell them about these problems and they must decide for themselves. At least they will not find that I have married them when they are small so they cannot change it.'

The results of my weaving class in terms of cloth were certainly small. Some students never even mastered the simple basic principles while the brightest had no time to get further than the first stages. But it was in this class, in the peace of a shared pursuit, that I really began to get to know these young men and friendship and understanding grew between us. And it was very often during these hours, while I was sitting beside them wrestling with tangled warps, that questions of great interest and importance were mentioned casually between us, and once mentioned freely discussed.

DUSK, VICTORIA AND THE CAMEROON MOUNTAINS

CHAPTER IV

The Mountain

To a large extent Mount Cameroon dominated all our lives as,
on clear days, it dominated the inland landscape. Not physically
impressive, lying like a great stranded whale up the centre of the
slender territory, it was deceptive in its bulk giving no indication
of its great height, 13,350 ft. For much of the time it was invisible,
brooding behind a haze of heat or grey veils of rain, but we always
knew it was there; at its reappearance after many days in the new
clarity of very early morning a student, or Ebenezer, would appear
on my verandah saying:

'Madam, Mr Dickson says to look at the mountain.'

I would stop whatever I was doing and rush out on to the games
field to catch a glimpse of the great barrier floating in the clouds
high above the banana plantation, tinged an ethereal pink in the

rising sun: or blue, maybe, the heart-catching blue that comes from an atmosphere washed in recent rain.

At the seaward end of the gigantic mass rose the pointed beauty of the Little Cameroon, its outline faintly fretted by the forests that climbed right to the top. The Little Cameroon presented to the outward eye the perfect mystical symbol of a mountain, tapering gently up from its base to a small conical summit; indeed this point was what every mountain-top should be, a square of open ground some yards each way balanced seemingly on the highest branches of the trees which moved around it and fell steeply on either side into impenetrable ravines. It was a difficult mountain to climb, its sides being deeply intersected by gullies and ridges, all thickly forested, which made the finding of any path to the top exhausting and hard. By comparison the greater mountain with its recognized route and climber's huts, and its clear, open higher reaches, requiring no great skill to overcome, seemed to hold no terrors. Nevertheless it was Mount Cameroon itself which filled our minds; it was Mount Cameroon which was haunted by the 'Half Man', a spirit much feared by all the local people. Mount Cameroon affected us personally during our five years at its foot, brooding, enormous, amorphous, it was often unseen but always felt.

For the students the knowledge that the climb of the mountain lay between them and their return home cast a shadow across the course. They, too, on clear days, would crowd to the windows to gaze on it, their expressive faces mirroring clearly their feelings; doubt and anxiety generally but sometimes determination. Even the outwardly sophisticated nursed a deep feeling of apprehension: the spirits might not be the spirits of their tribe or community but doubts remained. Might it not be true, after all, that the highest slopes were white with human bones? Who knew whether the spirits would discriminate between a Nigerian and a Cameroonian? The material props to life change very rapidly and adaptation is a matter of the mind; the mechanical toys of other nations are quickly mastered by any people and Nigerians, in particular, bring a great zest and enthusiasm to this game, but the things of the heart, the thoughts of the souls of men, are much slower to change and much more hesitant about acceptance or rejection of strange spiritual beliefs.

Yet this particular mountain had no apparent physical dangers to occasion such fears. No precipices or cliffs hung over dizzy depths, no towering peaks glittered forbiddingly with ice or snow. The slopes, forested to about a third of their height, seemed from the base gentle and open. They were not, in fact, so gentle; much labour and sweat was needed to scale them. It was however a snobbery among the young and still adventurous British to have climbed the mountain: there was even a record established of something like eight hours up and back from Buea, the Government Station at 3,000 ft. A beer bottle, or rather several beer bottles, buried in the ground at the top held the names of all those who had satisfied themselves by getting there; and in the third hut (German built—British neglected) there was a kind of visitors' book, an extension of the system of books housed in sentry boxes at the doors of senior officers in colonial territories, in which one could make it plain to all coming after that one had called on the mountain.

Two names, however, were not contained in this book or in these bottles, the two most distinguished conquerors of Mount Cameroon, Richard Burton and Mary Kingsley.

It was always surprising to think that Richard Burton had been the first European to get to the top of our mountain, for his fame and his name were both made in the Middle East, which he always preferred to Africa, a country he disliked and whose inhabitants he despised.

Early in December 1861 Burton, with a party which included Alfred Saker, famous leader of the Baptist Mission, and Gustav Mann, a native of Brunswick and a gardener from the Royal Gardens at Kew, left Victoria for the mountain. We were very familiar with the name Mann's Spring, an area on the seaward flank of the mountain where there was the only source of water and good pastureland, which the Veterinary Department was trying to develop as a cattle ranch. Here Burton and Saker had visualized a sanatorium where sufferers from malaria and exhausted missionaries could recuperate in the clear air of the mountain. But ninety years later the only approach to Mann's Spring was still a difficult climb on foot, undertaken from time to time by the wife of the officer in charge of the ranch, her baby carried in a basket on the head of one of her porters. We had sometimes thought of climbing the mountain with the students by this route as a change from the recognized and straightforward path which led up from Buea, but circumstances and the large détour involved, over country much less well known than the other, deterred us.

Mann had gone on before the main party to prepare camp at the

Spring and to recruit carriers for the climbers. The whole expedition was a very much more arduous undertaking than it later became and the party were away for three or four weeks. They had difficulty in getting porters and were asked a large sum of money by a Bakweri village through which they passed for permission to ascend the mountain—£500. This Burton refused although Mann, who visualized a more permanent relationship with the Bakweri and the mountain than Burton was likely to have, would have preferred to have given some sort of present. In the event, although it meant that their loads had to go up in shifts because of a shortage of manpower, the refusal had no disastrous consequences. The Bakweri had taken a sporting chance and they were not too surprised when it did not come off.

The day came when the whole party were encamped within reasonable distance of the main peak and Burton took advantage of an opportunity to climb it alone while the others were occupied with scientific observations or, in the case of his immediate companion, suffering from a sprained ankle. He admits that 'there was perhaps a little malice in my wish to win', and he thought himself to be the first man to stand upon the summit, certainly the first European. He does not tell how his companions reacted to his stealing a march on them: maybe there was less competition for the honour of defeating unknown peaks in those days than there is now.

He heaped up a cairn and put a fragment of *Punch* in it. Later on, when the party ascended as a group, they hoisted the Union Jack, drank a bottle of champagne and left two sixpences in an empty bottle!

Burton talks a lot about snow on Mount Cameroon and appears to have no doubt at all that there were times when the top was white. He says of this snow, 'from May to July and from September to October the appearance is common, at other times rare', and cites two instances: Saker and Mann in February 1860 saw the peak white from Victoria and in the same month in 1862 a Captain Perry of H.M.S. *Griffon* saw the peak all covered with snow. Albert Calvert, also, writing in 1914 about the mountain, says 'hoar frost is frequent and snow fairly so'. The climate may have changed since the 1860s but certainly in the 1950s there was never any question of the mountain having snow on it. We often discussed Burton's views and, once or twice, we ourselves saw a pure white blanket spilling over the top which nevertheless turned out to be only mist.

We had exciting evidence, however, that he was correct when he said Mount Cameroon was the 'only mountain on the continent whose fires are not extinguished'. There had been an eruption in 1923 which occasioned alarm in Buea. The lava stream had, in fact, gone down the seaward slope cutting a swath through the forest, and the petrified black river still lay like an angry scar from the crater to the shore. Though we used to joke about another eruption we did not take it very seriously and were therefore astonished when, one morning in 1954, we saw the mountain smoking. At first it seemed possible that this might be due to fires started by hunters, but as the smoke continued to ascend steadily and in increasing volume, news spread that the mountain was once more alive. Those who lived on its slopes began to eye their possessions and calculate how best they might be moved in a hurry: we, who lived on the seashore, took a more academic interest in the phenomenon, feeling that we should have plenty of warning if catastrophe were to occur. So perhaps thought the inhabitants of Pompeii! In the event we were luckier than they; the mountain smoked for some days and at night a faint glow was visible in the sky above it, but after a while the smoke decreased, then died away, and life went on unheeding until the next time.

The other climber was a very sympathetic one. Mary Kingsley reached the top of Mount Cameroon in September 1895, in the last fury of the rainy season. She reached it alone, having found it impossible to persuade her porters to accompany her on the last lap of the journey, and though she found bottles there, left by German officers, she did not touch them but put her visiting card among the rocks on the cairn, 'as a civility'.

The climb took her a week, five nights of which were spent on the open mountain. The huts which the Germans built to assist climbers must have been after her time for she makes no mention of them. She had to walk from sea level, indeed from the sea twenty-three miles away, in torrential rain. She started up the 'magnificent' new Government road holding up an umbrella and trying to keep her heavily braided skirts out of the mud. After five minutes, however, she was anathematizing the road, 'of all truely awful things to walk on, that road, when I was on it, was the worst'. It was barely begun then; half a century later it was tarmac all the way to Buea, 3,000 feet up on the side of the mountain, and we always did this part of the journey on wheels. But there were still moments when we felt about it as she had: of all the awful roads to drive on this road, and its extension up into Nigeria, was the worst.

The umbrella did not last very long. The road extended only a few miles and shortly after they had plunged into the bush there was a stream to be crossed. Mary Kingsley, seeing that it was not her fate to be dry, solemnly folded up the umbrella, handed it to her boy, and waded across. Thereafter she speaks occasionally of having to stop and wring out the hem of her skirts because the damp weight impeded her, and it seems probable that she was never again really dry till she returned to Victoria eight days later. She refused the offer of a hot bath at Buea because there were no doors to the house, only curtains, and she felt it unsuitable to bathe with so little protection.

What is so astonishing is not her courage nor her physical endurance but her enormous and evident enjoyment. She felt at home here in a way that she never did in Europe, and no accident or incident could upset her pleasure.

On the first·day above Buea the cook gave notice after an hour. 'What cook would not?' she remarks. Camping in the forest that evening, in pouring rain, she had to show her men how to make a fire in wet weather. They had become completely demoralized by the nightmare in which they were living and the disconcerting revelation that this woman just did not intend to be turned from her objective. When next day it was discovered that there was not enough water in the loads and no more to be had on the mountain (though it continued to rain with unabated vigour), she was convinced that this had been arranged on purpose to turn her back. This she had no intention of doing, and she spent the day exploring the great rock face above the forest belt while a reliable messenger went back to Buea with a note to the German officer there requesting that more water be sent up to her. She tried to get one of her boys to come with her on her exploration but to her request he replied: 'Softly, softly still hurts the snail,' so she left him.

After a difficult day in which she lost all the boys and eventually found them again only to discover that the cook (still with her) had sent all the food down to Buea to be cooked, she twice, that night, fell into the fire and but for the extreme dampness of her clothing and gallant rescue by one of the boys would have been badly burned. The next night her blanket stuck to a sun blister on one cheek and starting up suddenly at the onset of a terrible storm she tore off all the skin. To anyone else this would have been a major disaster, and such an injury would almost certainly have gone septic and caused a great deal of trouble; but we never hear of it again, and there is no indication at all that it caused Mary to alter one iota of her plans. It is to the credit of her porters that they did in fact stay with her in such unfavourable circumstances, and that, every evening, when they had her safely in camp and out of mischief, a fire started and some hot food inside them, they became exceedingly cheerful, singing and telling tales of their own heroism and the cowardice of their friends down below.

It is a little sad to think that when, on September 26th, she eventually reached the summit it was shrouded in mist and a hurricane was raging. She herself was disgusted, and said she felt no exultation at reaching the top but only annoyance that she could not see the view and the unexplored mountain range behind Calabar. However she never repined and having left the visiting card as a fleeting reminder of her call she turned round and came down again.

Coming down was much quicker, on the whole, but no easier than going up. Mary came down a good deal of the way on her back and again it seems extraordinary that she broke no bones. Nowadays only the most foolhardy, and they in the face of deep official disapproval, would consider climbing the mountain in such a season and under such circumstances.

I made my personal call on the mountain very early in my life in Africa and in a fashion which I never forgot. At this time I was not married but was prospecting both Africa and my future husband to see whether I could live with both of them. I was staying in Buea in the guest room of the Basel Mission, where Ali brought my morning tea and boiled my hot water in a kerosene tin just outside my door every dawn.

It was on a Saturday afternoon in February 1951 that the weekly passenger plane from Douala to Paris crashed on Mount Cameroon, although it was not until much later in the evening that we knew that it was even missing. And even then the news was only that it had failed to reach Abidjan and no one knew what had become of it. The weekend is no time for a crisis in a British territory; impossible that sports, siestas or bridge should be disturbed.

On Sunday morning, while I waited in his house, Alec went down to the police station to find out if there was any news of the aeroplane.

It was a lovely morning. Behind the house the mountain rose, russet pink, into a pale blue sky. It was impossible to think that up there might be death and destruction.

I heard the car coming up the hill and knew from the way it was being driven that there was news—bad news; it sounded agitated and breathless.

The 'boys', Andrew, Ali and David, came out too as it drew up to hear the report.

'It's on the mountain. A hunter brought down news this morning that he had seen a great fire. A small party of African police are going up but no one else. The bigger party won't be ready till tomorrow. They say everybody is dead, but the hunter admits he was afraid to go near so we can't really know. I hate to think of women, perhaps badly hurt and wanting to speak to someone in their own language, having no one but six young policemen. I've asked permission to go. Will you come?'

It had not occurred to me while listening to him that I would be asked to go too, and I am sure that it had not occurred to authority. But I had been an emergency nurse during the war, a junior skivvy concerned mainly with washing and cleaning, and I could not refuse.

'Yes,' I said, and hoped for the best.

But I wondered, and wonder still, why no Senior Police Officer accompanied the constables, for whom the mountain in itself, without the fear and horror of death at the top, was a considerable ordeal. And why it was so difficult to find any responsible British official concerned enough to give us permission to go. One was asleep and could not be wakened; one was playing tennis and could not be disturbed; one was engaged in a pre-lunch party and was not interested. But he was anxious to be rid of us so he said we could go and turned back to his guests.

We went into the kitchen and told Andrew that the Sunday lunch would not now be needed; would he come with us, we asked? That went for David and Ali too. To their great credit they began at once to get ready. Andrew was old and crabbed and had probably never climbed a mountain before; David was young, gangling and timid. Only Ali, slow-witted but faithful and fearless, knew something of mountains.

It seemed unreal to be stripping the beds and making up three emergency bundles in the blankets for the boys to carry on their heads while the Station slumbered round us in Sabbath sunshine. Up there people lay either dead or dying; in Douala the French prepared to fly in a rescue party, but here no one seemed interested or concerned save with the niceties of diplomatic protocol: who should meet the French at the airport and had Lagos been informed. Did no one of our own colour feel impelled to go and help, I wondered. In this I maligned my own people for, though I did not know it until two days later, down in Victoria the young employees of the Development Corporation were getting together a rescue party as well equipped as possible. When they arrived up at Buea some hours later they were told that their help was not required. Enough was being done. Six young policemen had left to go up— and the two of us.

And Andrew, David and Ali. They carried the headloads, the blankets into which had gone water bottles, some food (principally bread and bananas), warm jerseys, a bottle of whisky, a flashlight and what medical supplies we could rake up at short notice on a Sunday. They were theatrically inadequate when we considered what we might find on the mountain: a pot of vaseline, some Elastoplast, an old sheet for tearing into bandages, aspirin. I had on one of my nicer cotton frocks and a pair of light shoes but in the urgency of getting away there seemed to be no time to go back to the Mission to change. It was about twelve o'clock and we had seven thousand feet to climb.

The plane had crashed on a far shoulder of the mountain, away from all recognized paths, so it was not going to be simple to reach it. We must have a guide and he could only be found in a village called Bonakanda, the home village of the hunter who had reported the fire. It lay about one and a half hours' walk along the foot of the mountain and after that we might have about four hours' climb. Already the police had been away one hour in front of us, so we must go fast if we were to catch up with them. But first we must go to the local Chief and ask his advice about guides and routes and tell him what we were doing.

After we had hammered on his door for some moments in the sultry quiet of midday, Chief Endeli came to open it himself. With courtesy and an expansive gesture he ushered us into his sitting room where we explained why we had come. Here we had a piece of good luck. In this house, at this very moment, was the hunter who had seen the crash. Chief Endeli instructed him to go back up the mountain again and lead us to the aeroplane, and he accepted this with no sign of emotion.

All this while the day had been getting hotter and darker and suddenly, with a terrific crash, a tornado burst over the mountain. The heavens opened and the rain poured down in a solid silver sheet. It was impossible to start out in such weather and for one hour, trying not to think what conditions must be like seven thousand feet above us, we sat and listened to the rolling thunder outside and the endless repetition of the Chief's favourite gramophone record, the 'Cuckoo Waltz', within.

As suddenly as it had begun the rain stopped and the sun came out. Steam rose in clouds off the heating earth and vegetation. We said goodbye and set out. Andrew, David and Ali put their loads on their heads, the guide went off in front at a fast walk and we straggled out behind him in a long line. The air was fresh and sparkling; on our left the mountain rose, its top concealed from us by the dense tropical forest which we were skirting; on our right the land fell away three thousand feet to the sea, and far down on the horizon we could see the faint glimmer of the municipal buildings in Douala, beyond the frontier in the French Cameroons. We went as fast as we could, for it was already late to be starting on a mountain climb

VILLAGE ON THE SLOPES OF THE MOUNTAIN

and in our minds were unspoken thoughts about the difficulties of caring for desperately burned human beings, in darkness, on open volcanic rock.

So we made Bonakanda in one hour, sweating and stumbling for neither of us was in training for such expeditions, and already I regretted not having changed my Sunday shoes. Andrew, too, was showing signs of wear, and David, suspecting now that we should almost certainly have to sleep on the mountain, was becoming very nervous. Only Ali plodded on tireless and undisturbed.

At Bonakanda we found the police. They, too, were getting nervous and, through some oversight, had forgotten to bring any sort of lamp. A small crowd of chattering villagers was reassuring them with all the old tales of mountain ghosts.

Aware that we would be unmoved by fear of ghosts the police tried to dissuade us from going farther that day by assuring us that elephant had been seen in large numbers across the path which we must travel and that they were very dangerous. Anger now flared up in Alec. It seemed that no one at all cared what sort of conditions the victims of this disaster faced; each man wanted only to be left to his own comfort, to help yes, but in his own time and in the easiest fashion. Something of this he told the police then and there; it left them unaffected morally but when they saw that we intended to go on and that I, a woman, was prepared to face both ghosts and elephants they recognized that here were people who needed their help immediately, so they cheerfully borrowed some lamps and got ready to come with us. I did not tell them how very afraid I was of both elephants and ghosts, and most of all of what we should find when we reached the aircraft.

Now it was real jungle and we began to climb straight up from the village through dripping, tangled bushes and trees. The path was narrow and slippery with decaying vegetation after the rain. We could see only a few feet in front or behind; it would have been perfectly possible to walk round a corner into an elephant. Alec and I climbed in silence, reserving all our strength, but the Africans sang and shouted to keep off the ghouls and reassure their own troubled minds. Whenever I slipped, which I did very often for my light Sunday shoes had not been made for this kind of work, a voice behind me would say: 'Sorry too much,' and the faithful Ali put out a helping hand. Up and up and up. The undergrowth cleared and the great jungle trees took over, towering up two hundred feet, shutting out the sky. Even the Africans were silent here, overawed by the queer cathedral twilight.

After an hour we sat down to rest and have some food. Here we discovered that Andrew was not with us—and neither was his headload. As it had contained most of the food this loss was a blow. Still, we had bananas and water and all the medical supplies. Andrew would be afraid on his own in the forest, but the path back to Bonakanda was clear and well defined and we had no doubt that he would arrive safely.

On and on and on. Now the trees gave way to open hillside, grassland interspersed with rock. Here we began to be joined by Bakweri hunters, fierce wild men who roamed the mountain and were not afraid of it. They looked at us with open curiosity and contempt so that we felt glad of the cheerful, solid police who had now quite regained their normal spirits. They trusted that the presence of two Europeans was sufficient insurance against the appearance of ghosts, and we were aware their robust physical strength was well worth having at hand now that we were wearying and the mountain growing wilder and more inhospitable. Now, too, the cold began to strike. When we sat down to rest, as we had to do at more and more frequent intervals, the sweat would quickly dry and evaporate and a deadly chill penetrate our bones. It was getting dusk and David had not been seen for a long time. David carried our warm socks and jerseys, so his disappearance was serious. But Ali, resourceful in such emergencies, borrowed a cloak from one of the police (who willingly gave it up) and wrapped me in its thick serge folds.

It was about now, with dark creeping on and the mountain getting wilder and more rocky, that Alec and I began to face the implications of the climb. What were we going to do when, in a very short time from now, we perhaps found ourselves faced by dead or dying or desperately wounded men and women? In gasping breaths I began to say over and over again the Lord's Prayer—in French. It was an inaccurate, ungraceful translation which never seemed to get beyond the first few petitions, but it comforted me.

It was quite dark when we arrived. The ground flattened out and the police hurricane lamps glimmered and flickered on high outcrops of lava rock. It was not difficult to find the aeroplane, though it would not have been recognizable in normal times as such. A huge circle of earth had been burned completely black and bits of metal, engine, luggage, clothing lay scattered in a radius of many yards all about it. In the centre a small heap of twisted metal represented all that remained of the body of the aircraft. It must have hit the outcrop of rock beside which it lay with tremendous force and exploded into flames.

At first I could not see any bodies. Everything looked inanimate, blackened, burned. Then I saw that the dark brown wooden lay figures which sprawled in grotesque attitudes among the charred stubble had once been human. What colour, race or sex we could no longer distinguish. There were twenty-nine of them: all dead.

We had still a night to get through. It was very dark and bitterly cold, we stood on an open shoulder of the mountain at ten thousand feet, and there was only a little grass hut, built by hunters, for shelter. Already it seemed overcrowded with seven hunters and a dog crouching round the fire in the middle of the floor but we bent double at the low entrance and squeezed in. When the last policeman was sitting with his back to the door there were sixteen of us in this precarious shelter. By the light of the flames the hunters looked wilder than ever. They ignored us and talked loudly to each other in a strange, barbaric tongue, casting glances at me and bursting at intervals into maniacal laughter. All our food, our warm clothes, our toilet articles were with the absent Andrew and David. Ali's load contained medicine, bananas, a bottle of water and a bottle of whisky. We dared not produce the latter because of the effect that it might have on the hunters.

Outside the wind rose and the thunder began to roll and crack among the rocks. It was indeed a night for ghosts. Gradually, one after another, the Africans wrapped themselves in their blankets or cloaks and stretched out, head to tail, around the dying fire. I shivered in my cotton dress and the one blanket that had survived the climb, but it was no moment for squeamishness or prudery. Stretched out between Ali and Alec I took off my shoes and thankfully rested my sore, chilled feet on the warm back of the nearest hunter.

There was barely room for us all; and, as the night crept on and the unearthly chill of the small hours penetrated the hut and overcame the life of the dying fire, we imperceptibly drew closer and closer, all of us, black and white alike, conscious of the need for warmth and reassurance.

It was not a bad night, better, in many ways, than the long

succession of nights to come when I was to wake in a sweat from exaggerated nightmares. But the dawn, though bleak and early, was heartily welcome. We breakfasted on the last banana and combed our hair with our fingers. I looked sadly at the remains of my shoes and the resourceful Ali produced a piece of rag and tied it round them in an attempt to keep upper and sole together. We walked across to the wreckage and those inhuman roasted bodies.

How curiously the human mind behaves in time of crisis. I was conscious neither of shock nor of revulsion, only a complete detachment and a feeling that these corpses were in no way related to people as I knew them. The police appeared entirely unaffected. The spirits of the dead they might fear in the darkness but the bodies from which the spirits had departed were outworn furniture, no more awesome than the half-burnt shoes and despatch cases which lay scattered around.

It was a terrible journey back. Going downhill, slipping and stumbling with muscles of agonizing soreness; the knowledge that the crisis was over, and after all we had been of no use; a gnawing hunger and an aching tiredness. Very often my feet refused to obey and I sat down on the uneven path. Each time to get up and go on again seemed more than my exhausted body could bear.

When we staggered into Bonakanda the people came out to stare at us as we passed through.

'Any man alive?' they said, and we shook our heads and went on because to stop would have made further progress impossible.

It seemed that a lifetime had passed and we were in another world when, at last, we passed Chief Endeli's house where the 'Cuckoo Waltz' still played as it had done only twenty-four hours before.

We were not warmly received. A feeling of shame pervaded the station, now back to its Monday morning activity.

'Well, we knew there was no one alive,' they said, though this had not been known with any certainty.

'Did you see the gold?' they asked, and this seemed to be of more importance than the people: it now appeared that the aircraft had been carrying bullion.

Then came the French. For them it was, of course, a major disaster and they brought a large group of experts and authorities to enquire into causes and to make arrangements about the bodies. As soon as the immaculately clad, senior French officials arrived it became obvious that they, at least, expected that some official on the British side would have been up the mountain to ascertain what had happened. So a summons came to Alec to go up to the Commissioner's residence.

Next day we left on a trip to the North and I was glad to be away from it all. Away from the wrangles that went on; from the tragic absurdity and gallantry of these many Frenchmen, most of them of sedentary occupations and unsuitable clothing, all making their arduous way up to the scene of the disaster; from the difficulties of bringing down what remained of the bodies to be flown back to Paris, with the local Bakweri asking enormous sums of money to carry the stretchers; and, finally, from the distribution round the station of bottles of red wine to all those who had been of help. It was, for me, a disturbing revelation of what life in a remote tropical territory could do to the values of my own people.

It was a year later, by now married and in an official capacity, that I met the mountain again. It now became a regular part of our life, climbed once a month by our students, casting its shadow before it in anxiety, mine as much as theirs.

On the morning of the mountain ascent (the climax of every course at Man O' War Bay), up very early preparing sandwiches and breakfast for some of the staff by the flickering light of a hurricane lamp, chivvying a sleepy Ebenezer, counting and re-counting the items to go into a rucksack: food, matches, jersey, socks, water-bottle, etc., I would be aware of lorries revving up at the big house and the shouts and clatter of the students. At last all would be ready and we made our way over the grass to the assembly point. Everyone climbed into the two big lorries, sitting on wooden planks stretched from side to side. Some shouted cheerfully to me:

'I'll bring you back a rock from the top of the mountain, Ma'; some smiled rather weakly; some could not even bring themselves to smile.

They wore a wonderful assortment of clothes. Official issue was a thick jersey, a blanket, a mackintosh cape and canvas hockey boots, but they could (and did) wear also whatever of their own clothing they felt they needed. So Northerners would appear in their long white 'nightgowns', *rigas*, worn over the top of everything else; some preferred to climb in bare feet and carried their boots on their heads or round their necks; headgear varied from a towel wrapped turbanwise round the head to a cloth cap or a smart panama, but all these assorted garments were worn with a jaunty aplomb which somehow gave them style and panache in spite of their oddity. The lorries trundled off out of sight among the bananas, a forest of pink palms fluttering at me from the back.

That was the setting out. How different was the return.

Late in the afternoon of the second day we would begin to listen for them. I would become nervous and forgetful about my household tasks, an ear always cocked for the rumble of the lorries, half my mind on the success or failure of the expedition now, for better or worse, over. But this time it was often not the heavy crashing of gears that came first to my ear but, very faint and far away, a sound of singing. Gradually it came nearer, a triumphant, full-throated roar accompanied by a ringing bugle, the treasured possession of one of our Nigerian instructors. As the lorries turned the corner and drew up beside me this wonderful sound would rise to a magnificent climax, a sound full of achievement, relief, and the enormous pride of men who had vanquished something they had secretly believed unvanquishable and had come home to tell the tale. I heard this sound many times during my years at Man O' War Bay and it never failed to turn my heart over and fill my eyes with tears.

But now they poured off the lorry. Everyone had come out to witness this triumphant return, cooks, drivers, staff who had not been on the expedition. Everyone embraced everyone else; cries and laughter echoed all round:

'Did you get to the top?'

'Well done, oh, well done.'

'So you come back, ha! I think you lose yourself on this mountain.'

'You saw the Half Man?'

'Ma, I brought you these everlasting flowers from the very top.'

'Madam, I didn't get to the top, but I DID get to Hut 2.'

I wrung their hands, sometimes embraced them too: congratulated, commiserated, comforted, cheered, until even the weaker brethren, who had fallen by the wayside, felt that they too shared something of this triumph which was not entirely an individual one but also a group effort.

Before the courses ever started we were well aware of the dangers of the mountain. Our experience with the French aircraft had given us a lively appreciation of the difficulties of the climb and we had been very conscious that without hunters, guides or huts that night might well have been disastrous for us too.

Course by course, however, the mountain expedition went well. A varying number of students reached the top and all got some way up. At this stage I had no real fears about Mount Cameroon, those were reserved for the sea. When I watched the course set out across the bay on an expedition I felt genuinely unhappy until they had arrived safely back again. Against the immensity of the Atlantic, with its rolling swell, our canoes looked very frail and tiny; there were sharks in these waters, and the dangers of a man panicking in a small boat seemed much greater than any case of hysteria on the mountain could be. But when tragedy struck again—the first time for us at Man O' War Bay—it came on the mountain and took an unexpected form. In one ascent, within an hour of each other, two separate students collapsed and died of fright. Quite what happened was never very clear, but a form of hysteria seized each young man, a combination of fatigue, cold and mental fear. For many this was the first time that they had experienced the sensations produced by cold, and the shivers down the spine, the discolouration of finger-tips, eyes watering, ears tingling, all seemed portents of approaching dissolution. Each lad, at a given moment, began to shout 'I want to die'—and did so.

At the inquest the Medical Officer gave his view that death was due to exposure, but it was exposure to fear not cold. The knowledge that psychology is giving us only today of how closely sickness and accident are associated with the will has always been apparent to Africans. We had terrible evidence now that fear could destroy a man if he lacked the determination to overcome it.

The repercussions nearly meant the end of Man O' War Bay and of our time in Nigeria. Reactions in the Nigerian press were very unfavourable; public opinion in Victoria was very hostile; life became a nightmare lived in a whirl of telegrams to be despatched and received. We discussed endlessly and futilely all possible pre-cautions against such an unpredictable disaster, I did my shopping in Victoria very conscious of curious looks and whispered comments. One of the two dead young men had been a Cameroonian and local opinion was composed of a combination of genuine tragedy and a savage exaltation that their mountain had, after all, repelled strangers. Political opinion in Lagos was asking what mountain climbing had to do with leadership, and the relationship, which seemed obvious to us, was, in fact, not easy to explain without becoming involved in abstracts. Governmental opinion generally, in the manner of all governments, was merely anxious to cover itself against any charge of responsibility and we well knew that we could expect no open official backing.

In all this, however, one man stood four square behind us, our boss, E. R. Chadwick, Commissioner for Community Development, Eastern Region. It was his faith and imagination which had enabled Man O' War Bay to start at all and now that we were in trouble he did not desert us but gave us his full and public support. And it was in a large measure due to him that we found ourselves, when the furore had subsided, with permission to continue the courses.

We had always been vaguely conscious that the chief job on the mountain expedition was not guiding the students to the summit but giving them the heart to get there. Quite how important the psychological aspect was became apparent on the next course. It seemed possible that there would be no students at all: news travels fast, and for the already fearful this disaster was ample confirmation of their fears. Cancellations began to come in from all over the country. When the day came thirty-six, instead of the usual fifty or sixty, arrived. Morale was very low and, from the beginning, it was obvious that fear of the mountain overshadowed everything else. We, too, were very concerned. What should be our policy? If we abandoned the mountain expedition then, all over Nigeria the news would go around that the mountain had won, that after all the spirits were the more powerful. Yet we could not make the climb compulsory in this instance and so risk a repetition of the disaster. We decided to ask for volunteers; the question was would we get any?

There was a school of thought among the staff which advocated a gradual introduction to the mountain, so the students went on picnics to the lower slopes. The result was disastrous, they became progressively more afraid each time. Another faction felt it was better to say: 'All right, if you don't want to climb, don't climb, but you'll look very foolish when you get back home and are asked whether you had the courage to go up or not.' Both theories, however, fell to the ground when on the night before the climb the Army Physical Training Instructor, on loan from the West Africa Command for that season, reported that he declined to go. This was defection in face of the enemy and, in an Instructor and one looked up to as a brave man by the students, could only have the most disastrous results on the morale of the very small group of volunteers who had agreed to climb.

My husband acted at once. The instructor was summoned to an interview, the position was carefully explained to him and he was told that we could not tolerate, at this delicate stage, having a deserter on the compound; either he must reconsider his decision and go up with the party or he must leave Man O' War Bay, at once, tonight. He was a senior N.C.O. so he understood perfectly both what was expected of him and the possible consequences if he refused. He chose to leave.

His things were quickly packed and a Land Rover drew up in front of our house to take him into Victoria. It was a solemn moment. The fate of much more than this one man hung in the balance. My husband said: 'Goodbye, Sgt-Major.'

'Goodbye, Sir.'

The scared faces of Ebenezer and Lucas hovered in the darkness beyond the verandah; the rest of the African staff, aware that they by acquiescence in this dismissal had taken for themselves a vital decision, stood stiffly at attention. The culprit turned on his heel and went out into the night. He climbed into the Land Rover and we all waited, caught in a breathless moment, for the sound of the engine and departure. Nothing happened. In a few seconds the driver's face appeared in the door.

'You come help me push,' he said. 'This engine no go start at all.'

There were also on this course two exceptionally good men. Two of the best that we ever had, and we had very many. One was an Ibo, Ogbonnaya Okoro, and one a Northerner, Dauda Haruna Kwoi. It was Okoro, leader of his section, who when asked in a Treasure Hunt some days before the mountain ascent to produce an example of 'guts', came up to my husband and whispered: 'I will get all my section to the top of the mountain.' It was Dauda, of frail physique and already (though we did not know it) suffering from tuberculosis, who by his example of Christian courage and love gave many of his weaker brethren the ability to overcome their own fears. Out of the fifteen who volunteered to climb Mount Cameroon eight came from the section containing these two men, with the remaining seven from all the other three sections.

The two days and a night that the party was on the mountain were very anxious ones. We, along with the students who were left and the staff who remained to carry on some kind of normal programme, found our eyes turning constantly to the east where the mountain lay concealed behind its banks of cloud. When, on the first evening, the sky cleared and the mountain was revealed bathed in the pale pink innocence of a lovely sunset we drew together, without speaking, to gaze at it and pray. We had no words at this moment to voice our hopes or our fears. With the quick, instinctive feeling, based on affection, which West African servants have with those they serve, Lucas and Ebenezer made it plain as they gave us our meals and went about the house that they, too, were anxious, that this was their concern as well as ours.

It was not possible to get any news. We must wait until we heard the lorries rumbling on the road. Would they be silent, defeated and deflated, or would we hear them singing again as they had sung, so very long ago, before the accident?

They came before I was prepared for them. I had steeled myself to wait until the latest possible hour, and then suddenly I heard it. The roar that told me all was well. The triumph such as we had never had. The lorries were on us and there was no need to ask anything. One look at the grinning faces which surrounded us, one sound of the swinging verse made up to celebrate:

> *There are very many mountains in the Cameroons,*
> *You got to climb or you shame.*

and I was overwhelmed.

'We did it, Ma.'

'*Kai*, Ma, we look down here to see you from the top.'

'Madam, I put my name in the bottle as I said I would.' I did not cry, but I found it difficult to speak.

.   .   .   .   .

But the mountain had not finished with us. For two years after this our students went up and down without any untoward incident and we began to take the expeditions for granted. Then, in April 1954, we had a course for schoolboys from the major secondary schools of all Nigeria.

This was the first time we had had boys and it was not certain how they would react. Some of the exercises which we had done with young men were very arduous and it was felt that the boys would have neither the physical nor mental development to cope with them.

HENRY OBINECHE, SCHOOLBOY

This course, also, was shorter than usual because it had to fit in with the school holidays.

However, our activities were well known by now and bush telegraph had carried news of them all round the country. The schoolboys were indignant at having their course curtailed; they had boasted before they left school of the terrors they were going to face and the dangers to be overcome and now these terrors and dangers had been watered down! Some of us wondered if they could reach the top of the mountain, memories of the tragedy two years before came back and we were not sure if these untried youngsters were capable of the endurance needed. It was also late in the season, with the possibility of bad weather descending suddenly.

When something of all this was mentioned to the boys, however, it was obvious that they were going to feel badly cheated if they were not allowed to attempt the climb.

'But, Sir, what will my companions say to me when I return?'

'But that is what I came for, Sir. How can I go back and say I have not been to the top of Mount Cameroon?'

So great had been the swing in public opinion in these two years that students now came willing and anxious to climb the mountain. It was a test of manhood, something to boast about to lesser men.

The first party of thirty-one did the climb in record time and got twenty-nine of its members to the top. The second party was not so lucky. In it there were two boys from different regions, Eugene Labinjo from the West and Henry Obineche, an Easterner. Eugene

MOSES ADENIJI, SCHOOLBOY

was the son of a Salvation Army official; he had lived most of his life in towns, Lagos and Benin. He was a cheerful, willing lad, a follower rather than a leader, and he had a hobby which interested him very much—photography. Henry was quite a different character. Physically small and disfigured by a terrible scald that scarred one side of his face, he had a brilliant brain. His great interests were Botany and Natural History, and at school he had been conducting an experiment with bats, sticking Elastoplast over their ears in an attempt to find the means whereby they controlled their flight. He was not content to accept knowledge, as are many young Africans, but sought it for himself, peering, collecting, experimenting.

When the party reached the top of the mountain the weather had begun to change from clear sunshine to swirling mist. Sgt-Major Riga Addingi, in charge of the group at this stage, having got them all to Hut 3, would have preferred to return at once rather than continue the few hundred yards to the buried bottle which marked the official top. But the boys felt that this would snatch their whole triumph from them and lay them open to the jeers of their fellows

85

who had packed the bottle with names two days before. So Addingi consented to go on; the boys were told to keep together and on no account to wander. The group moved on to the summit.

It was not until they were already on their way back that it was discovered that Henry and Eugene were missing. Sending the party down to Hut 2 with a junior instructor Addingi took John Lukom, the mountain guide, and returned to the top. It was bitterly cold by now and there was a swirling mist. Addingi had a very powerful voice which he used to the full but the whipping wind drove it back on him. Mount Cameroon, unlike its smaller namesake, has a summit which is not a true summit at all. A rolling plateau, broken by small ridges each appearing higher than its neighbour, stretches over a considerable area. The ground is wild and full of volcanic clefts and hummocks. A man could search there all day and still not find another man.

Hoping against hope that the boys had been playing an unpleasant trick and were even now at Hut 2, Addingi and John came down again. By an unfortunate coincidence the three British instructors who had started out with the party had all fallen sick and this was an added burden for Addingi. However there was no better man in Nigeria and he dealt with the emergency with sense and responsibility.

When the news reached Man O' War Bay and I had, a second time, to prepare my husband for a search party of this nature, I could not believe it. Some nightmare too terrible to contemplate seemed to have us in its grip. We were acutely conscious that the decision to let the boys climb the mountain at all had only been taken late in the course and under pressure. If only we had insisted on the simpler alternative! But it was too late for second thoughts and this time I had many things to do. Mr Awolowo, the leader of the Action Group and Premier of Western Nigeria, and nine of his leading politicians were coming to lunch to see the Centre. They had already started out that morning and could not be reached with a message. It was out of the question that any able-bodied man be spared from the search, so I must entertain them. And the sixty-eight boys who were not lost must be kept employed.

This time, though a sense of shock pervaded the atmosphere, there was none of the terror and abandon that took hold of the course after the first tragedy. This was something we all faced together

and the boys made it plain in many touching ways that they understood how terrible an occurrence this was for us.

At noon Mr Awolowo and his nine satellites stepped from their
fleet of cars, their voluminous robes making them appear twice the
size of normal men. My heart failed me for a moment when I thought
of the difficulties there might be in explaining to a Nigerian politician
what had happened and why his reception committee had diminished
to a wife and our elderly administrative officer.

I need not have worried. I have never known a Nigerian to
fail in courtesy and resource in time of need and Mr Awolowo was
no exception. He had already been told what had happened and he
at once laid himself out to be sympathetic and pleasant. Lunch
went off well and afterwards he addressed the boys, telling them
that he hoped this crisis would not deter them from continuing to
overcome the difficult things in life, and that he and his colleagues
looked to young men of their sort to make the leaders of the future
Nigeria. They lined the path as he drove away and cheered him
enthusiastically; I, feeling like a tightrope walker who has just safely
made the platform at the end of his wire, had time to think again of
this terrible thing that had happened to us.

Two days later the cars came back after dark and the boys
crowded down the stairs of the big house, their anxious faces illumin-
ated by kerosene lamps. I knew even before my husband spoke that
the search had been useless. There was a defeated air over the little
convoy. Unshaven, grey and tired he climbed out and shook his head.

I think the next week was the worst of my life. Again the miserable
business of sending off cables to parents, schools, Governors and
other interested officials; the receiving of sympathy and condemnation in return, both equally hard to bear; handing in our resignation;
seeing off the rest of the lads, whose course had now come to an end,
all except four who had been near Henry and Eugene when they
disappeared and would be needed for an inquest; arranging for the
search to be continued by the Bakweri hunters and for a reward to
be offered—dead or alive. We were sure they were dead, and somehow, this time, our greatest emotion was personal grief for the
boys themselves. We could not bear to visualize them, lost, afraid,
two small boys (for all their seventeen years) alone on the immensity
of the mountain. We hardly spoke to each other at meals; each knew
the other's thoughts and had no words to help.

One incident only lightened this time of waiting. Handing

dishes to us at table one day Ebenezer indicated that he had something to say. He got it out with difficulty but when we understood
him what he said was this. Master was in trouble, very bad trouble.
Because it was trouble with the mountain, which was susceptible to
juju, there might be ways of dealing with it. He, Ebenezer, and one
of the drivers had clubbed together and paid ten shillings to a local
'doctor' for a spell to bring the boys back again. We were very
touched, ten shillings was a large sum of money by Ebenezer's
standards and he did not part with money easily. I felt an irrational
and wholly pagan hope that the spell might work.

On the eighth day the telephone rang. A laconic voice said:

'This is the Cameroons Development Corporation. We have just
received a wireless message from our farthest plantation on the far
side of the mountain. It says: "Two Man O' War Bay boys found—
send transport." '

That was all. I flew down to the jetty where my husband was
working sadly with the boats.

'They're found, oh, they're found!'

He looked absolutely stunned, then in a funny sort of croak
he said:

'Are they dead?'

I did not know! The message had not said, nobody knew. We
rushed up and rang the Cameroons Development Corporation. 'No,'
they said, 'we can't tell you. There's only radio communication with
that plantation once every twenty-four hours and we can't get at
them till tomorrow morning. Sorry!'

'They *must* be alive,' I said. 'Surely they'd have said if it were
bodies.'

I could see that my husband could hardly bear to hope. We
looked at each other with tears streaming down our faces and started
to get together blankets and pillows to put in the Land Rover that
would go out to pick them up.

The plantation in question, Idenau, lay about forty miles along
the coast from us round the foot of the mountain. It was the remotest
of all the C.D.C.'s estates and to get there the Land Rover must be
abandoned after about thirty-five miles, a river crossed, and the
rest completed on foot.

I heard later from my husband of that journey. I think we were
both sure that, by some miracle, they were alive, against all the odds,
against all the probabilities. I know that I felt so and my husband

told me that all the way out to Idenau he was going over in his mind how he would greet them. He felt that nothing would be adequate except an embrace, that he must fling his arms round their necks and weep over them. Yet when he walked into the plantation dispensary and two small figures rose to their feet and said: 'Hullo, Sir,' something in his Anglo-Saxon background made it impossible for him to do more than say:

'Henry! Eugene! Get into that car!'

It was an astonishing story which they told when we got them back.

Henry had determined, before he came to the course at all, that he would take back to the school museum some plants and rocks from the very top of the mountain. When Sgt-Major Addingi said that the group was to go to the top very quickly and all together, under his eye, Henry saw his chance of collecting his specimens slipping away. So, very discreetly, when they saw the opportunity, he and Eugene, who was determined to have a photograph of himself at the summit, hid behind a rock. They meant to linger only a moment or two, but somehow Henry's plants took longer to find than he had thought and when they turned round to rejoin the party the mist had come down and they were lost. They shouted, but only the echo of their voices came back to them; they ran here and there but only succeeded (as it afterwards turned out) in increasing the distance between themselves and Addingi now searching for them.

At this point, with remarkable discipline and common sense in the circumstances, they decided to sit down and consider the situation. First, however, they prayed together and sang a hymn. Henry was a Roman Catholic and Eugene Salvation Army but their prayer was simply that of two believers to God for help and the hymn was one which we had taught them at Man O' War Bay. It began, with an irony that they did not perceive, 'Now as I go upon my chosen way'.

They then assessed their possessions: pitifully few because, alas, all extras had been left at the hut where the night had been spent. They had no knives, no matches, no food; both had macintosh capes and jerseys over their shirts and shorts, and Eugene had a packet of biscuits in his pocket. Henry had his specimens and little else. The weather had now deteriorated and the top of the mountain was wrapped in a black and terrifying cloud. A bitter wind shrieked round these two small figures, whipping their garments about their legs and catching their breath from between their lips. There was a terrible desolation about the landscape when the mist was rent apart for a few seconds, it had the appearance of some lunar terrain, devoid of any life. During one of the momentary partings of the cloud they glimpsed, far below them, the sea. 'We'll go down there,' they said to each other, Henry adding that it would be easy to get along the coast till they reached Man O' War Bay. So they set off, and even at this stage and in these circumstances Eugene still had it in his mind that he must be back for the visit of his Western Region Prime Minister the next day. Only eight days later did they, and we, discover that they had chosen to come down the wrong side of the mountain, a side uninhabited and unexplored.

That night they spent on the bare mountain crouched together in the shelter of some rocks. They were barefoot by now, the hard volcanic outcrops had torn their shoes to pieces. But, though they clung to each other for warmth and comfort, they did not think of giving up and they prayed before they slept.

The next day was not a good one. The mountain was still wreathed in mist which made it impossible for them to achieve any sense of direction. The enormous whaleback did not descend uniformly but undulated in ridges so that in the blanketing cloud they were often confused by the sensation that they were going uphill. They had no food or water and the cold was intense.

'But we said to each other that this was a crisis and we had been taught to meet these things at Man O' War Bay,' said Henry to us afterwards. 'And we felt we couldn't let the staff down.'

After a moment he added: 'We were often disappointed—but we never despaired.'

The next day they reached the forest and with it some degree of shelter from the wind. But both boys were town boys, as utterly unacquainted with the jungle as any seventeen-year-old British boy would be. They tried to climb a tree to find out which direction they should go in, but the highest trees soared two hundred feet above them and to climb was impossible. They found a stream and began to follow it remembering that all rivers run to the sea, but it disappeared into the ground. They found elephant tracks and tried to walk in them hoping it would lead to a banana plantation, but the tracks vanished. All this time they ate only grass, though now they had plenty moisture in the sodden vegetation. And they still prayed.

The next day was Saturday and they wandered all day without, apparently, coming any nearer help. I do not think either of them thought of death though both were bewildered and afraid; they were also still concerned that they had failed to get back to the Centre and conscious that the staff would wonder where they were. And, very strongly, they seemed to have the feeling that all this was an opportunity to put into practice the qualities of self-reliance, responsibility, leadership and courage which had been stressed during the course. Both were most certainly very afraid but, this time, fear was mastered by faith and by the conviction that they were expected to overcome the terrors they were undergoing.

On Sunday, when they awoke from an uneasy sleep much disturbed by bad dreams, they said to each other:

'This is Sunday so we must not work; we'll rest and pray.'

Henry told us this casually, unaware that he was saying anything extraordinary; and we felt ashamed that we, in circumstances so much less dire, should often have broken the Sabbath, while these two, with death beside them, never even considered doing so. All that day they sat under a tree and rested and prayed and told each other stories.

On Monday they rose up again, refreshed, and set off. Henry had still in his hand the specimens from the top of the mountain which he had paid so dearly for. It was only the next day, when he saw and managed to catch a chameleon, that he threw them away. Two or three times now they thought themselves near a village and hastened to the spot where they could hear chattering, only to find that it was monkeys, some of them very large.

On the eighth day after they had got lost, in the afternoon, they thought they heard the sound of chopping and coming into a clearing they found an old man cutting wood. They must have looked to him like visitants from another planet clad, as they were, in long black capes and hoods and leaning heavily on sticks to take the weight off their cut and weary feet. He took them at once to the British Manager. This man must have been one of the very few in all Nigeria and the Cameroons who did not know that two boys were missing on the mountain. His estate was so isolated that he only rarely heard local news, and Henry and Eugene merely told him that they had got lost and wanted to get back to Man O' War Bay. So in his next radio report to his headquarters he stated that they were there but had no idea that he was making news, that everyone had given them up for dead.

Though they both suffered physically for some weeks after this incredible adventure, their legs swelling up and their stomachs having difficulty in adjusting to proper food, neither seemed to have any mental ill-effects. Indeed of all those concerned they seemed the least affected, having never doubted for a moment that they would manage to return. Their whole faith can be found in the background to the words of the telegram sent off by Eugene to his family the day after he was recovered:

'Safely back at Man O' War Bay. Rejoice with me.'

CHAPTER V

First Aid

CROWN BIRD

THE disaster on the mountain, which happened on the Fifth Course, had shown that it was not enough to teach First Aid in the accepted manner, a lecture followed by practical demonstration. This certainly equipped all our young Africans to pass an examination, and even to tell someone else what to do, but bore no relation to their own reactions to a genuine accident. It is, in fact, in the nature of accidents that they happen in difficult circumstances and when there are no bandages conveniently to hand, and this is especially true in a country such as Nigeria where the familiar injunction, 'Send for the doctor', may be totally unrealistic and the nearest doctor many miles away. It is much more likely that the patient must be prepared for a difficult journey, carried slung from a pole or in some jolting vehicle, to the nearest dispensary or hospital. Rarely is it possible for him to lie quietly in his bed while medical aid comes out to him. So the young Nigerian training in First Aid must be ready to take much greater responsibility and to carry his assistance much further than would be necessary in Europe. At the same time he finds it harder to do the simpler things. He is generally quite prepared to be responsible for some major dressing which involves the use of a good deal of abracadabra but not so ready to clean a simple cut and leave it to nature to heal. There is a feeling, which is common I believe to human nature everywhere, that pills and ointments have magic properties over and above their medicinal ones, and not to use them requires great restraint and understanding.

But there was another side to the teaching of First Aid which

93

was very strongly brought out by the mountain accident. Then, although every man had had training in Artificial Respiration, when it came to the test many refused to help, because they themselves felt tired, because the man was not of their tribe, because they were cold and wanted to be near the fire and other reasons equally trivial. It is not enough to know how to do something, the willingness to use this training must also be there and a sense of the obligation to give back in help to others the skills which one has acquired, perhaps at first only as assets for oneself.

The instinct in Africa is to leave the site of an accident as quickly as possible because it may involve one with the police, or because the people concerned have no close claim of family or clan. There is no stigma attached to such behaviour, it is the sensible thing to do, and it is only gradually that a social conscience is being built up. Europeans are shocked when they first encounter this attitude. It is right to be shocked, but such behaviour is not confined to countries outside Europe. Not long ago, in Britain, a young man was attacked by a gang and severely wounded in front of a bus full of passengers, none of whom went to his aid. How often when a woman has a fall in a busy street is she left to struggle to her feet without assistance. There must be the heart to help as well as the knowledge how to do so.

In the third year of Man O' War Bay we found ourselves without a member of the staff equipped to teach First Aid and my husband asked me if I would do so. Though properly qualified I was reluctant, doubting my ability to teach these young men successfully in a subject which was, for me, much more complicated than my gentle weaving class, but in reality I had no option for there was no other instructor available.

I began in the most orthodox fashion, clutching my Red Cross handbook to me and surrounded by miles of triangular bandages and efficient home-made splints. My sessions took place in the afternoon on the verandah of the big house; the students had always had a physically strenuous morning, it was hot, the sea glittered and sparkled. I used to notice heads nodding as I explained how to set a broken bone, and there was an inclination among those with the largest notebooks to launch upon lazy academic discussions about medical terms; there was no flourish in talking about 'breathing' when 'respiration' had such a fine impressive ring. But the real shock came with the tests at the end of the course. All my students could tell me, in fine resounding words, how to deal with any form of injury but presented with a simulated casualty they were pitiful. The gulf between words and action was immense, in their minds what they wrote down in their notebooks appeared to bear no relation to the reality of a wounded man suffering from pain and shock.

I was appalled and went in to tell my husband that the whole undertaking was a complete failure. As usual he was both constructive and encouraging; we discussed very thoroughly what we felt to be the reasons for our inability to bring home to the young men the human side of First Aid as well as the purely technical and I determined, with his permission, to attempt a totally different approach with the next course.

A month later we gathered again on the verandah of the big house. Thirty faces, some of them already somnolent, gazed at me and the blackboard. Thirty notebooks lay open ready to take down my words of wisdom.

'First Aid,' I began, 'is the very first help we can give in the case of accident. We may not be doctors or nurses but there are certain things that we can all do to help when we are present in a crisis. Perhaps the first and most important thing is that we should be willing to help at all; that we should be ready to take responsibility, and be prepared to act quickly and think clearly.'

I had been talking for about five minutes when a piercing scream interrupted me and there was a crashing, tearing sound just out of sight round the corner of the house. The atmosphere became electric.

'Something's happened,' I said wildly and obviously. 'Come on, we'd better see what it is.' I am not a very good actress, but they were not thinking about me at that moment. In a flash they were off down the stairs and streaming round the corner.

I went after them.

When I got there Sam (at that time helping Ebenezer) was lying groaning on the ground clutching one leg in which there was a large gash losing a good deal of blood. His eyes were rolled up, and when asked what had happened he indicated with moans and sighs that he had been climbing the tree and had fallen off. Africans are good natural actors and Sam put everything he had into the performance. He was completely surrounded by students, none of whom were doing anything to help him, and a splendid argument had started up as to what, in fact, they ought to do.

'Come on,' I said briskly, 'what are we going to do about him? What's happened to him anyway?'

At this the more alert began to pull themselves together. Two rushed off for a basin of water and a towel; Gabriel bent down and began to manipulate the injured limb in a manner which would quickly have rendered any fracture compound; Humphrey and Ekpo had the bright idea of going for a blanket to make into a stretcher.

At the moment when they turned the corner of the house out of sight someone said:

'Why, this is not blood at all!'

Everybody stopped and looked at me. Slow smiles of relief and comprehension began to spread over their faces, the more enterprising looked a little smug, the timid began to look rather ashamed, Sam continued to moan and groan having worked himself into his part and being reluctant to abandon the limelight. We got the blackboard brought down under the tree where we all were and I continued the lesson; but with a great difference. I now had a thoroughly stirred-up class ready to talk and argue and listen with interest. I had an object lesson right at hand; everybody had seen Gabriel pull the leg about and recognized the justice in the observations about humanity in dealing with a patient, that it was not just a limb but a limb attached to a man. When the case was developed a little more it was obvious that the accident would have to have been reported to my husband, as Principal, that Sam's wife should have been told and that she was going to make a terrible fuss so some way must be found of keeping her occupied, boiling water for instance or getting their room ready for Sam to go back to. All these points and many more which for other courses had had no reality suddenly took on fresh importance because they were put practically as applying to someone we knew and it was an easier step to go from there to the wider application than to come the other way round.

It was also a satisfactory jolt to the pride of the one or two who had made it plain that they already knew how to deal with the injured and who now stood revealed as no better than their ignorant fellows in time of emergency; and it showed me clearly which of the young men were genuinely ready to help, which were quick thinking and sensible, which felt it easier to be just a little behind the leaders at a time like this, and which preferred to be out of it altogether. This was invaluable information when arranging future exercises.

One of the pleasures in teaching these young men was their responsiveness. Of course, those who came were selected for this very quality, nevertheless it is, I think, true of most Nigerians that they are avid for knowledge. They were also easily fooled! It would not have been possible in Europe to use a false accident again in the same course with any success, but at Man O' War Bay we could repeat the ruse in different forms constantly and each time the students' sense of the present made them feel that this emergency was genuine; and each time, when they discovered that it was yet another exercise, their humour and the openness of their natures made them join with us in enjoying the successful stage management of the crisis and ready to go forward with gusto to whatever might happen next. And even if some of them did suspect that everything was not as it seemed this same warm openness of nature made them ready to co-operate for my sake and the sake of the course in general. I believe that they began to acquire a feeling of expectancy and urgency about life which made them begin to look at their own problems in a new and more exciting way and awoke them to the possibility of their finding solutions.

This, in turn, began to give me an insight that I had not had before into the conditions in which many of them would have to perform the things I taught them. These differed so widely from my own preconceived ideas that I saw that this was not a one-way traffic but that I, too, had things to learn from them. I began to feel that I laid great emphasis on common sense in dealing with accidents while at the same time expecting them to adhere to a formula. Sometimes their common sense did not work out as it should, but at others they confounded us with their logicality. In one arranged emergency a party hurrying to an outbreak of typhoid fever in nearby labour lines was discovered to be carrying both mosquito nets and machetes (a West African cutlass). My husband asked what the nets were for.

'Why, to catch the mosquito that is spreading the typhoid,' they said.

We ridiculed this and went on to the machetes, calculated (we thought) to spread panic among an already disorganized group of men and women.

'But we must build an isolation camp and that we can do straightaway if we have our machetes,' confounding us with practical realities.

I began to realize from the questions which they asked me that when they returned home there would be no neat triangular bandages and ready-made splints in a bush village; that Africa is a tropical country where people wear fewer clothes than we do and that the familiar injunction to tear up one's petticoat for a bandage was not possible when both patient and rescuer might be wearing the minimum; that many villages already possessed local remedies for certain types of injury and that I would be wise to consider whether any of those could still be used while rejecting the obviously unhygienic. The forest contained larger leaves than our forests do, leaves which fulfil many useful purposes and could fulfil many more if we did not make the mystique of First Aid so rigid that only the prescribed dressing would do and a man might bleed to death because of a lack of imagination.

Gradually I went to my classes with less and less equipment and, eventually, with none at all. When the cry went up that Sgt Agbaji, our senior police instructor, had slipped on the jetty and broken his leg it was the students' job to find, borrow or improvise whatever apparatus they needed. I, too, had to be on the alert to criticize or praise or suggest alternatives to whatever they might decide to use.

This policy had its moments of disaster also. Somehow it was always the decent chap who offered his blanket as a stretcher and found himself holding two disconnected strips, hopelessly torn by the muscular weight of Sgt Agbaji, and complaining that helpfulness did not pay. On one occasion L/Cpl Ekechuku, after a severe manhandling by an enthusiastic team who were trying to lever him up the sheer side of our grotto with a broken thigh, said very firmly to me:

'Madam, I cannot go on,' and got up and walked away leaving his dismayed rescuers feeling rather ashamed of themselves. They felt even more ashamed when told that they need never have attempted to take him up the cliff if they had thought of fetching a canoe and sending him round to the jetty by sea.

All this, however, created an atmosphere of enterprise. The students began to have a feeling that things were expected of them and to pay lip service, at least, to the idea that a man should help his fellow-man in trouble whenever possible.

The pendulum could also swing in the other direction. I have found an energetic rescuer assuring a patient with a badly burned arm that he had had the same thing himself last week and look at him now! On a long mountain walk one enterprising young man did a faint on his party and watched with interest their reactions to his need. He then reported them to me. Unfortunately the staff member in charge of the expedition was not amused and told me coldly that my First Aid classes were getting out of hand.

If this responsiveness was rewarding it was also frightening. Their very eagerness to learn made the students uncritical and my words were accepted as the final judgment on every question. At first this was flattering but in time it led me to search my own knowledge very closely and to be careful to be as truthful and honest as possible. It was terrifying to hear, solemnly repeated as true, something said in error and to know that, unless corrected, the student concerned would himself go back to a place where his own word was listened to with avid eagerness, so that my mistake would be endlessly repeated, multiplied and believed.

There were deeper problems too. Europeans have a background and an ethic which has built up a morality about helping other people. But in Africa to help is not taken for granted. 'Why should we?' they would sometimes ask me, and this brought up the whole problem of motives for action. Why should one help a man who does not belong to one's immediate family or tribe? One, moreover, whom to help might bring harm on the helper, for undoubtedly there could be unpleasant complications with the police if a man became involved as a witness in an accident.

We had an answer, we believed in the teachings of Christ, and it is the background of Christian civilization in Europe which has made men feel that they owe help to other men. But what does one say to the Moslem whose own religion leads him to think that the blind and the maimed should be left as they are to provide outlets for the charity of other men?

There are other, less worthy but nevertheless powerful, motives which could be used. Nationalism was one. He was not a true national-ist who was not prepared to give his service to his fellow-citizens; but this is a motive which stops short at the border as religion does not. More and more my husband and I came to feel that in the kind of training which we were attempting the foundations went very deep and that we, ourselves, should look to our own faith so that we could, at least, make it plain what were the motives which influenced us.

As time went on and I became better at working out situations

which really tested the students and gave the minimum opportunity
for shirking or sheltering behind other people, I began to feel that
the courses were a success. Perhaps one of the reasons for this success
was that they were fun for us all. The African staff, who gallantly
agreed to act any kind of body in any sort of circumstances, were
wonderful. They did not have a very easy time and were often
roughly handled but they entered into the spirit wholeheartedly and,
at the end of a session, could give a shattering and highly entertaining
account of their treatment from the patient's point of view.

'What you think I am?' Riga Addingi would say indignantly.
'You think I'm piece of meat? Or perhaps you I think I'm already
dead so it no go matter how you carry me? You bring me up that
mountain side standing on my head so I feel better you leave me die
in peace down below. Pah! You U.S. useless!'

I would hold no brief for the quality of our First Aid. Some
of it was very poor and, I fear, any full time Red Cross instructor
would have turned grey at the sight of some of our treatments. We
had little time within a programme full of other more exciting,
strenuous and interesting activities. So we concentrated on arousing
interest in what could be done to help a fellow in distress, particularly in villages where accidents with fire and water were very
common and, unless someone on the spot could give assistance,
there would be no aid at all, and on opening the eyes of our young
men to the need and the part that they could play. I began to get
enquiries about a full Red Cross training (with a certificate attached),
and some went back and did, in fact, take such courses.

Then letters started to arrive telling of emergencies dealt with
promptly and self-confidently, and, when due allowance had been
made for the wonderful West African use of words, enough remained
to convince us that a public opinion was gradually being built up
among our old students.

'Last Wednesday, as I was passing on a bicycle, one mile from
home, I heard a sudden cry by the bank of a river. I rushed to see
the cause, but behold, a girl of five years drowning. She was in
company of another elder girl ten years. The salvation was that
it was still water. I jumped down and dived. I brought her to the
shore unconscious, but applied serious respiration which after
ten minutes she survived. For this the Headmaster has allowed
me to introduce life saving in the school.'

So wrote one of my old students, and another described a more hair-raising experience:

'In April last year an accident occurred in which two people were buried alive under the concrete storeyed building they were breaking. People present were all in a panic and didn't know what to do, but I managed to get some of them to remove the concrete covering them and by means of the double-bowline lowered them down from the storeyed house.'

I, too, found that I was having fun. On one of our leaves my husband persuaded me to attend a Casualties Union course outside London. This was a revelation to me in the art of simulating wounds and symptoms and when we returned to the Cameroons my baggage was full of flesh-coloured plasticine, collodion, grease-paint and recipes for making up gallons of sticky blood!

However, there were two sides to realism, I presently realized.

VICTORIA

My students were entranced by this magic and prepared to offer me large bribes to reveal the secret; the British were less enamoured. On one occasion, using myself as a victim, ready to burst on the class fresh from a terrible disaster, I came into our sitting room to try the effect first on my husband. He had a young member of staff with him who took one look at me and before I could explain rushed across, helped me gently into a chair and then went out and was sick on the verandah. He found it hard to forgive me for inadvertently revealing that he had a queasy stomach.

It also proved too time-consuming in our already overcrowded lives to coach my victims in all the refinements of authentic reaction to symptoms and treatment. The natural Nigerian gift for drama led to an abandon in the players which made nonsense of any exercise purporting to be completely realistic. So I returned to the cruder but adequately satisfactory performances of earlier days with an occasional *pièce de résistance* with myself as the central character.

CHAPTER VI

The Sea

RETURNING FROM BIMBIA

IF THE mountain dominated our eastward horizon to the west
our eyes and thoughts were occupied by the sea. Framed in the horns
of the bay it stretched, unimpeded, from our rocky shores to the
coast of South America. There were days when, standing on the end
of the little promontory that ran down from our house and gazing
into a remote, clear distance, I felt stirrings of the same astonishment
and awe at the immensity of water which took hold of our young
Northern students when they, for the first time, saw the sea. This
enormousness, however, which might so easily have been overwhelming, was reduced to human size by the proportions and
situation of our bay. We were enclosed by it, protected from the
rages of storms and the fierceness of untamed waters; we looked out
from a position of safety, aware that we were poised on the edge of
perils but also, smugly, aware that they could not get at us unless
we went to seek them. I would have been content never to have done
this, for I was much more afraid of adventures by sea than of adventures by land, but my husband was not content to lose a trial of
strength by default. The sea must be used so that in pitting themselves against it our students might find courage and comradeship.

Many of them did not like it much more than I did!

'When I saw the sea I thought I had come to my death,' wrote
one afterwards; and some discovered, with astonishment and shame,
that the sea barred no holds in the struggle and could force them to be
publicly and humiliatingly sick.

NACHTIGAL LIGHTHOUSE

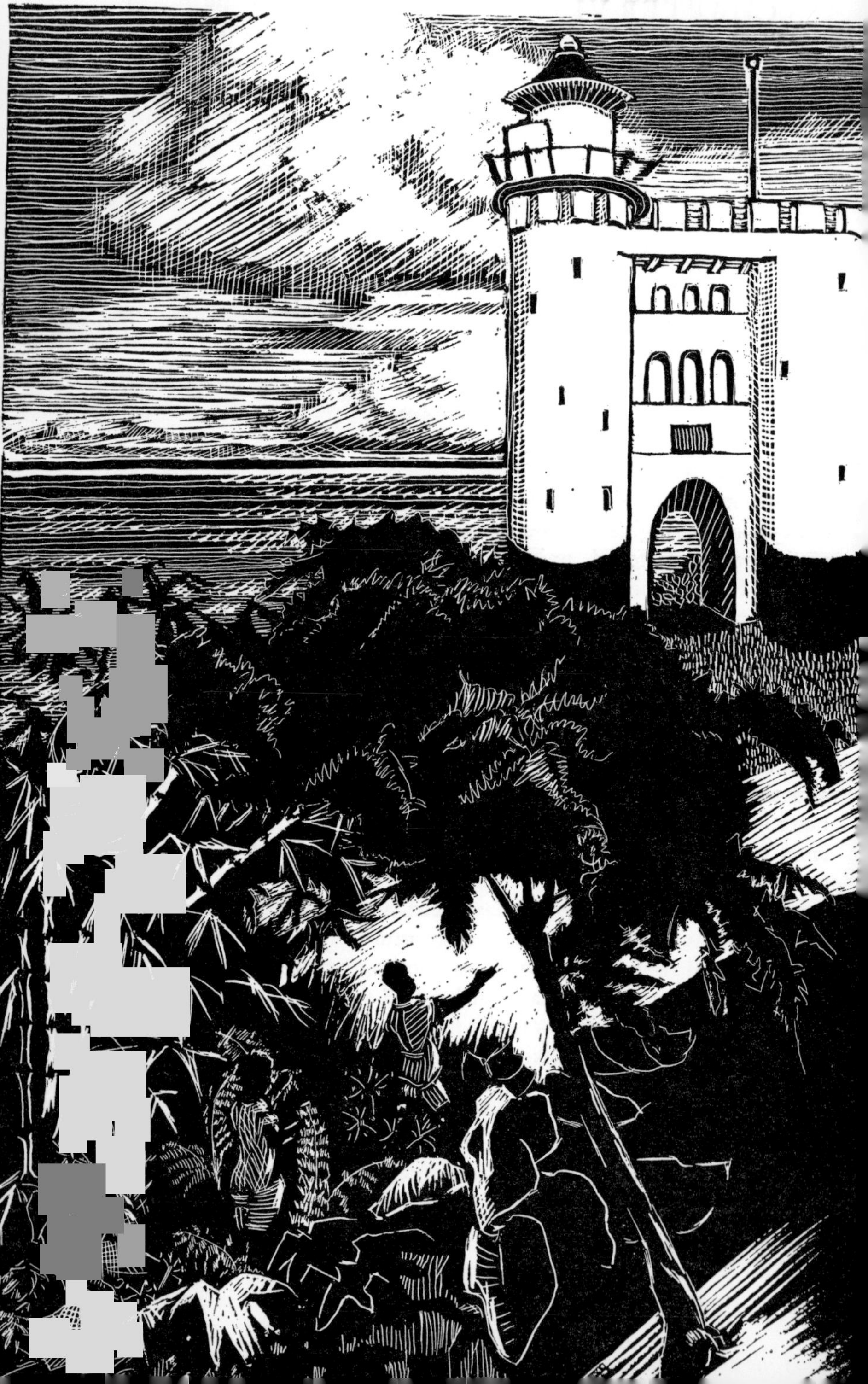

But this came some time later, at first it was enough that every man must learn to swim. Of course many could do so already, since those from the creeks and coast of Southern Nigeria are accustomed to the water from the day they are born, but on each course about half our students had never been into any kind of water and were uncertain of their ability to overcome this new element. I used to stand concealed among the giant ferns on the cliff-top above the jetty and watch the first timid steps which they took over the rocky shore into the sea. For some even this was too much. Tata, from the remote interior near Kano, could not bring himself to touch the water; he was genuinely and terribly afraid. He used to come down to our house after dark and beg my husband to give an order that would exempt him from swimming. This my husband would not do but he spent many hours of his precious spare moments taking Tata, by himself, to a secluded beach where they could wrestle with this fear. It was, partially at least, overcome in the end and Tata passed his first swimming test, but I think he went back to his own dry, arid country with a sigh of relief and the hope that he might never again be called on to take to the water. He was an exception, however, and I was constantly astonished not by their slowness or reluctance but by the speed with which they mastered this fear and the ease with which they learned to swim.

We had a good collection of canoes, some made locally and some bequeathed to us. Of the latter our pride and joy was a very large one, capable of carrying thirty men, which had been captured by the Customs from smugglers a few weeks before our first course started and given to us for the nominal sum of £1. One of our young staff had had the good idea of painting these vessels with designs, as they are often painted in Western Nigeria, and with white, blue, red and aluminium paint we covered them with elaborate and eye-catching patterns. Each had a name, some of them the names of old smuggling or slaving vessels known to have used Man O' War Bay in the last century, and these canoes with the addition of two old life-boats, handsomely presented to us by interested Companies, formed our little fleet.

The first canoe expedition took place within the bay, to visit the lighthouse called after Dr Nachtigal which was built on the seaward side of the right-hand horn. The lighthouse was German-built and took the form of a little castle such as might be found on the banks of the Rhine. Invisible from inland, it looked from the sea

romantic and misplaced, its twin castellated towers at variance
with the luxuriant tropical jungle which lay behind it. It seemed,
nevertheless, a good memorial for Dr Nachtigal.

The students assembled up at the big house and collected life-
jackets and paddles from the store, then they marched, singing,
down to the boats. They sang because it was a natural way for them
to express their feelings, because we encouraged them too, and
because, after all, they were enjoying life. As they passed me, standing
by the path to watch them, their irrepressible good humour rippled
out in jokes.

'We go die-oh, Ma.'

'Madam, I make my will before I go on this adventure.'

I joined in at the end of the line and marched down, too, for
this was one of the expeditions on which I could also go.

Getting into canoes when half the crew have never been off dry
land before is not a very easy exercise and tempers were frayed,
some precious hats destroyed, and friendships strained before we
were able to push off. Each boat had a sprinkling of seasoned canoemen to help it along and the steersman was always, at this stage,
one of our staff. Steering a canoe is a very much more difficult art
than it appears; I have stood for a long time on the cliffs watching
a boat which had gone out on a fishing investigation go round and
round in circles in the middle of the bay because no one had thought
to make sure that at least one of the crew knew how to handle the
steering oar!

All the students wore life-jackets. They were of an old type,
two square boxes encased in brown canvas hung on chest and back
and, isolated above these twin protuberances, I saw some rather
nervous faces as we cast off and made for the opposite shore. Paddles
waved and dipped wildly and a certain amount of water managed to
find its way on board to the accompaniment of disgusted exclamations:

'My friend, you make me wet!'

Gradually, however, as we still remained seaborne after the first
five minutes and the canoe was making recognizable progress in the
right direction, the more fearful began to relax and ply their paddles
with more rhythm and vigour. Those among us for whom the sea
was a known element began to sing and the song was taken up by the
whole crew. A favourite was Paul Robeson's canoe song from
Sanders of the River, 'Ei-ee-oh-ko'.

So we progressed, in growing triumph, across the bay, three or four canoeloads of young men, their songs echoing and re-echoing from boat to boat, the unco-ordinated spider's legs of the paddles slowly finding unity and pattern. Behind us a surprising view of our camp perched on the height of the cliffs and backed by the mass of the mountain, fish eagles gliding scornfully overhead and barracuda (maybe) as scornfully below, before us the whole vista of the open sea but, because we knew that we were not being asked to brave its terrors today, it was possible to hold up our heads and to appear, outwardly at least, unafraid. There is no doubt that some feeling was communicated to us all which we would have found it hard to define; sea and sun and the confinement in a small boat at the mercy of both drew us together in a moment of affection and pride. We felt we had conquered though we had as yet met no difficulties; we were aware of our common humanity in the face of the unpredictable; and it seemed that we had started on a journey of much more importance and significance than crossing the bay to visit a lighthouse.

Even this, however, was quite exciting. We left the canoes at the lighthouse-keeper's beach which lay inland from Cape Nachtigal, itself within the shelter of the bay, and took the path through the forest for some distance to reach the sea coast. This was a true jungle path, overhung by trees, slippery underfoot and permitting only single file. Monkeys leapt about in the branches and toucans uttered their extraordinary cry. Once away from the shore the path twisted so that it was impossible to see far in front or behind and we might well have been tramping through untamed forests remote from any human contact. So it was with a certain relief as well as astonishment that we came round the last corner and saw the lighthouse. Pure white and glistening it came straight out of a fairy tale and needed only a long-haired princess leaning out of the top window to complete the illusion. What vision it conjured up for the African, whose background did not contain Rapunzel, I did not know. As many of them had never seen a lighthouse before perhaps they accepted it as the recognized pattern of European lighthouses. For them the fact of a light to warn ships at sea and the mechanics of its working were far more fascinating than its architectural extravagance.

We were allowed to go over the lighthouse and see how everything worked. Mr Bada, the keeper, showed us the huge cylinders of gas which kept the light going and explained the automatic devices for producing the correct flash. We climbed up one of the towers and looked from the top over the long swells breaking on the rocks below. Now we were exposed to the Atlantic and could see its size and power. On the right, twenty miles away, lay the Spanish island of Fernando Po. If the weather was clear and the island visible it also offered a sight full of romance, for the mountain peak is from this side conical and the veils of distance coloured it a beautiful blue.

Fernando Po had played a significant part in the history of the Cameroons; it was there that the first missionaries from the West Indies, returning with the Gospel to Africa as a thank-offering for the abolition of slavery, had landed in the nineteenth century; and from there that they had later set sail, led by Alfred Saker, for the mainland of the Cameroons to get away from the overpowering Catholicism of Spain.

Nowadays smugglers came over with Spanish wines, and the island had for us the attraction of the unattainable. It was then very difficult to get permission to visit it and all our efforts to do so, either alone or with the students, met with refusal. Later this changed and at least one course was able to make such a visit, but by that time we were no longer in Africa so, for us, Fernando Po remained until the end an island of fantasy and imagination.

This impression was heightened, if anything, by the exploits of two young men from the Development Corporation who, at this time, achieved the impossible and visited Santa Isabel. We woke up one morning to hear Ebenezer repeating, from the bush telegraph, some fantastic tale of a European who had 'gone for Spain'. When we later got more details the story began to take shape. Making careful preparations these two young men had hired a canoe and a fisherman crew and had set sail one Saturday evening from Victoria to Fernando Po. Sensibly they went by night because by day the sun-scorched stretch of sea in such a boat could have proved unbearable. The tale said that they wore palm beach suits and sat in the centre of the canoe in some kind of folding chair while their intrepid paddlers headed out into the night. But this I cannot vouch for though it makes a pleasant embellishment.

In the middle of the next morning, to the astonishment of the population and the confusion of the Gendarmerie, their small craft pulled into the harbour of Santa Isabel and drew alongside the jetty. The two young men, in by now somewhat crumpled palm beach suits, rose up, produced their British passports and explained that they had come for a visit. After an initial sojourn in the police station they became temporary heroes and were taken to the hearts of the crowd which had collected. Treated to magnificent meals, bouquets and a football match they were returned next day in an official launch.

Both the Cameroons Government and their own Corporation met them coldly. The age of adventure was definitely over for these two organizations and not even a wink of amusement could be detected administratively. Later we were told that the Spanish, too, had not delayed sending over a message to say that once was enough for this kind of thing and that any future adventurers would be greeted with a good deal less cordiality and a considerable fine.

I always enjoyed the return from expeditions such as this to Nachtigal. Night falls early in the tropics and the sky would be turning a wonderful pink; perhaps already a star would be out above the mountain, itself visible in the calm and pure evening air. The boats moved smoothly through the water and we all sang. It is the singing that is my most powerful memory; those deep, rich voices, full of a robust sanity, so that though the songs they sang were often the nostalgic spirituals of their enslaved ancestors yet they gave them a swing and confidence which did not look back but forward into the future.

As we drew near our own jetty my husband would suddenly give the order: 'Everybody overboard.'

A look of horror appeared on fifty per cent of the faces confronting me. Their belief that they had successfully surmounted another hazard was rudely shattered. Had they heard aright? Unfortunately they had! One or two of the braver souls leapt in at once and discovered that their life-belts did, in fact, hold them up (the object of the exercise); from their vantage point in the water they then exhorted or jeered at those less courageous. I have not forgotten my stunned admiration on one such occasion when the wife of a young British officer attached to us for the duration of a course went over the side herself, fully clad, to show an example. I was prepared to do many things for the cause—but not this!

The next expedition was a longer one and involved going outside the bay into the open sea, round the left-hand point and up the next inlet to a village called Bimbia. Bimbia had, in the days before Victoria grew up, been a place of some importance and Man O' War Bay itself was situated on the edge of the plantation known locally as 'Bimbia Banana'. The village had other claims to fame, some good

SWIMMING

some bad. It possessed a famous racing canoe which, once a year, appeared at the Empire Day regatta at Victoria to race against the long canoe belonging to the fishing community on one of the islands. These boats were very slender and carried a fabulous number of men. But the Bimbians had gradually lost the competitive spirit of their ancestors and the canoe was not entered for the only Regatta which I actually attended: Government had been asked for a large sum of money, over £100, by the Bimbia Chief to put their boat in a state of repair, it having lain out all the year utterly neglected, and had very properly refused.

When we first came to Man O' War Bay it had seemed that Bimbia, our nearest rural community, would be a very good place to try to help. So, armed with spades and headpans, the students set out one day to assist the Bimbians in constructing latrines. The understanding was that so many young men would be provided by the village to work with ours, and the whole project had been discussed with Chief and people beforehand to make sure that they wanted the latrines and were prepared to work with us. Apparently they repented when the time came for, while the students sweated and worked in the heat of the day, the villagers sat in the shade watching and assuring them that, while enjoying seeing others work, they had no intention of using the finished object. Was not the beach available to them? After two or three frustrating days the project was called off.

However, Bimbia was not erased from our visiting list altogether and expeditions still went round by sea, beached their boats at the village and returned overland, while half the course, having started overland, picked up the boats at Bimbia and returned by sea. I saw only the beginning and the end of these outings and they caused me some of my most anxious moments. Down at the jetty, with laughter and discipline, in the hot sunshine, as they piled into the canoes the men all looked lifesize and our seamen, Maurice Dienne (affectionately known as Ab-le-sea-man), 'Blackie' Nelson and Thomas, competent and efficient. Half the accompanying British staff always knew about boats and the other half could be trusted to look as if they did and not add to panic in an emergency.

I waved them off and they shouted and laughed as they pulled away from the wharf. But when I got up to our house and went to the cliff's edge to watch the canoes round the corner and begin to strike across the bay there seemed to have been a change in scale.

Now it was the sea which looked large and self-confident and the canoes scratching across its surface like water beetles all too easily a prey to adverse circumstances. Even the binoculars could not help to restore the balance though for a moment they gave back individuality to the occupants of the boats.

I watched these toy vessels creep slowly out towards the open water, rising and falling as they began to meet the swell and sometimes hesitating as an unaccustomed paddler realized whither he was bound and momentarily lost his nerve. I could have thrown a stone and sunk them all, or so it seemed, and now even the illusion of speed was gone and I could barely tell that they were moving, so much more powerful was the counter movement of the sea. At last the small black speck, hardly distinguishable as boat or rock, disappeared from the corner of the bay where my eyes had strained to find it and I was released from my personal compunction to keep them safe by sympathetic effort; I could go back to the house and pretend to forget them.

The hot afternoon drowsed by with time to do some of the hundred jobs so constantly left undone until something in the colour of the sun told me that the moment had come to look again, to help the other party returning round the point and back to home.

This could be a genuine agony. If there were no moving speck upon the sea I wondered what had happened to them. Were those rocks that I could just distinguish really rocks, or were they changing place and gradually enlarging? Alas, no. But now, truly this time, the long shape of a canoe had materialized beyond the point. And so began again my anguished (and unnecessary) assistance. There was a strong tide running round this point and a heavy swell; if the party had miscalculated their time it could be a difficult and frightening job to get the boat into the calm and safety of the bay. I watched my speck move two paddle strokes forward and then slide one back. It seemed to me, my view hideously contracted by distance and perspective, that they were slipping nearer and still nearer to the spraying waves breaking on the rocks. Surely an hour had gone and they were no farther forward than when I had first glimpsed them! But time, like distance, had got out of hand. Nevertheless the struggle was sometimes hard and I do not think that anyone ever knew how much I suffered on my promontory bringing home the boats by prayer and will-power.

But oh, the relief when they did, at last, turn the corner and begin to enlarge! Signs of movement became visible, the black spot materialized into a recognizable shape, thin spidery lines detached themselves from its sides and became paddles, heads rose up, and then a faint, thin thread of sound. Good heavens, they were singing, and I had imagined them half paralysed with fright! Then the glorious moment when they saw me first and the canoe swayed perilously while a forest of paddles was lifted in the air to wave. I rushed into the house and tore a sheet off the bed, a table-cloth, anything, and waved it madly back in an ecstasy of relief.

One night, however, my fears materialized and the canoe did not come back. The land party arrived safely but, though we strained our eyes to seaward, there was not a sign of life coming round the distant cliffs. As the sun began to set my husband decided that a search party must go out while there was still light to see if they had been driven on the rocks at any point. So a canoe was manned by staff, both black and white, and set off across the bay. This time I watched with keen and well-founded anxiety while they crept over a sea of molten gold and disappeared from sight. Night fell, rapidly as it always does, and the routine of baths and meals went on as usual. The remaining staff gathered in my house to wait for news which we knew must come overland as no one could bring a canoe round from Bimbia after dark. Suddenly, the telephone rang. I picked it up, my hand trembling, to hear a voice say: '*Ici Douala, ici Douala, est ce que Mme Dickson est là?*'

In such moments one does not think of probabilities or possibilities, all my anxieties rushed to focus on Douala in the French Cameroons. I knew that it was Alec; that something disastrous had happened.

'*Oui,*' I said, even my reasonable French deserting me. '*Oui, je suis Mme Dickson.*' Pause. Then my husband's voice saying:

'Darling, we couldn't make it. We got picked up by a launch and taken to Douala. I'm all right. . . .' Click, the line went dead.

I wasted some seconds trying to get it back again then turned to the others.

'Something's happened,' I said. 'They're all in Douala. That was Alec.'

I stopped. Something was wrong. They were not taking it as

they should, indeed they did not seem to be looking at me at all but through the window behind me, and one or two of them were even—smiling. It was monstrous. I turned round and at that precise moment my husband leapt through the open French doors and enveloped me in his waterproof cape. I do not believe he was ashamed of such a heartless leg-pull and everybody else seemed to find it infinitely amusing. If I had not been so completely wrapped up in my own anxieties I might have heard that his call was on our internal telephone system and that he was speaking from the big house less than a hundred yards away. The missing canoemen had been found, they had failed to overcome the tide at the point and been forced to return to Bimbia. Arrangements for the safe keeping of the canoe overnight had delayed them and the rescue party arrived just as they were leaving for the walk back overland.

The major sea expedition of each course came in the third week and involved spending a night on an uninhabited island. This was usually Mondole or Casement Island, the largest of the many in Victoria Bay. In the latter half of the nineteenth century when Britain had a Consul appointed to the Oil Rivers Protectorate who also took an interest in the affairs of the Cameroons (at that time still unaffiliated) two, at least, of these men had a house on this island, a pleasant change of scenery from the low-lying swamps of Calabar.

Sir Harry Johnstone, who was Consul in 1885, persuaded the Foreign Office to let him live on Mondole. He had a prefabricated house sent out in sections from Liverpool which contained a blue room, a red room and a green room. Sir Harry believed that the men who were making Africa their life work should, if possible, not live in boxes, constantly in a state of transition, but should look upon the country as their home, and live as comfortably as they would in their own land. Seventy years later, in different circumstances, we too had to make the decision whether or not our home was Africa and, all unwittingly, followed in Sir Harry's footsteps. We saw too many people living from one Leave to another, scarcely unpacking either physically or mentally in the months between. We decided to take out our wedding presents and our books, though they ran the risk of damage and loss, and to do our very best to create a proper home in the little house at Man O' War Bay. I am sure it was the right decision, and that one of the reasons for our success in a job that was often heartbreaking was the fact that we made for ourselves a true centre of strength and affection in our bungalow on the cliffs which enabled us to concentrate all our love and service in the country in which we lived instead of draining some of it away in longings for a different life elsewhere.

Sir Harry Johnstone's occupation of Mondole Island had been completely forgotten, but not so that of Sir Roger Casement who next lived there and the name Casement was still interchangeable with Mondole in the title of the island. Casement was, in fact, attached to the Survey Department of the Oil Rivers Province between 1892 and 1895, but his work was really that of an intelligence agent keeping an eye on the Germans in the Cameroons and the French on other frontiers of Nigeria. There is no actual record of his living on the island which, one must presume, came under German sovereignty by then along with the mainland, but it seems unlikely that his name would have lingered on attached to this specific lump of rock unless he had, at some time, inhabited it. He loved Africa when he first went out there as an idealistic young man and I am afraid it would have distressed and saddened him to know that we told our students something of his story as a traitor. For them, as indeed for us, it was a remote and ancient tale with no particular significance except that it added a certain interest and glamour to the expedition.

My husband believed that as many interesting side-lights as possible should be added to outings of this sort. A sea journey and a night spent in the open might be enough to sustain the interest of young Englishmen but for our Africans, for some of whom the former was a penance and the latter a not unusual phenomenon, adventure pure and simple was not necessarily exhilarating or welcome. So each section was set an exercise consisting of a survey of the island: information about the site of Casement's house, water supply, possibilities of present-day use as a training centre, types of fruit and fish, etc. Armed with this and provisions of all kinds, against ghosts and wild beasts as well as the more ordinary hazards of rain, hunger and cold, the crew set off in fine style, taking with them the life-boat as well as the canoes.

Writing in their log books after the return from this expedition the students would often give a vivid account of what it had meant to them.

'And the Commissioner came specially to receive the charts we had made of this island which had never been visited since Sir

Casement died,' wrote one. He may have got his facts wrong but the true spirit of romance was there all right.

Describing the rounding of the point on the way home in a rough sea another wrote: 'Then a great shape rose out of the sea, the mast creaks, a young man rose up before me unconsciously in terror. Though I did not fear anything afterwards I would not agree to part with my life-belt.' I cannot think that in such straits anyone asked him to part with his life-belt.

All sorts of extraordinary objects came home from these journeys. Very often the boats themselves presented a strange appearance when they rounded Cape Nachtigal, seeming to have grown some kind of forest on board, Birnam woods coming to Dunsinane. As they approached I could see that palm branches had been cut and arranged as a shady canopy over the paddlers and rowers. By a curious coincidence the songs that floated over the waters out of these decorated vessels were hymns, giving an Easter flavour to the whole cavalcade that contrasted strangely with the visual image of hot sun, heavy jungle and shining black bodies. Easter may be universal but for me these hymns conjured up daffodils, thin dark trees caught in a veil of green and the cool fresh smell of spring.

As they clambered on to the jetty I was presented with a variety of gifts. One, I remember, was a tiny coconut palm which was duly and ceremoniously planted by the donor outside our house. There were jars with crabs in them and little fish; curious stones and pieces of seaweed; stems of green bananas. The latter caused us to be very nearly embroiled in a lawsuit on one occasion. Bananas grow wild as well as cultivated all over this part of the world and fruit found on an uninhabited island was naturally assumed to be the property of the finder. Naturally but, as it turned out, wrongly. Some days later we received a formal complaint that some of our students had stolen bananas of very great value from a family who claimed ancient rights over the island. While contending that the price set on two small stems of bananas was far too high we had no means of disputing the actual title to the island and agreed to pay a reasonable sum in compensation. Our friends, who thought that they had here an admirable opportunity for money-making, at first refused our offer and it looked for a while as though we were going to be involved in an unpleasant row. However, the matter was eventually settled, to their satisfaction if not very much to ours.

Many of these trophies were eventually taken home by the

Northern students along with beer bottles filled with sea water, and in schools all over the Northern Region geography took on a new dimension when the teacher produced in class shells from the shore and allowed the more adventurous to sip from a bottle which proved that the sea was actually salt. One teacher told us that for many years he had been instructing that the higher one went the colder the air became—without in the least believing it himself. Of course, as one got nearer the sun the atmosphere warmed! Now he had climbed Mount Cameroon and found, to his great astonishment, that he became progressively cooler as he went up and was shivering on the summit.

'Now I shall be able to tell them that I *know* this to be true,' he said.

Some evenings we all went night fishing and this, though a profitless occupation so far as we were concerned (I never knew anything to be caught), looked quite wonderful. The canoes were all equipped with a very powerful light which hung over the bow, or perhaps the stern, with the object of attracting the fish, which could then be netted or speared. So our little bay suddenly developed a relationship to the Grand Canal; brightly-lit vessels slid quietly about in the darkness under the brilliant stars, soft laughter and voices floated across the water, and sudden skirmishes denoted either a false alarm about the approach of fish or a miscalculation on the part of an uncertain paddler. Perhaps it was the atmosphere of barely subdued bustle and enjoyment which warned the fish that the bay was not safe that night, or perhaps we did not take the whole operation seriously enough to be successful.

On the other hand our professional fishermen did sometimes manage to catch fish, often a shark, and then there was great excitement. The news would quickly fly round the compound that there was shark on the jetty and all work stopped at once. The labourers simply flung down their tools wherever they happened to be and ran to participate in the carving up. As a source of extra and free food this windfall was very valuable. It also gave rise to all kinds of jealousies, rivalries, even physical assault, and the responsibility for seeing that the division was fairly done had to be put into the hands of one of the senior employees. No work at all was possible for the next hour or two while every man watched with a gimlet eye the portions put aside for himself and for his neighbours. Even there it did not always end and on one occasion my cook, who had two wives, came running desperately to ask me to go and stop them fighting over the lumps of shark allocated to him. I, however, felt very strongly (though perhaps smugly) that this was an internal domestic affair in which I could take no part.

For some days after this I would, every now and then, become conscious of an abominable smell wafting over from my kitchen, where I knew quite well that no fish ought to be. I would rush across indignantly and fling open the door of the ancient oven. Sure enough it was full of unmentionable odds and ends of shark drying in among our evening meal or next day's batch of bread. When summoned, Lucas managed always to look extremely surprised and give the impression that he had no idea at all how his oven came to present such a curious appearance. Ebenezer, also, the culprit according to the cook, became very huffy and stood much upon his dignity. What happened in the kitchen was no affair of his; he had his pantry and I could see for myself that it was completely fishless, how should he know what Lucas did with his oven? A running battle went on between us until the shark was finally disposed of some days later. I watched the oven cleared and the fish removed; I showed my displeasure strongly and unmistakably; nevertheless some hours later the tell-tale smell would send me out again in a fury to hear the same tale of wronged innocence.

It never seemed to occur to my staff that they were doomed to discovery by the extraordinary pungent smell of drying shark in a tropic country. To be fair I must also admit that never once did either the dinner or the bread taste of its grisly companion. African cooks have some very powerful juju which enables them to produce excellent meals under impossible conditions using tools which are practically prehistoric and with foodstuffs whose taste they themselves neither understand nor care about.

Every year on Empire Day there were canoe races at Victoria but it was only in our fourth year that we thought of entering a crew. The course under training in May 1954 was a very good one on the sea and they were keen to test themselves out against local competition. Some, that is, were keen; there were always the few difficult students who found no interest in others doing the things which they themselves were not good at.

As the day grew nearer excitement rose. I dyed all the triangular bandages (by now discarded as First Aid appliances) bright pink and blue so the crews could wear them round their heads as distinguishing marks. How beautiful these vivid crude colours looked above their shining dark faces and glistening black chests! This was the first time that Man O' War Bay as an entity had taken on the rest of the world and we were all anxious that our canoes should do well.

The races took place very early in the morning before the sun had got too hot, and this meant a rise at dawn for us because the students were going to walk the four miles into Victoria. It was one of the perfect mornings that come when the season is changing, clear, sunny and blue. At the last moment, when the boats had been seen off on their journey round by sea, and everyone was lined up ready to start, there was a crisis. Down the steps of the big house came one or two of the more difficult students dressed to kill in their own clothes, 'co-respondent' shoes, dark glasses, natty panama hats. It had been decided, and everybody knew this, that shorts and singlets would be worn by all students and staff because we were going to the races as a Centre and not as a scattering of individuals.

There was silence while the course surveyed the culprits and the culprits looked defiantly at the course. I could feel my husband coming steadily to the boil beside me. The renegades had chosen their moment well; we were already a little late and we all knew that if we were not present at the other end when the starting gun went off no one would wait for us.

Riga Addingi saved the day. He cast one scornful look at the little band (by now slightly uneasy) and in two seconds his description of their clothing produced a roar of laughter among the rank and file. Ridicule is difficult to outface and Addingi had made it plain that the course did not wish to be associated on this occasion with anyone so conspicuously overdressed; if they came they came alone. As the two lines swung out of the compound, singing lustily, the rebels were observed to fall in quietly behind, indistinguishable from all the rest in singlet and shorts.

I went by car. It seemed rather shameful and I had been prepared to walk with them as my husband was doing but when offered a lift in the Land Rover I weakened and accepted it with pleasure. So I was down on the beach at Victoria some time before the contingent arrived.

There was great excitement. All the children of the neighbourhood were swarming round, examining the canoes, trying to sell cigarettes and nuts from round trays balanced on their curly heads, fighting and laughing; the women had on their best dresses, vivid cloths draped round their ample forms and enclosing firmly on their backs a nodding black infant. Surprisingly, many of the competing crews were female, highly-skilled paddlers although their enormous buttocks appeared to overwhelm their narrow craft. Wild administrative chaos was the order of the day on the beach, and it was quite impossible to tell what was meant to be happening. To my relief the Man O' War Bay life-boat, its attendant canoes clustered round it, was riding the swell out beside the official starting launch.

Presently a splendid noise was heard which sent the children scurrying up on to the road. Swinging along the causeway which emerges out of the forest came the students, led by Cpl Iloba playing the bugle. This ringing martial noise, backed by full-throated singing, gave an impression of triumph, before ever the races had begun, that I hoped would unnerve our opponents. We knew them of old and were already rivals: the men of Bimbia, though not today in their immense racing canoe.

The races were rowed in heats. The canoes started some distance out at sea and rowed to the beach through the surf. On the beach, surrounded by his court, stood old Chief Manga Williams, and the winning crew was that which first got a man to touch him. This may have been a good idea to begin with and was intended, I have no doubt, to make absolutely clear who had won, but as tempers rose and the crowds increased it all but ended disastrously for the old Chief.

The excitement was tremendous when the heats started. Far out at sea a row of bobbing, brilliant bandages indicated which crew was ours. At first they hardly seemed to move at all after the gun had gone, then rapidly they began to enlarge, paddling furiously and rocking perilously when they ran into the surf. In the bow each boat carried a juju emblem, a palm branch or a decorated stick, and behind it crouched the man who would leap on to the beach in the mad race for Chief Manga Williams. The steersmen yelled encouragement, Iloba lifted up his bugle and blew a wild tan-tan-tara. The spray broke and glittered, the children screamed, supporters began to fight; nearer they came and nearer, waves and paddles thundering upon the beach, till at last the racers leapt for shore and flung themselves through the crowd to reach the Chief.

We lost one heat, but L/Cpl Ekechuku's crew won theirs and were in the final. Their opponents were the men of Bimbia who looked upon the race as theirs by right and despised us anyway as foreign amateurs. They felt it beneath them to compete with us and paddled out to the start with contemptuous ease.

By now the whole course was gathered in a solid phalanx round the bugler, even the desert Northerner who had no interest in boats and had been discovered sitting smoking behind the Post Office. If lungs and good-will could bring our crew in first then we were ready.

They came flashing in, charging on to the beach, prow to prow, and the two racers leapt ashore. But the Chief—where was he? Surrounded as he was by his followers and Bimbian supporters, our man could not get through to him. Nothing loath the students flung themselves into the path of his rival. Pandemonium broke out, and the Chief was overwhelmed, buried beneath a scrum of conflicting bodies; all over the beach fights were going on.

The bugle now had to be used as a rallying cry and physical force was needed to separate some of the more joyful contestants. When, eventually, the crowd was reduced to order and it had been discovered that Chief Manga Williams was suffering from no worse than shock and a slight heart attack, it was impossible to ascertain who had won the race. We were sure that we had, and if not that it was dirty work which had foiled us at the last moment. The Bimbians were practically apoplectic with anger at the very idea that the result might be in question. This was their race and, whatever the appearances, they were the winners. The dilemma was resolved by a statesmanlike decision on the part of the Chief who elected to divide the prize money. It was as well; both sides were prepared to die for their rights!

So we formed up in two long lines and marched side by side to the Chief's house where he handed over thirty shillings to the captain of each canoe. And if our bugle blew a defiant and mocking note, and the looks that the Bimbians cast in our direction were more belligerent than congratulatory, no one really noticed or cared.

We spent our thirty shillings on a group photograph, to be treasured in the days to come, and on bottles of beer with which the whole course celebrated a famous victory later that evening.

If memories of past happiness, of deeds performed and dangers overcome in the company of others with whom a temporary community of aim has revealed a glimpse of the power and possibilities of friendship, give a man a background and basis from which to face the future with strength and confidence as I am sure they do, then, among many other things, we gave our students shared experiences which would play a part, however humble, in their view of the future.

PART TWO

'BETTER MEN'

ZARIA MARKET

CHAPTER VII

Sgt-Major
Riga Addingi
Queen's Own
Nigeria Regiment

VISITORS to Man O' War Bay as they watched the students engaging in strenuous activity and noted the physical characteristics which distinguished the different tribal groups used often to ask us the same question.

'Tell me, where do the best men come from? Which region sends the highest percentage of successes?'

At the very beginning, when we ourselves were still inexperienced, we used to try to answer this question. We would consider the traits which appeared in men from the same area or tribe and attempt to show that, perhaps, one or another was more receptive to this kind of training. But as time went on and more and more young men passed through our hands, as we began to be wiser and to see deeper, we came to the conclusion that the good Lord had divided His gifts very equally, that there were brave men and cowards, good men and bad in every tribe. It was not possible to make generalizations about any one section of the very large population (32 million) from which our students were drawn, and we were often surprised, long after a man had left us, by actions on his part which we had not anticipated.

It is true that there were certain tribal and regional characteristics, as there are in peoples everywhere, and that problems of background and tradition could, in some cases, determine ultimately whether a man was able to carry out what he had learnt when he returned. The men from Sokoto, one of the farthest away of all the provinces in the North-West, were stubborn and tightly closed against new ideas; the men from Bornu, in the remote North-East, were difficult, fighting men and fiercely individual; the Ibo from the South was talkative and ebullient; the Western Yoruba more sophisticated; these and other superficial distinctions were easy to make. But when, beneath the stress of shared strains and undertakings, we grew to know our students better and a man's individual character and ability began to dominate his heredity and family traits, then we saw that the Ibo who talked too much could also work, that the man from Bornu, once convinced that communal action was a good thing, could bring his vehement independent energy to bear on it with great effect; the man from Sokoto, who had resisted all our blandishments when in the South, could go home and try to practise what we thought he had never learnt, and the sophisticated Yoruba was capable of considerable sacrifice of dignity and outward show. Of course this did not always happen, it did not even happen very frequently, but often enough to make the job worthwhile and working with these young men a fascinating and rewarding occupation. Courage and cowardice, pride and humility were, in the end, evenly distributed.

There were the few who went back home to be a spectacular success, like the young Emir of Wushishi who was found by the District Officer up to his knees in mud making bricks with his people. There were those, also few, who were spectacular failures, like the young Tiv clerk who ended up in prison for embezzlement. But the real backbone of the work was the great mass of decent, cheerful young men who went back to their towns and villages—as policemen, teachers, coal miners, politicians, clerks, co-operative assistants, students, railway workers, adult education organizers, commercial employees, and a dozen other jobs—and who tried, not always perhaps very successfully or ably, to put into practice something of what they had learned. Sgt-Major Riga Addingi, Physical Training Instructor in 1954, had a slogan which he passed on to every course that season and which became part of the tradition of Man O' War Bay. It was a good slogan and one which the students accepted as expressing perfectly what we all aimed at in the courses: 'Better Men.' I am perfectly certain that many of them, years afterwards, when faced with a difficult decision, thought of Sgt-Major Addingi and his rallying cry, 'Better Men', and resolved to do the right thing even if it meant hardship.

It is not possible to mention more than a few of all the young men who came to us and who, subsequently, remained in touch with us. I have taken one or two whose stories are, for one reason or another, of special interest; but I would like to record our affection and admiration for the very great numbers of our students and staff whom we grew to think of as friends and to assure them that it is lack of space and not lack of love which prevents me mentioning them all by name.

It is a reasonably simple matter to find staff for any course to teach a special skill, when all that is required is that the instructor should know his subject and be able to impart it to others in a convincing manner. When, however, it is hoped that the students will leave the course not only with a certain amount of technical ability but also with a new attitude of mind and a sharpened awareness of spirit, then what is asked of the teacher is something much greater than straightforward knowledge and this makes him the more difficult to find. He has to agree that it is correct to try to open men's minds in this fashion and he must feel that the ultimate aim of this endeavour is worthwhile; but even believing this is not sufficient, he must be able to influence men by virtue of his own character and personality, for the ideas he is hoping to propagate are caught, not taught. He needed, for our special job, to love his fellows and be prepared to put up with them twenty-four hours a day, often in very trying circumstances. Such qualities are not easy to find.

For some time, because our methods and ideas were new and strange, we had wondered if it was going to be possible to get Nigerian staff who understood these ideas sufficiently to be able to inspire them in their own people. We were asking a lot and we knew it. We had both Africans and British who failed entirely; we had some who tried conscientiously but yet made little impression; but, gradually, as the scheme became known, the quality of the staff rose until, in the end, we were recruiting first-class African staff. They were seconded from the Army, the Police and the Marine; sometimes they were lent for a season, sometimes only for one or two courses; one, L/Cpl Ekechuku of the Nigeria Police, was seconded to us for several seasons and became a pillar of strength. It seems invidious to mention one more than the others but C.S.M. Riga Addingi, who came to us from the Nigeria Regiment in 1954, was undoubtedly the best instructor, black or white, that we ever had.

Riga Addingi was a Tiv from the 'Middle Belt' which lies

between the Eastern and Northern Regions below the River Benue. The Tiv are a people who have resisted Muslim penetration and retained their individuality in the face of pressure from North and South. They are strong, stocky men, famous as carriers, with heavily cicatriced faces; the women have the most beautiful patterns embossed in the flesh of their backs and breasts. Riga was the eldest son of a farmer who expected him to follow in his footsteps on the land and saw no need for the boy to have any education. This did not suit the son and at an early age he ran away from home and joined the Army. He must, even then, have had an exceptional character for he could not fail to recognize that he might be forfeiting the family's good-will—and this means a great deal in Africa. The Army accepted him and he began to lead the ordinary life of a soldier. He found himself, however, at a disadvantage because he spoke only his own language, Tiv, and he could neither read nor write. The *lingua franca* of the North, and of the Army, is Hausa and this he set himself to learn. Having learnt it he was still irked by his illiteracy; his family had forgiven him and he wanted to be able to communicate with them but he could only do this by having his letters written for him, which was expensive and fretted his independent spirit. And when letters came back at long intervals he must get a friend to read them out which was done perfunctorily, or with a too immediate interest in the Addingi family affairs. So many nights, by the light of a hurricane lamp or a candle, Riga sat up while his companions slept, sweating over the books he had managed to borrow, teaching himself to read. All this had to be done without loss of keenness and efficiency during the daytime, for he was determined to outstrip his contemporaries and could not afford to be thought lazy or sleepy-headed. But at last the day came when he managed laboriously to trace out his first letter to his family and to read theirs to him without the intermediacy of a friend. Perhaps he never quite lost the thrill of this first triumph for, many years later when we came to know him, he was still a tremendous letter writer.

About the same time he got promotion and began to rise in his profession and he recognized that to remain bilingual in Hausa and Tiv when the universal language of the whole of Southern Nigeria was English might prevent his reaching the goals he had set himself. So his evenings were now devoted to teaching himself English, and then to learning to read and write in that language too.

He came to us as a Physical Training Instructor, very highly recommended by the Army. A succession of poor instructors with good testimonials had made us wary and we received Addingi cautiously. He far transcended his recommendations. Cheerful, robust, courageous, disciplined, he was one of those rare men who possess the ability to inspire others. He could lead his fellows—the timid, the effete, the conventional, as well as the adventurous—in feats of physical and spiritual sweat and courage of which they had not thought themselves capable. He could show highly educated young teachers that there were other values in life than the accumulation of knowledge, and they believed him when they would have believed no one else.

'Grammar,' said Sgt-Major, with the utmost contempt, signifying by this one word all superficial learning, 'Grammar! U S—useless! Now I show you what makes a man,' and he would launch into his P.T. lesson, in himself a superb example of the virtues (not only physical) which make a man, whether he knows anything about grammar or not. The astonishing thing was that his students accepted his judgment. Though a few days before meeting him they would have said that 'grammar' and everything it stood for—higher education, a white-collar job, freedom from any kind of humiliating labour—were the most important attributes of a gentleman, the contact with Riga Addingi brought with it complete recognition that here, with none of their superior advantages, was a man who far outstripped them all in character and capacity, and, to their credit, they loved him.

When the season came to an end Riga spent many hours writing letters to those of his students who lived within reasonable distance of the railway line which he must travel back to his army depot in Northern Nigeria. The message received by each man read: 'I shall pass through your station at [indicating the time whether day or night]. You will be there.' And so they were. His journey, nearly one thousand miles, became a triumphal progress; at all hours of the day and night young men trekked to the railway line to greet him. Only one failed, because his letter arrived a day too late. We saw him shortly afterwards and he told us of his great disappointment at missing this chance to greet the Sgt-Major.

This, then, was a man on whom we could rely utterly. His loyalty and courage were beyond question and his robust humanity gave him the power to impart his own virtues in some measure to others.

It had long been his ambition to see Britain and we hoped very much that his excellent service at Man O' War Bay would weight the scales in his favour if he were ever to be under consideration for any overseas course. So we were delighted when, some time after we had left Nigeria, a letter arrived at our home in Edinburgh telling us that Addingi was en route for the United Kingdom to spend three months at Aldershot on an advanced Army Physical Training Course.

The Army sent him in one of their own planes which arrived in this country ten days before the course was due to begin. We thought of him at Woolwich, for the first time in surroundings which bore no resemblance to anything he had ever known, and asked if it were possible to bring him up to Scotland on a visit. Permission was given and a place found for him on an overnight bus.

Sgt-Major was finding life very strange. Reality so rarely coincides with imagination for any of us. His English, which in Nigeria was rich and racy, seemed in England to have become hesitant and incomprehensible. Food was foreign and unpleasant and he was having a good deal of trouble eating and digesting it. The climate was cold and the temperament of the strangers who swarmed around him was, apparently, cold too. He was lost, missing the accustomed structure of society and the warm friendliness which permitted total strangers to accost each other without taboo. People were kind when he did approach them to ask the way, which he did frequently, but when he produced a notebook in which he wished to record the names and addresses of all who had helped him they became silent and evasive and slid off with nervous looks. Nevertheless he retained his kindliness and his essential common sense; he had come to see what we were like in our own country and he recognized that all the surprise at strange behaviour was not necessarily on his side.

On the bus, however, something of his feeling of exasperation at our aloofness broke out. It was a company which supplied hostesses on their long-distance coaches and, shortly after the start from King's Cross, she began her duties.

'I'm Jeannie McClintock, your hostess. Are you quite comfortable? The first stop will be Stamford where you can get out if you wish. What about another rug? Are you sure that you're quite warm enough?'

She went round each passenger ascertaining his or her wants but always when it came to Riga she lost courage and, with a quick, uncertain smile, passed on to the next man. He must have looked formidable to her, a big black man in army uniform with a fiercely cicatriced face. She had been asked to look after him and had been warned that his English might not be very good so she felt that she had an excuse for not addressing him directly. Riga, on the other hand, had a growing feeling that he was missing something; here he was, in a closed community where people were making an effort, however stilted, to be friendly and, for some reason that he could not wholly understand, he was being left out.

So when, on her third or fourth round, Jeannie McClintock was handing out cardboard boxes of food and did so to him without the customary word of good wishes for a hearty meal, he burst out:

'Why you no speak to me? You think I speak French? You think I talk German? You speak to all these people but you never speak to me.'

Jeannie McClintock was confused and surprised by this vehement attack but she recognized both the justice of the accusation and the fact that she was, probably, depriving her most appreciative customer of the benefit of her mothering. Henceforward she spoke to him and so did many of his fellow-passengers; when he left the bus at Edinburgh next morning it was obvious that he had made many friends.

This ability to break down normal barriers and make men forget that differences of colour, race and education, ordinarily supposed insuperable, lay between them and him was shown many times during his stay in Great Britain. We saw it ourselves when we took him round Scotland in those first ten days. In villages in the remote Western Highlands, where black men are rare and surprising, Riga Addingi quickly established a rapport: in Aldershot, where no one takes any notice of students from abroad, he earned golden opinions and made many friends.

One evening, a particularly beautiful one, we arrived at Kyle of Lochalsh. The hills of Skye, a wonderful distant blue, rose on the other side of a sparkling, glinting sea. It was May and the light lingered on long after (so Riga thought) the proper time for darkness. We went for a walk, climbing down below the little town to where some boys were playing shinty on a piece of rough ground beside the sea. As we descended the path more small boys materialized and began to follow us, keeping a safe distance in case the black man should do anything untoward. To Sgt-Major small boys of any kind were of interest and in a short time he, too, was hanging back endeavouring to engage them in conversation.

When we reached the shinty ground my husband and I wandered on, content to enjoy the evening and admire the wonderful scenery. Sgt-Major Addingi, with his small following, stopped to watch the game. Five minutes later we turned and saw that the game had stopped and Riga was surrounded by small boys. He was beginning to strip off his heavy coat and khaki battledress; some of the boys were, rather slowly, taking off their jackets.

'Now make I show you,' we heard Riga say, and he launched himself into a perfect handspring on the heather. 'Now you, and you, and you, Tom!'

One after another the small boys followed suit until a full-blown physical training session was being held on the shinty ground. One or two of the bigger boys, however, stood out against the persuasive charm of this black stranger, lounging on the perimeter with hands in pockets, constituting a dangerous opposition to Sgt-Major's authority. He was too good a teacher to permit this and presently we heard:

'You big boys, why you no go do 'em? You be no good! U S useless! You only fit stand there and drink tea!'

I held my breath, horrified at the possibility that these dour fifteen-year-olds might answer in such a way as to shrivel all Riga's confidence in the essential brotherhood of black and white. There was nothing we could do and we waited in extreme apprehension. For a few seconds there was silence, then the biggest of the boys slowly took his hands out of his pockets, removed his jacket and began to practise a forward roll. The rest followed his example. For one evening in this Scottish village roles were reversed and a black man gave back to these children, to their enormous surprise, something of what their forbears had given to his people.

Very conscious of his good fortune in being sent to Britain Riga was anxious to know how much money had been spent on him by both his own Government and ours. We could not tell him exactly but we were able to let him know the probable price of the air fare. His reaction was one all too seldom found among recipients of Government grants.

'*Kai*, I must work hard if they go spend all that money on me!'

This word '*Kai*' and another 'Kpash', the latter an expression of amazement, the former equivalent to 'Fancy that', amused us very much. He used them frequently and with a wonderful rich and fruity vehemence which seems impossible for a European voice. He became very attached to my mother, whom he called 'Ma' from the first moment of introduction, and when, at his request, she showed him photographs of her sons and grandsons he exclaimed in admiration:

'*Kai*, Ma, you done try too much!'

Sgt-Major Riga Addingi is again immersed in the daily duties of a C.S.M. seconded to a boys' training unit, but he writes faithfully and often. We are mutually in each other's debt for if he owes us anything for the experience which his visit to Britain brought him we recognize that we owe to him a large portion of our ultimate success at Man O' War Bay. His last letter retailed with pride the presentation to him of Long Service and Good Conduct medals. We wrote back, delighted:

'*Kai*, *Kpash*, you done try too much!'

GBOKO

CHAPTER VIII

Dauda Haruna Kwoi, M.H.A., M.B.E.
Ogbonnaya Okoro

THE Sixth Course, which took place in May–June 1952, was a very difficult one. The month before the two young men had died on Mount Cameroon and an atmosphere of alarm and despondency had spread over Man O' War Bay making the students nervous and jumpy, and infecting the staff with a certain amount of indecision. We all knew that this course was a vital one in the life of the Centre; we could not afford to have any more accidents, but neither could we afford to go back on our previous assertions that there was nothing on the mountain which could not be overcome by courage and physical effort. We must go on, walking a tightrope between success and failure.

The first weaving lesson took place the morning after the students had arrived. I noticed a Northerner who did not seem to be making very much progress with the disentangling of his thread and the setting up of the loom. Because the atmosphere was tense and uncertain I spoke louder and more heartily than usual, teasing and shaming the clumsy ones without taking much account of the reasons behind their failures. When I came to the Northerner he bore my mockery with a smile and did not tell me why he found this particular lesson so difficult. It was only later that I learnt that, on the journey, his spectacles had been mislaid in the lorry and without them his sight, for fine work, was very bad.

This was Dauda Haruna Kwoi, a man of gentle kindliness, honourable and courageous.

He was of frail physique, having suffered for a long time with a weak chest; tall and thin, rather paler in colour than many of our students, with his oval shaven head set most beautifully on a slender neck. His smile was full of humour and compassion and he was incapable of malice or bitterness; a Christian, he represented Christian interests as a nominated member of the Northern Region House of Assembly. It was no light thing for a man in such an august position to come on a course of this nature, and Dauda Kwoi had volunteered to come because he felt he ought to know something of what was going on at this place Man O' War Bay.

Originally his family had come from much farther north than Kwoi, which is in the middle of Nigeria, but his father had been a convert to Christianity and had had to leave his home because of the fury of his family and neighbours to come to live in a district which was not Moslem but pagan. I used often to look at Dauda, who took his Christianity very seriously and was prepared to suffer for it, and think how far we, in the safe security of a traditionally Christian democracy, had forgotten the realities of our faith.

In the same section, wearing the same green shirt which distinguished the group of eight as 'Section 1', was a young Ibo. Robust, self-assured, exuberant, he too had an interesting background. He was working on a daily pay basis for the Public Works Department when the Regional Community Development Officer noticed him at a meeting of local African staff called to hear an address on Community Development. Recognizing in the young man qualities of leadership which could take him a long way from the humble job he now occupied, and also the zest and ability which he, nevertheless, brought to that job, Mr Chadwick decided that he must go to Man O' War Bay. The Public Works Department refused to release him on pay which meant that if the young man came on a course he lost his job. Mr Chadwick, however, said: 'Let him go,' and himself made it possible for money to be found so that he could come to us: his judgment of character proved correct, the young Ibo took his chance and went on to make a position for himself. Ogbonnaya Okoro recognized opportunity when it knocked and leapt to make the most of it.

From the first he was a natural leader. Of splendid physique, unafraid physically or spiritually, he quickly made an impression and, in a course of fearful, hesitant men, his section alone presented a united front. There were weak members, but such is the effect of assurance and courage that they felt themselves braver than their normal wont because section public opinion and the confidence of their leader made them so.

Ogbonnaya Okoro and Dauda Kwoi became firm friends. This was remarkable not only because these two men differed so greatly in character, background and the nature of their abilities, but because one was an Ibo and the other a Hausa, and friendship between these two peoples is rare. The Ibo, for the most part, gains his opinions about the Hausa from the itinerant traders who travel about the country selling small merchandise, and thinks of them as two-faced wheedlers from a backward country; the Hausa, on the other hand, is conscious that in his own region he has, until very recently, had to rely entirely on Southerners for most of the skilled jobs, for clerks in offices, train drivers, signalmen, overseers and foremen. Many of these are Ibos, a people who are energetic and adventurous, who spill out from their own region to gain prestige and make money all over Nigeria. Pride and the knowledge that his people are to some extent dependent technically on these Southerners leads the Hausa to despise them, and community feeling would make it hard for an individual Hausaman to own to having an Ibo friend. On every course we used to set as the subject for an essay, 'Is real friendship possible between North and South?' These essays were written in a quiet hour before supper and after a strenuous day, and we hoped that in the writing of them a little time was given for reflection about the underlying ideas which were the foundations of the activities undertaken; they certainly gave us some insight into the understanding, or otherwise, which individuals had of the things we tried to teach them. Sometimes the answer to the question of friendship was 'yes' but with a note of highmindedness which made us feel that the writer was saying what he thought would be acceptable rather than what he felt to be the truth. But quite often the answer was an uncompromising 'no', which came as something of a shock when we had watched young men from both regions climbing, swimming and working together in apparent amity.

It seems probable that, for Okoro at least, the friendship between himself and Dauda was dramatized at the start as a 'good thing'. But to pay lip service to an ideal is often no bad beginning to the growth of genuine feeling for it, and these two men quickly found in each other not just national characteristics which they were determined to admire, but personal traits which drew them together. The courageous determination of the Northerner to undertake physical tasks far beyond his frail strength roused a protective admiration in the tough Ibo, and both, men of integrity, respected each other's methods of meeting the difficult problems of everyday life; a gentle resolution on the one hand, an outspoken strength on the other.

On the mountain climb, fraught with tensions and undercurrents, it was the section containing these two men which supplied eight of the fifteen volunteers who had agreed to climb at all; seven of them under the leadership of Okoro got to the very summit, Dauda reaching the second hut at 10,000 feet, a magnificent effort of endurance.

They had told us when the course came to an end that they intended to exchange visits during their next vacations. We recognized that this project presented difficulties, not only of immense travelling distances but also of all kinds of intangible obstacles, and wondered in our hearts if it would ever turn out to be more than a dream. Dauda Haruna went back to organize Adult Literacy classes in Kwoi and to continue his work in the Northern House of Assembly, where he spoke with refreshing frankness of his time at Man O' War Bay; Ogbonnaya Okoro was appointed Educational Assistant in the Eastern Region and proceeded to justify the help he had received.

However, this was not the end. Next year, when Okoro's annual leave was due to come round, Dauda wrote to ask him if he would come to spend it in Kwoi. It was not a simple matter for either of them. When it became known in Kwoi that Mallam Dauda had invited an Ibo to stay he was sent for by the Emir.

'What is this I hear?' said the old man. 'It is told me that you have asked an Ibo, a Southerner, to stay with you here in Kwoi. My son, you cannot do this. I must forbid you. We cannot have a man of that tribe here among us influencing our children and spying on our people. You must write at once, Dauda Haruna, and tell him that he must not come.'

To which Dauda answered, with a sweetness which concealed determination:

'This man is my friend. He will come here as my friend seeing only good and wishing no evil. When I went away to this training in the South last year I learnt many things. I learnt that God made all men to have the same hopes and fears, the same thoughts and desires, whatever their tribe. I learnt that it is possible for men who come from different nations to be friends, and that it is good that they should be so for how otherwise are we to build up a world of peace for our children? I want to show my friend that this love is real and to let him see and know my children and my people, and how can I do this unless I ask him into my home?'

The Emir was unconvinced, but Dauda was a man respected among his own people and he was not to be swayed by adverse public opinion. So, reluctantly, he was dismissed with an admonition that he, Dauda, was answerable for the good behaviour of the stranger.

HAUSAMAN

Okoro, on the other hand, when asked by his fellow-clerks where he intended to spend his leave, had to put up with a good deal of mockery and unpleasantness at the idea that he should go to stay with some Hausaman in a remote village in the uncivilized North. Why did he not go to Onitsha or to Lagos, the big cities of the South where there was plenty of life?

So Okoro arrived one day by lorry in Kwoi after a long journey by rail and then a dusty, bumpy one by road. The country was much more open than he had been accustomed to, rolling lands with outcrops of rock which became on the horizon fantastic, piled-up hills. The village, with its round mud huts each enclosed by a high wall within its own compound and the square palace of the Emir in the centre, was quite different from his own sprawling Ibo villages of oblong, palm-thatched houses facing on to the street and the focus of bustling, energetic life. The handsome shy children who watched the arrival of this stranger turned away when he greeted them, unlike the impudent, cheerful rascals of his own town; dignified, withdrawn men in towering turbans and long flowing robes, squatting in circles in grave discussion, had none of the pushing friendliness to which he was used; but Dauda's welcome, at any rate, left nothing to be desired and Dauda's wife and children took him warmly into their home.

It was not in Okoro's nature to stay quietly behind the walls of his friend's compound for fear of offending the village. He felt, as do many young men in Nigeria today, that he carried a banner for Progress and there was no point in carrying a banner unless it was well seen. Dauda, in his own way, understood this fighting spirit in his friend and respected it, so when Okoro suggested next morning that they go out together and start some community development in which the village could gradually join them he agreed, though he must have had many qualms about the outcome. He also suggested a starting point; a small gully ran through the centre of the village which, in the rainy season, filled with water, making a difficult obstacle for the women and children and, even in the dry season, causing lorries considerable trouble. They could construct two culverts substantial enough to carry a lorry and provide dry walking for men and women. Difficulties did not occur to Okoro as daunting factors but as challenges to his spirit and ingenuity and he genuinely loved people, especially children, and could not imagine that they might fail to respond; Dauda was always prepared to stake everything on what he felt to be right, and he felt this to be right: so they sallied forth.

No doubt, at first, the children came out of curiosity to see what this monster, the Ibo whom their mothers frightened them with, was like, but they stayed because he charmed them and within a week work on two culverts was proceeding apace with ample help from the delighted children. As the first culvert was finished the word 'Victoria' was written into the wet cement as a reminder that the original inspiration had been found in the Cameroons. When, next year, we visited Kwoi we drove proudly over this culvert and saw 'Victoria' cut deeply into its side.

That was not the end of the story. As the week drew to a close and the time came for Okoro to return to his home the Emir sent again for Dauda. He went, with the same simple dignity as he had gone before, ready to accept either praise or censure. The old man looked at him for some time before he spoke, then he said:

NORTHERN HOUSE

'Mallam Dauda, I would like to meet your friend, the Ibo. He is a good man and has done much for our people. We did not wish him to come but now we see that what you said about him is true, he is a friend. We would ask you to ask him if he would not like to leave his own country and come here to live with us in Kwoi, for we see that he has much to teach us.'

It was not in Dauda's nature to triumph, but he must have smiled gently to himself and been proud of his friend. Okoro came in to greet the Emir who repeated the invitation to stay. It was not possible for him to accept but he left Kwoi having struck a resounding blow for friendship between North and South.

When the Northern Region's delegation to the Constitutional Conference in London in the summer of 1953 was made up Dauda Haruna was included. He and a pastor from the Plateau Province represented the minority of Christians in a predominantly Moslem region and thus gave the delegation an appearance of broad-minded solidarity.

We were on leave in London at this time and made contact with Dauda to ask him to visit us. He had not much time to spare but said that it was possible to get off one afternoon and that he would very much like to do some shopping. Would Madam agree to go shopping with him? I was delighted and called at their hotel in the centre of London about two o'clock one afternoon.

I had forgotten in the months since we had seen him what a charming appearance Dauda presented and when he came into the lounge, clad in a long blue robe with a small embroidered cap on his head, I was struck afresh by the look of transparent goodness and kindliness which illumined his handsome face. He always wore the graceful robes which have become associated with the Moslem Northerner, though he was a Christian, saying that a man's faith was a matter of his heart and his actions, and not of his clothes.

We went out into the street and I began to question him as to what he wanted to buy. I was a little alarmed when he replied:

'Something for my wife, Madam. And then something for each of the children.'

'And how many children are there, Dauda?'

'Ten, Madam.'

Thunderstruck, I stopped in the street and exclaimed:

'But, Dauda, have you money for all this?'

West Africans can be prodigal in generosity themselves and

sometimes take it for granted that others are the same. I had, for a fleeting second, a vision of Dauda's purchases being heavily sub-sidized by myself. It was an unworthy thought and I should not have entertained it. Dauda dived into the folds of his gown and, after wrestling with them for some seconds, produced a thick, khaki money-bag of the kind used in banks. This afterwards proved to be full of sixpences and contained all his allowance of English money, several pounds. I never discovered why some official had thought it right to give a stranger from Nigeria all his money in sixpences; it seemed senseless and was certainly a nuisance. When, at the jewellery counter of a large store, Dauda had chosen with very good taste a gold link necklace for his wife and we proceeded to count out over £2 in sixpences to pay for it, the girl who had served us thought us not only 'foreign' but 'queer' into the bargain.

It was walking through the household linen department that Dauda suddenly caught sight of blankets. Africans find it difficult to resist blankets, that invaluable piece of material which can act as a covering, a shelter, protection against the weather, bed and home rolled into one, and his eyes lit up. They were of all kinds and sizes; pink, fluffy and enormous, small and light in green or yellow, white blankets, grey blankets, blue blankets, single and double. They were very beautiful and had I been an African with a love of blankets in my blood I, too, would have felt impelled to buy one. As it was I felt my responsibility as guardian of Dauda's purse weigh heavily upon me and foresaw all kinds of complications if he made such a bulky purchase.

'But you can't, Dauda,' I exclaimed when he stopped to examine them more closely. 'You came by air and you're only allowed a certain amount of luggage. It's impossible to take back anything so big and heavy.'

He turned to me with his enchanting smile, laced now with a hint of mischief.

'It is true, Madam, that I brought a large suitcase with me and I could not take back another one, but you see it was really empty because I knew I should want to buy many things in England. So I can easily take this blanket if I wish.'

I knew then that we were lost, and in a few moments Dauda became the proud possessor of one of the largest and pinkest and fluffiest blankets on show and we grandly paid for it in sixpences. A year later, in his home in Kwoi, we saw him for the last time. Already the tuberculosis that was to make his remaining years a valiant struggle against ill-health and hospital treatment was beginning to take hold of him. When we arrived, unexpectedly, at the door of his compound and waited in the outer room of his house while he rose from his bed to greet us I noticed round his wife's dark throat the gold necklace we had purchased for her in London, and, when Dauda threw open the door of his room and came out to meet us, I could see, discarded on the bed that he had just risen from, the lovely pink blanket.

But there was one more incident on our London shopping expedition. As we wandered through the crowded store, gazing at a delectable array of tempting objects, Dauda suddenly said loudly and without warning:

'Please, Madam, show me a Jew.'

I was flabbergasted and glanced hastily around hoping that we had not offended anyone. Dauda repeated: 'I want to see a Jew.' I began to try to explain that it was not so simple as he seemed to expect, to point out a Jew, and that they did not differ so greatly in features from those who were not Jews. He was puzzled and admitted that he had imagined them to be a different colour from the English and as easily distinguishable as Africans or Chinese. The explanation of the place of the Jews and their history then became so involved that I thought it better to delay it until we returned home for tea when my husband could make things clearer than I could. This we did and when, at the end of a long exposition of Jewish history, the difficulties of their being both a race and a religion, and other complicated matters, my husband said: 'Why do you want to know, Dauda? There aren't any Jews in Africa,' we got a very surprising reply.

'My people are Christian as you know, and we have our church in Kwoi. We are poor and have not much to give but every year we have a collection for the London Mission to the Jews. Last year we collected twenty pounds and so I wished to see the people to whom we were sending this money to help to save them.'

I thought, with a feeling of intense relief, of the prosperous Jewish women whom I might have pointed out to him in the store and whose furs and jewels must have made him wonder what benefit the pennies of Kwoi could accomplish here. My husband's first thought was one of indignation that the congregation at Kwoi, most of whom would be of pagan origin and among the poorest and lowliest of peoples, whose pennies would be hardly earned and greatly valued and to whom £20 would represent a small fortune, should be induced to send their money to the aid of a community which, even among the converts to Christianity, must number some who were very rich.

But, on looking again at Dauda's calm face, we had second thoughts. Here was his community, very poor, a minority in a region where a different faith held sway, accustomed to thinking of themselves as the underprivileged and backward, yet every year they had the opportunity to contribute to a group which they felt to be even more underprivileged than themselves, and this, too, in London, that fabulous city which represented all that was most opulent in the world. The feeling that they, too, the Christians of Kwoi, could give to others help which was needed lifted them up and gave them the opportunity, which they otherwise almost completely lacked, of exercising the Christian duty of helping those more impoverished than themselves. The use to which the money was put was of no great consequence; what mattered was the spirit in which it was given, that of true Christian charity. We felt humbled, and ashamed of our own niggardly giving out of what must have seemed to these people immense material wealth.

Dauda Haruna Kwoi died in 1957; in him we lost a true friend and his people lost a good and wise man. Before he died he saw the Queen visit Nigeria, an event which gave him immense pleasure, and received from her the M.B.E. 'It was good that I did not get my M.B.E. last year,' he wrote. 'This made it possible for me to get it from the Queen herself directly. She gave it me with her own hand and then shook hands with me.' A few months later he was dead.

His death was a blow to Ogbonnaya Okoro, for the two men had remained friends, though their opportunities for meeting were rare. Dauda's family wrote to his Ibo friend and told him that the face of Kwoi had been changed by many development projects the initiative for which they, at least, attributed to the famous visit in 1953. Okoro, himself, had his own difficulties to face; ambitious and flamboyant with a basic integrity which he, rightly, dramatized, he made enemies. He was without the pull which higher education and well-placed friends can give in a new country and the nature of his temperament made him out-spoken about his rivals and, occasionally, indiscreet in his actions. He was a man of his country and his time, struggling for a different and a better way of life though without clearly discerning what the shape of that life might be. He was also capable of great courage.

Some months after leaving Man O' War Bay, while he was Education Assistant to the Native Authority in Afikpo in the Eastern Region, a women's riot took place in that district. Women's riots are a favourite political weapon with the Ibo, and Ibo women can be formidable. The British District Officer or Police Officer faced with the serried ranks of these large, determined females, their offspring on their backs, is in a dilemma. His background and tradition forbids him to use force against a woman, either personally or by ordering his subordinates to do so; the women, well aware of this psychological prohibition, will listen to no words or threats until their object is attained, and either camp around the wretched officer's stronghold until he is forced to make concessions or actively invade whatever location is their objective. This happened in Afikpo. Some women had been jailed for riot and assault and five hundred of their fellows decided (or were incited) to demand their release. They crowded up to the Government station and settled down outside the District Office. Any attempt to talk with them by the District Officer was met with shouts and insults, and an effort by the police to remove them resulted in bad tempers on both sides. The women spent the night outside the District Office, dancing and singing, aware that they were in a strong position and determined to maintain it.

The next morning, when there was still no sign of slackening on the part of the women and the work of the station had become thoroughly disrupted, Okoro said he would try to make them see reason. This was a courageous act; he had no means of telling whether the women would listen to him and, indeed, because he was one of their own people and on the side of the law, they might well have become infuriated and harmed him physically.

He stepped out on to the verandah and tried to address the brightly-clad crowd in front of him. Delighted to have a focus for their indignation, the women shouted him down, jeering and insulting. Patiently and calmly all through a long and sweaty afternoon he argued with them, gradually wearing them down and compelling them to listen to him. At last it began to be obvious that he was winning their confidence; they started to talk in sensible terms and eventually agreed to send a delegation to the District Officer to discuss their complaint. This they did and so far had the mood changed that it was now possible for the District Officer to come to a reasonable agreement with the leaders and the crowd dispersed quietly to their homes. We would not have known of this story had the District Officer not told us himself.

These two young men were remarkable before they ever came to Man O' War Bay. I like to think that what we did for them was to give each one a greater understanding of his own powers and qualities and to focus attention on the ways in which they could be used to benefit others.

BAUCHI HILLS

CHAPTER IX

Johnson Chukwuemeka Obi—Andrew Maduku

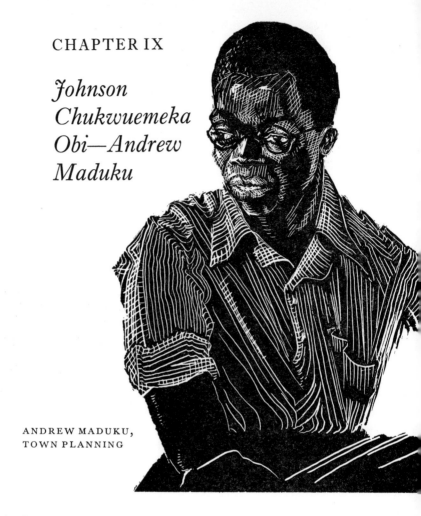

ANDREW MADUKU,
TOWN PLANNING

JOHNSON OBI, who came on the Fourth Course in 1952, was an
Ibo from the Eastern Region. Obi is a common name in this part of
Nigeria and we had many students whose surname it was, so we
generally used their Christian names to distinguish them.

Johnson was a good student; he belonged to the middle category
of ordinary, decent, young men who did what they were asked to do
and tried hard but who were less easily remembered than the outstandingly brilliant or the despairingly bad. He enjoyed his course
and went back to his job with the Eastern Region Co-operative
Department, satisfied that he had earned a reasonable report. The

first test came sooner than he had expected. The Registrar of Co-operative Societies, Eastern Region, had sent Johnson to Man O' War Bay because he saw in him all the potentialities of an up-and-coming young man, and with the idea that, if he did well on the course, there would be an exacting job waiting for him to tackle on his return. The Co-operative Inspector who had originally been posted to this particular station had resigned rather than accept the transfer and now Johnson was called into the office and told that he was to go to Tombel in Bakossi.

Bakossi, in the Kumba Division of the Southern Cameroons, was at that time beyond the reach of ordinary travellers. There was no road to it and the final part of the journey had to be done on foot with all baggage headloaded. The country was wild and very primitive, hilly, rocky, swampy in parts. The soil was exceedingly fertile but the small patches that man had managed to subdue were in constant danger of being swallowed up by jungle and bush. The people were backward, lazy and easy-going. It was possible to live off the natural products of the luxuriant soil and the efforts required to better their position by struggling against the fecundity of nature to clear ground for cash crops did not seem worthwhile. It was a remote, forgotten spot where a man could easily be submerged beneath the passive resistance of the inhabitants to change, and his own frustrations.

Johnson was young in the Co-operative service and was just beginning to build up a life for himself. He was furnishing a room with taste and style, he had begun to cultivate a circle of friends, his own people were among the most virile and active in Nigeria and he was on the threshold of launching out, a young adult with an assured career, within a community of which he was an integral part and whose workings he understood. The stories which he heard from friends of the difficulties of life in Bakossi lost nothing in the telling, and he was aware that in a rapidly developing society out of sight could often mean out of mind. He was appalled at the thought of this posting and the privations it would entail and dissolving into tears he begged to be excused.

The Registrar, a man of kindliness and insight with a concern for his young staff, explained that it had been in his mind when he nominated Obi for our course that he might be prepared on return to tackle an uncongenial job. He hoped that, having learned at Man O' War Bay to overcome difficulties, Obi would be ready to carry this lesson into his ordinary life; if he refused to go to Bakossi no one would force him to do so but both his own officer and the staff at Man O' War Bay would be deeply disappointed.

It was a hard decision for Johnson to be faced with, just when he thought that he had done with hardship for a while and could enjoy the bright lights and cheerful fellowship of his own region. He could have refused, many of his colleagues would have done so preferring to risk promotion for the sake of comfort, but Johnson pulled himself together and agreed to go.

He wrote and told us what had happened to him before he set off into the wilds and asked, unselfconsciously in the endearing fashion of his people, for our prayers; then he disappeared from our ken. Life outside the jungle went on as usual and no news came out of Bakossi. After some months, however, there was another letter, this time altogether different in tone. He wrote cheerfully of difficulties overcome, nine new Co-operatives set up, some miles added to the much-desired road system; he had become a personality in the area. More important he wrote with self-confidence and assurance, aware that he had triumphed over arduous conditions. When his tour came to an end he had earned the commendation and added responsibility that awaited him. Perhaps also he had discovered an ability in himself to go further than he had before thought possible, and maybe his sympathetic Senior Officer, in training him through hardship for a higher position within the Co-operative Department had, like many a parent and patron before him, reckoned without realizing the ultimate effect on a young man of finding himself confident and capable with all the world before him.

At any rate we had a letter, one day in 1955, addressed to our home in Edinburgh, telling us that Johnson had obtained a Central Government Bursary and was coming to the University of Hull to take a degree in Economics, with the hope of going on to be a Chartered Accountant. Arriving in winter his first impressions were of cold, of the kindness of the British and their keenness to help the stranger; but he noted also that people would not sit beside him in a bus unless there was no other seat vacant, and that ladies declined to dance with dark gentlemen even if they were without a partner. These things hurt and surprised him, but he was ready now to balance good and bad and even prepared to attempt to alter some of the things he disliked by public-spirited action on his own part. He had come a long way from the boy who wept because he was being posted out of his own region to a difficult and isolated job.

His letters from Hull in the first year, written in impeccable and idiomatic English, were full of the enterprise, vitality and enjoyment that are the hallmarks of the young Nigerian student. He had not a great deal of surplus money but this did not deter him from seeing as much of the country as he could in his free time. He earned the extra cash for this by doing all kinds of odd jobs, and about this time turned up in Edinburgh to see Scotland—a trip paid for by his working on nightshift in a biscuit factory and using his days and his pay for bus tours round the Lowlands. He visited a great variety of places inside Britain and spent many of his vacations on the Continent, visiting Spain, Germany, Holland, Belgium and France where he spent a week as the guest of the family of a French friend whom he had met in Hull. These tours he called his 'hop abouts' and they contributed greatly to the balanced and sensible view which he began to develop about the people of Britain. He was not unusual in his initiative, our other ex-students who came to the United Kingdom to study also displayed this curiosity and enterprise, taking themselves to many out-of-the-way places with a charming gaiety and confidence, one on a pilgrimage to Lourdes, another to a weekend in Paris, a third round Sweden and Norway.

While in Grimsby on a visit Johnson was asked to address the Local Council of Women and he wrote with humour and appreciation of their reception of him:

> 'Sixty venerable ladies formed my audience and what a strange audience for me who, at one time, could hardly look a girl in the face. I made sure my mother saw a picture of me taken on that occasion by the local newspaper (to throw back her taunts about my shyness). I felt very flattered by the ovation at the end of it all.'

I wonder if the Grimsby ladies, being addressed by a young Ibo, in a tongue not his own, who a few years before would have been horrified at such a prospect, realized how astonishing a feat of adaptation he was performing.

It was in 1956 that he began to sign his letters with the African second name which his parents had given him. He became 'Chukwuemeka', and Johnson was relegated to an initial in his signature. Perhaps, as with many of us, residence among people of another nation made him feel more strongly nationalist than before; perhaps it was a response to the wind of independence sweeping over the world; perhaps a sign that a different personality had emerged out of all this experience: whatever the motives which led him to make the change it marked a stage in his development. He was now a young man accepting his own background and proud of it; ready still for friendship, but friendship between equals. The letters were no longer those of a student to his old master but had become communications between colleagues whose interests touched at many points. He had from the beginning paid a good deal of attention to the interracial problems of the University, and he belonged to the Anglo-African Society. Hull had a large number of Nigerian students (between 80 and 100), and, in some ways, this made it more difficult for them to become part of the life of the University. Chukwuemeka (as we now call him) set himself the task of enlarging the activities of the Society and bringing together black and white. In 1958 he was elected a member of the Students' Council and writing to tell us of this he related also something of the history of his efforts in this direction:

'Relations between the African and the British students in 1955 were anything but cordial and close because the number of Africans here was large enough that they could form a little community of their own and withdraw into that small community. They did not mix with the "local" boys either in the games clubs or other social activities of the University, such as participating in the debates or even coming to the concerts or other dramatic shows. Reasons for this: the difference in upbringing and cultures—I refer, for instance, to the natural difficulty of an African to appreciate classical music. Then there is the difference in age. With an average of 5–10 years' difference in age, and given the African's sensitiveness to age, it was difficult for our boys to enter warmly into or appreciate the jokes and pranks of the English students. There is, of course, the fact that we are not equally responsive to the same jokes; what may tickle me to death may not even touch the outer fringes of the other chap's humour.

On the part of the British students, some of them were meeting Africans at close range for the first time. In some cases they were bashful to mix with us, or had first to overcome their accumulated prejudices (based on what picture of the Africans they had had painted for them).

Whatever we have been able to achieve in the Anglo-African Society has been due to personal contact mainly. For instance in my 1st and 2nd years I belonged to a number of societies and games clubs and mixed with the boys—and girls. Then last year a Nigerian pal of mine came in and he being a particularly good mixer made a lot of friends within a short time. Some of the friends he talked into joining the Society. Then there were two particularly friendly English members whose attitude charmed the hearts of the Africans they came in contact with. In short all along it has been mainly personal relationships that have the greatest impact on the attitude of potential members. Then we found that calypso music and high-life dancing are very much admired by the British students—and of course by the Africans. This lighter side of the Society's activities drew in quite a few.

I don't want to give the impression that it has been smooth sailing for the Society all the time or that the Society alone has been responsible for the changed social atmosphere here. Generally the Africans are coming forward to contest for officers in the University Union and as officers of the Union their prestige and social standing are enhanced—with good effects on the Africans.'

J. Chukwuemeka Obi got his degree with Honours and hoped to go to take his articles with a firm of Chartered Accountants. While I am sure that all the basic elements of his character were already formed before he came to Man O' War Bay as a student I would like to think that somewhere, on the mountain or sweating with pick and shovel, in the comradeship of games and laughter or in serious discussion, we lighted the fire which made it possible for him to accept Bakossi and then to go forward to such a full and balanced life.

Andrew Maduku came on the Eleventh Course sent from the Township Office, Sapele, in the Western Region, where he was in training as a building inspector. A small man, wearing spectacles, he gave no great promise of being athletically outstanding, and, on a course with the record number of seventy-four students, it seemed perfectly possible that he might be swamped and remain one of the rank and file making little impression. That this was not so was due not to any special physical ability on Andrew's part but to his alive, interested and kindly mind. He came ready to co-operate and pre-pared to believe that the things he would be asked to do were reasonable and constructive; he knew the object of the course and was anxious to profit from it.

Man O' War Bay had now been in existence three years and

had survived one disaster and many difficulties; news of its activities had travelled round Nigeria and public opinion among young men was gradually changing from fear and suspicion to an adventurous interest. It might have altered more rapidly had returning students not been so anxious to enhance their own reputations as men of courage and resource and in doing so exaggerated the difficulties which they did have to face into dangers requiring life and death decisions! The time had not yet come when volunteers asked to be sent on a course, but now, when nominated, they complied with faintly pleasurable anticipation. Many circumstances combined to make this course, the Eleventh, the best we had yet had. A first-class African staff were welded into a team by two previous courses that season together: C.S.M. Riga Addingi and Sgt (now Asst. Inspector) Atanda Agbaji were both men of the very highest calibre; Cpl Iloba, Nigeria Police, had been a student before staying on as an instructor and so knew the programme from two differing points of view; L/Cpl (now Sub-Inspector) Ekechuku, also of the police, had been with us for several seasons and understood thoroughly what the object of the training was; and, on the sea, Able Seaman Maurice Dienne gave admirable and highly skilled service. It was a good time of year, the extreme heat was past and the rains not yet upon us; the days were clear and sunny with an occasional shower which freshened the air. There had been a sudden decision by the Administration to close the only road into Nigeria because of its appalling condition which necessitated us flying in most of the students at short notice and at enormous expense: this, for nearly all of them their first time in the air, started them off with the feeling that they were already adventurous and courageous and prepared to tackle anything. Finally there was the new feeling which was spreading over the country that Man O' War Bay was, in fact, a good thing. So, in an atmosphere of cheerful co-operation, the course began well.

Of course there were 'incidents', life would have been unreal without them. One of our British colleagues deserted us on the first day without explanation; we were disconcerted at the primary roll-call to discover that we had a dear old man of 56 as one of the students, and at the other end of the scale there was a cheerful, unemployed boy of 17. Gabriel, the elderly gentleman, was also upset when he realized what was expected of him. A form had gone round his district asking for volunteers for a Community Development Course in the Cameroons and he had filled it up without any idea of the implications. He remained with us until it was possible to transport him back to Nigeria, and he and I watched many activities from the sidelines. Much later we climbed up a forest track in the Eastern Region to visit him and found, to our pleasure and astonishment, that this elderly man had taken to heart many of the things he had seen and heard and was making a real attempt to put them into practice.

This course we had decided to develop the singing and, under Sgt-Major Addingi, we really concentrated on learning and perfecting a repertoire of songs. The result was heart-stirring and, when during the last part of the course in the Eastern Region, helping local people to build a road and a bridge, we had a visit from the Lieut-Governor, that gentleman, no sentimentalist, was visibly moved to tears by the songs. It was here, too, that the students, on the final Sunday when they should have spent the time packing up and celebrating, volunteered to a man to finish the culvert which was still needed to complete their section of the road, a gesture which was unprecedented and which cut across all their usual ideas of privilege.

This, then, was the course which Andrew Maduku attended, one which, even for us who had seen others, had a special atmosphere. It gave Andrew memories which influenced many of his future decisions.

Sapele is a small township in the Delta area of the Western Region. Its chief occupation is timber which comes out of the huge surrounding forests and is floated down the river to Sapele where there are a saw-mill, a plyboard mill and other facilities. It is low, flat country without views; the roads lie through thickly wooded land and the towns and villages are unseen until almost underfoot. It could be a sinister country, dark and brooding, permeated still with echoes of the bloody history of Benin, but Andrew's warm welcome and his smiling face, the open peaceful stretches of the river and the handsome resthouse, dispelled any imaginary shivers that we may have had. All was not well, however; just as we had unloaded the car and prepared to settle in, another British official arrived and claimed the resthouse as his on a prior booking. Andrew, who considered himself our host, was disconcerted by this, as indeed we were too, and unsure what to suggest in exchange, but the day was fortunately saved by the kindly invitation of the United Africa Company to make use of an empty flat in one of their company houses.

Andrew had been busy since he had returned from Man O' War Bay. He had started a Boys' Club which went in for athletics and football, but which had the declared aim of bringing up the boys on the lines of good citizenship, future leadership and community development. In our more reticent framework it would be unusual to hear such aims stated publicly by a club leader little older than the boys he is training, we would smirk self-consciously and somehow feel that such a lad was 'peculiar'. The warmer and opener nature of the young Nigerian, and the particular stage in his country's development at which he now finds himself, makes it possible for him to say without shame or confusion many of the things which are in his heart. Andrew meant every word he said when he declared his intention of bringing the boys up on these lines, and the boys accepted from him the idea that civic duty and football went hand in hand—even though they preferred the football, and in 1955 succeeded in bringing home the local Cup. I was also amused and pleased at Andrew's tale of an incident in the street with a blind man. He did not relate the exact nature of the encounter, but merely told us that his restraint and lenience in dealing with the man had been remarked on afterwards. There had been jokes about Man O' War Bay being a toughening course, yet Andrew had come back soft. 'I told them,' he said, 'that the course is not supposed to make me hard to the blind and—la! Mrs Dickson's blind exercise was no joke. I remembered how I trembled thinking I would fall into a big pit.'

We went round the district to visit other ex-students, Andrew acting as our guide and friend. One evening, coming back along a dull, straight jungle road in heavy rain, we saw a strange sight, something we had never seen anywhere else in Nigeria. Running in single file along the grass verge, clad in shorts, wet with rain and shining with perspiration, were a dozen boys—training. We stopped the car and asked one of them what they were doing and who they were. The answer was a village boxing club run by a 'palm tapper' in his spare time. This was a rare enough event to be of great interest and Andrew promised to investigate further and do what he could to help them. He did not forget this promise as soon as our car had disappeared into the forest, but took the club under his wing and sent regular reports of their progress and development.

We had been away from Nigeria some months when a letter came from Andrew to say that he had succeeded in getting a scholarship to take a Town and Country Planning Diploma in Nottingham and would be in Britain in the autumn of 1955. It is a tremendous step into the future which many young Nigerians take when they decide to come to England. Most have very little idea what Britain is really like and many come from circumstances and background very far removed indeed from those in which they will find themselves over here. Yet all come with confidence, prepared to adapt themselves and ready to believe the best of us, though they may, at the last moment, have qualms about the wisdom of leaving their familiar surroundings.

Andrew left in a flurry of achievement and with the good wishes of a great many people. A senior members' training course for the Boys' Clubs of Sapele District had been arranged to take place in the week before he left; the responsibility was his and he intended it to be a grand affair. It was in his nature to take such things seriously and it was his farewell fling before departure into a different world. Boys came from all around and he had some well-known instructors including a boxer from the Gold Coast (as it then was) and a Nigerian athlete; the Principal Social Welfare Officer came from Lagos, it was a fitting finale. Andrew's own club scored the highest marks, closely followed by the 'palm tapper's' boxing club (who were very good at manual labour), so we also were well satisfied; indirectly Man O' War Bay had contributed largely to the development of both these organizations. Only one incident marred the day. The best boy in Andrew's team had marks deducted because he scratched himself in an unmentionable place in front of some women! They, the busybodies, without regard for the nervous frame of mind of a youngster engaged in an important test, reported him as behaving disgustingly. Andrew, rightly angered, wrote that they should have minded their own business!

Leaving home was painful, and there must have been moments when he regretted going. Many farewell parties were arranged for him, the Boys' Club played a football match in his honour—a favourite form of salutation in Nigeria—and defeated the combined Sapele clubs by 2—1. England seemed very far away, and for some of the older people it was as if he were taking his life in his hands with an equal chance of never returning.

So he came to Nottingham, finding Britain, as all his countrymen did, very cold. In the spring he wrote that 'winter seemed reluctant to pack bag and kit and depart finally', and he, too, found the bulk of the British reserved and difficult to get to know. Nevertheless he had seen the 'fires of adventure' at Man O' War Bay and recognized that these were found not only on mountains and at sea but also in adaptation to what is strange in everyday life and in keeping a curious and questing mind. Many of his comparisons were taken from that other outstanding experience; the top of Mount Cameroon was relatively warm compared to England in winter, he saw a book in a shop window and was excited because it was about 'our' Sir Roger Casement, on his own initiative he visited my mother in Edinburgh and told her how the Cameroons had changed his life.

We were, at this time, in the Middle East on a tedious and uneasy job, and something of the difficulties encountered must have permeated our letters to Andrew. It was a touching, and somehow proud, moment when he wrote to us in the terms which we had so often used in letters to him and his fellow-students. 'Shall I presume to council patience? Perhaps success might come in the end. Then joyfully we could keep to the immortal motto which has inspired so many Man O' War Bay students, "the impossible becomes possible".' It was salutary and strengthening to be reminded by our young men that we, too, had need of the principles which we had laid down for them. It was exhilarating to feel that they had grown up to equality with us and felt entitled to give back something of what they had received. Even the names by which he addressed us changed gradually as his confidence in our relationship developed. 'Dear Sir and Madam', the letters used to begin in the early days, to grow into 'Dear Mr and Mrs Dickson' as time went on and we became friends and not only mentors. And finally, with Andrew as with many others, the last hurdle was crossed and the letters started simply, 'Dear Alec and Mora'.

If I tried to analyse the friendships which developed between our students and ourselves I think one of the reasons for their continuance was this quality of growth. It was not a static relationship as between master and pupil; while ready to accept help and advice, to be taught the things which we knew and they did not, they did so without subservience, prepared themselves to offer help where their knowledge was the greater with every expectation of having that help accepted. This was a two-way traffic, both sides teaching, both sides learning. When difficulties beset Britain at the time of Suez, Andrew wrote with sense and sympathy in the name of his country, as a younger brother might to an older to whom he is bound by ties of affection and familiarity whatever the differences that divide them. Out of shared efforts in the Cameroons had come for us and many of our students a mutual respect which made us criticize each other from a basis of esteem rather than of prejudice.

PART THREE

THE FABULOUS JOURNEYS

THE ROAD TO THE NORTH

THE MAMFE ROAD

CHAPTER X

The Mamfe Road

ONCE every month, once every course, we made the four-hundred-mile journey from the Cameroons into Nigeria taking the students to participate in a village Do-it-Yourself, to show them Community Development at first hand and to give them the certain knowledge that many things were possible with hard work and combined effort. We felt it necessary to go into Eastern Nigeria for this because it was essential that our young men should work with a village, and not just for it, and in no place in the Cameroons was there the upsurge of village pride and virility which produced these conditions. In Eastern Nigeria, on the other hand, it would not only be the young Hausa Northerner who would be surprised to come round a corner and find four or five hundred men in the company of their chiefs and elders working frenziedly with headpan and hoe to make themselves a road, or a school, or a dispensary; we British also would find this an astonishing and exhilarating sight. For many of our students, who had either never believed this kind of work possible or had stood outside it because they were educated, it was a revelation of the opportunities for self-help and of the pride of achievement to be gained from communal labour.

These journeys were not easy ones to be lightly undertaken. There was only one road out of the Cameroons and because of its nature, precipitous and twisting, it was one-way traffic; vehicles went up into Nigeria on Monday, Wednesday and Friday and down on Tuesday, Thursday and Saturday. Sunday was a day on which only Governors or visiting U.N. missions travelled after due warning had been given of their direction of movement. This regulation applied for about 120 miles and meant that if anything went wrong and a car broke down within this area it might well have to wait over a whole day before it could continue the journey. When the rains came, those terrible Cameroons rains which give it the reputation of being the second wettest place in the world, portions of this road might well collapse, or bridges be washed away, and I have known it to be entirely closed for many months except on Saturday and Sunday, one day up the other down.

I started preparations for going on trek some time beforehand. Camp beds, bath, kit-bags and other purely travelling equipment were kept in readiness from one journey to another, but linen, china, food, cooking pots had all to be packed afresh each time. It was neither so complicated nor so intimidating as it sounds. My husband made a wonderful master-list of all we needed and we had special wooden boxes, known as 'chop boxes', into which it all fitted. But stores had to be taken according to the length of time we expected to be away and the location of the village we would be working in. It was perfectly possible that we might not be able to buy any dry stores, tea, sugar, flour, milk, butter, lard, etc., during the whole time we were away; moreover we might find that the village would not be able to supply us with much fresh food either, so we had to be prepared with substitutes for eggs, meat and vegetables. Petrol must go with us and kerosene for our lamps, and the lamps themselves; Ebenezer and Lucas came too and they brought also bedrolls, food and once, to my horror, an immensely weighty black cooking pot. All this—and ourselves too—had to be got into and on to our Chevrolet station wagon without breaking the springs. I prided myself on the ability to pack it like a complicated jig-saw puzzle, leaving no empty space but with things so disposed that in the event of an emergency the right things came out first.

When the morning dawned the routine was always the same—and in all the years I never got used to it.

We rose very early, in the candlelit darkness before the dawn. The lorries had all been packed the night before and at half past six they rumbled off into the sunrise, their sleepy passengers, our students, lolling on the hard wooden benches in the back. We returned to our house for breakfast and, when that was finished, packed the last of the pots and pans into their containers and put them in the car. I was always determined to start early, temperament and knowledge of the road ahead combining to make me feel that on such occasions it was fatal to be late. But my husband, sitting in the midst of a pile of papers all requiring his personal attention before he left, had no such intuitions.

At 10 a.m., having done and redone every last-minute job that I could possibly think of, eyeing with growing despair the pile of papers which still concealed my husband from the outer world, I would go out to the car to check up yet again that everything was all right. Sitting enthroned in the back seat was Ebenezer, an Ebenezer clad in a spotless best uniform, resplendent as we rarely saw him, ready to go.

'Oh, Ebenezer,' I cried. 'You'll get filthy on the road. Suppose we have to get out and push the car, you know it's been raining these last few days. Why wear your good uniform?'

Ebenezer never replied to this admonition; he just looked mulish. I do not suppose he could have put into words his reasons for wishing to travel in the maximum splendour but had he been able to they might have run something like this. At home everybody knew who he was, he had a certain position and standing as our steward; what he wore might reflect on us but it made no difference to his position. Now, however, he was going out on a great journey which would take him away from everyone he knew and from his own familiar background, so it behoved him to make it apparent, at a glance, that he was not just anybody but a man of importance. I have since, in my own country, had the very same feeling myself; but, at the time, I was always annoyed to find Ebenezer determined to travel in his best which, I knew quite well, would be ruined before the end of the journey. We would then be treated to the sight of our steward waiting on us in a torn singlet and filthy ancient shorts.

Thoroughly ruffled I returned to the sitting room determined to make my displeasure apparent to my husband by silent glowering: not that this made any impression at all. At 12 p.m. we ate the sandwiches which had been made for the journey in antagonistic silence. My harried husband, enjoying for the first time in three hectic weeks a spell of uninterrupted hours in which to catch up with necessary administration, must often have regretted that he had not sent me on with the lorries; he cannot have regretted it more than I did!

At 3 p.m. we went round the estate seeing that everybody remaining knew what they were to do in preparation for the next course, and I began to feel more cheerful knowing that the end was near. At 4 p.m. my husband said gaily:

'Well, shall we go? What are we waiting for?' The staff recognized this as an old joke and shouted back: 'We're waiting for master,' but I was no longer amused. We climbed into the car and set out on an eight-hour journey over one of the worst roads in West Africa.

It took me some twenty miles, until the roads forked below Buea and led away round the mountain to the north-east, to regain my temper and find myself able to speak again. By that time the relief of being actually embarked on the expedition combined with the beauty of the country in the late afternoon light had soothed me and I recognized that difficulties enough lay ahead without my adding to them.

Until now the road had lain between thick forests or banana plantations with only an occasional glimpse of the mountain before us, but not long after the fork it began to run parallel with the foothills of Mount Cameroon: the view opened out at this point and presently, from the top of a steep escarpment, we came on a breath-taking panorama over many miles of plantation and forest to the far horizon where the Oban hills floated, pale indigo, on the borders of Nigeria. This was the hour, when the sun began to lose its strength, that the country looked its most enchanting. A veil of many blues lay across it, pierced now and again by the rosy pink of a tree-trunk or a rock caressed by the setting sun. The shadows gave depth and definition to the landscape which it lacked in the flat blaze of midday; the rivers were full of laughing, shouting, bathing people and the red earth road was the highway for every kind of walker and the playground of innumerable naked children who waved shrimp-pink palms at us as we passed.

There is a legend to account for the pale palms and soles of the African. It was told me by a Nyasalander, Alec Nyasulu. When the Lord first created the world and made men and women to people it they were all black. So He decided to wash them before he finally started them on

YORUBA WOMAN

the business of living. There was a very big lake on the earth and to this lake the Lord brought all His created people and He told them to walk through it and come out on the other side, white. So they began to do so. But the Lord had created a great many people and gradually they used up the water which became less and less. At last, when the water was nearly all gone, there were still many people left. They were distressed to see that there was not going to be enough water to make them white, but there was nothing that could be done about it. So they walked through the little puddle that was left, bending down as they went to wet their palms also in the water. When they came out at the other side they were still black but the palms of their hands and the soles of their feet had become pale pink.

Now, watching those waving pink palms, we all relaxed, and even Ebenezer, sitting bolt upright behind me, consented to smile as a group of small boys shouted cheeky admonitions after us.

For sixty miles, until Kumba, the road behaved well. It had no unduly startling gradients and ran much of the time between high dark borders of trees; mysterious and rather sinister, this forest gave no indication of what lay inside it. Occasionally a terrible shriek issued out of it, a sound like a spirit dying in torment, but we rarely saw any sign of life and if there were exotic jungle flowers they did not grow along the road.

It was beginning to grow dark as we drove into Kumba. A scattered, ramshackle little town, it was important to me for several reasons. On the road out of the Cameroons I felt that once beyond Kumba we were irrevocably launched on the current journey. There was no longer any possibility of turning back in the face of difficulty; from now on the road was one-way only and we must go forward. On the journeys home Kumba held out welcoming arms as we drove out of the jungle and I felt that we had accomplished, once again, a major feat. But whichever way one entered it there was never the slightest doubt where the township limits began and ended. The main road might be bad, but the section through the town was appalling. The car leapt from crater to crater with grave danger to springs and the skulls of the passengers; even progressing at the minimum speed was agony and sometimes it was better to go fast in the hope that, becoming temporarily airborne, the Chevrolet might miss one or two of the intervening potholes.

We drove through the police post, out of Kumba, on to the

Mamfe road. It was nearly dark. Before us lay the forest, a gloomy, green pool into which the pale thread of the road curved and disappeared. A pregnant silence had fallen, the prelude to the noises of the night; my husband said to me: 'Will you drive?'

I always admired Lucas and Ebenezer for their stoicism in the face of what they must have felt to be mortal risks. After many such journeys taken together both they and I realized that I was quite safe, but the first time that they saw the wheel handed to a woman must have been a shock. Yet never by the flicker of an eyelid did they show any apprehension or indicate that they considered me unfitted for the task. Indeed, on one occasion later on in our acquaintance I did, in fact, land them in the jungle. The three of us were alone, driving through sudden rain which settled momentarily on the surface of the track concealing it. With no warning at all the car slid out of my control, turned a half-circle, and came to rest with its bonnet in a thicket of scrub. My heart had temporarily left me and was beating wildly somewhere in front of the steering wheel. I had an idea that Lucas and Ebenezer might well have fainted with fright and was afraid to turn round because of the deathly silence behind me. When I did do so there they were, sitting blandly upright as usual, waiting unconcernedly for me to back out again as if such a procedure were the most normal in the world. In that moment another bond of affection was added between us; without their complete faith in my ability to overcome any such trivial mishap I should have been incapable of driving another yard.

Now I took the wheel, put up a prayer, and we set off on the second stage. It was about 6.30 p.m. and, if we were lucky, we might make Mamfe at midnight. I knew that the car was very heavily loaded, that hazards innumerable lay in front, that we must arrive in Mamfe that night and that any accident could prove disastrous. Normally I should have despaired before ever beginning but one thing, a most curious one, gave me confidence; no sooner had he handed over to me than my husband promptly and peacefully fell asleep. I have never ceased to be grateful to him for this. The knowledge that he put this great responsibility into my hands with such perfect trust in me that he could then abandon everything and settle into undisturbed slumber acted as a tonic. And somehow Ebenezer's unsleeping, unmechanical eye watching unwearied over us both helped too.

The road unwound in the beam of the headlights like a much twisted pale ribbon. It began to climb steadily, now and then crossing rivers on precarious wooden bridges with a steep drop on the approach side and a rapid rise, quite without take-off, on the other. Only the knowledge that there was nothing coming in the opposite direction made it possible to take some of the corners at all. Sometimes it was not possible: rain coursing down the track and the day's traffic of heavily loaded lorries had churned the mud into a wallow. It was a horrible moment when the car lurched to a standstill, engine revving fiercely, back wheels turning hopelessly in a shower of mud, and we knew that we could get no farther. Hearts sank and there was a second's stillness, before we started to climb out, in which we felt unable to bear what lay ahead and I thought, with bitterness, of Ebenezer's fine, clean uniform.

There is a technique for getting a car out of mud wallows. It does not always work and one may have to invent, at last, new and better ways of overcoming the slippery resistance, but, at least, one starts off by a known method and with a certain amount of hope. For myself, I came to believe in a juju peculiarly my own. I recognized, after a time, that this was not a purely material struggle but, as so often in Africa, a tussle between opposing and very alive forces. The only thing that really mattered was endurance. If we could continue to annoy the vehicle with our efforts to move it for longer than it could bear to be annoyed then, reluctantly and with much groaning, it would eventually move on.

First, however, there came just pushing; violent revving in first gear, a concerted shout of 'Hoi' and all available shoulders behind the sunken wheel. Usually this resulted in us all being heavily sprayed with liquid earth and the wheel settling even deeper into its hole. Then we tried taking it by surprise and pushing from the front while revving the engine in reverse. Sometimes this worked, but often the only result was to make the whole car slide gracefully sideways into another and softer patch where it settled, seemingly irrevocably. Reluctantly we opened up and took out spade and machete. Ebenezer was despatched into the jungle to cut palm branches and dry sticks and the rest of us took it in turns to dig the level of the road round the back wheels down to their last resting place. If it were a daylight journey there might by now be a small crowd of bystanders, materializing out of the forests in the mysterious way of people all over the world when they smell trouble: or another traveller might have come up behind and be prepared, on a mutual basis, to help. But at night this seldom happened and the eerie sensation of isolation in a pool of light in the midst of dark and frightening jungle did nothing to help our fraying tempers. When enough vegetation, or rocks, had been collected these were carefully packed in front of the wheels to give them a little solid purchase and, girding ourselves spiritually and physically, we would try again. Sometimes, with the most painful slowness, we gained enough ground to make the next heave the final one. Often, with heart-breaking relentlessness, our precious packaging was ground down into the quagmire and we were no better off. If we carried expanded metal or a plank of wood this was the moment when it was discovered to be at the bottom of the luggage and the car had to be unpacked to get at it. If we did not carry either of these things this was the moment when we began to give up. It was at this instant that my juju came into action. Somehow I knew that the car felt it had won and was relaxing its efforts to remain static. If now, on the edge of despair, we could rally ourselves for a supreme effort it might do the trick. It was surprising how often it did, and there is no more joyful sensation than feeling under a straining shoulder, when despair has set in, the inching progress of a resistant mass of metal. We climbed in, filthy, damp, dead tired, but undefeated.

But the road held other hazards. The wooden bridges were neither very permanent nor very strong. Travelling by lorry was made tedious for the passengers by the number of times which they had to be decanted out to walk because a bridge could only hold up under the weight of an unloaded vehicle. Bridges with a weakness were marked by a crossbar on which was hung a bunch of palm leaves or other vegetation. This had, at least on my European mind, the extraordinary effect of being connected with witchcraft. One of these barred bridges looming up in the lights, its seemingly innocent bunch of straggling leafage proclaiming a warning, had a very sinister air to me. My heart gave a great thump and I quite expected to see a masked and painted witch-doctor leap out of the scrub at the side of the road. I disliked having to stop the car while Ebenezer climbed stiffly out to remove the barrier and felt all the while as if I were being ambushed and the jungle might disgorge at any moment its most deadly terrors. Maybe something of this arose from my very first journey up this road and the first time I saw this warning. I had no idea what it meant and was so new from Britain that my mind was still filled with imaginary pictures of the sinister and strange. My husband drew up to wait while the bar was removed, he turned to me and said: 'Well, darling, if we don't make it thank you for everything.' I did not know him well enough to recognize that he was joking and I am sure he had no idea of my mental turmoil. I believed him and thought that we might be going to our deaths—though what sort of death I did not get round to imagining. It was all over in a few seconds and we were on the other side intact, but I never really got over a feeling of acute unease when we came across this particular Public Works Department sign!

In the tornado season, that is twice a year in the short interval between wet and dry, it was not unknown to find a tree blown down right across the road. Usually these were the silk cotton trees whose great pale trunks rose one or two hundred feet into the air, buttressed at the foot with gigantic wings resembling the tail fins of some trans-world airliner, spreading at the very top into a flat umbrella of green. These huge trees, perhaps because of their great size, seemed to have a precarious hold upon the soil and to be easily uprooted in a high wind. Once down they presented a formidable problem to those whose job it was to keep the road in repair. The enormous trunks could be six to ten feet across, requiring highly efficient tools and equipment for their removal. These the Cameroonian did not possess, and if Government possessed them it kept them, for reasons of its own, away from the Mamfe road. The standard method of removal was for a fire to be lit under the trunk in the middle of the road and the foreman in charge and his mates then set up camp beside the fire and prepared for a long siege. The wood being green and, in this season, often very wet as well, the fire was reluctant to burn too briskly and the whole operation might take days, or even maybe weeks, before it was completed. It would not be unusual to find that the first fire, though it had divided the tree into two portions, had not really made removal any easier so a second, or third, or fourth, were lit at strategic points to make movable units.

Meanwhile the traffic had to manage as best it could. The P.W.D. labourers considered that their job was the tree—and there was no real urgency about that; what happened to the vehicles did not interest them. But it interested the lorry drivers. This road was the lifeline of the Cameroons, its only land link with Nigeria, and it carried a great volume of traffic. African passengers are accustomed to travelling without undue haste and with the certainty of many delays, but for the Ibo drivers there was money involved and every extra day on the road lost them trade. So the lorries took to the bush, a maddening, frustrating, ruinous thing to do—but the only one. By hand, by sheer bulldozing with the vehicle, a new road was made penetrating into the forest, round the end of the tree and back again to the main route. It was often damnably difficult but, surprisingly, it was invariably possible.

On one journey we came upon such a scene. It was on the verge of darkness and the fire under the great cotton tree glowed in the middle of the road. On the left-hand side there was what appeared at first sight to be an encampment; women and children surrounded by their goods, pots, boxes, mats and rolls, with hurricane lamps glimmering fitfully, sat about on the bank and in small groups in the forest. Farther into the bush there was a burst of light and the bulk of several large vehicles round which a group of men stood talking. They looked tired and dirty and when they saw us approaching glanced up without much interest. We got out to investigate. A temporary track, deep in mud, led off the road and into the jungle. Some hundred yards up this a five-ton lorry had become embedded at a point where obstacles on either side made it impossible to by-pass it. All efforts to get it out had only resulted in the creation of a fresh swamp. That other vehicles had used the improvised road before it was obvious for, if it could be moved a few yards, the rest of the track was reasonably hard. Two more lorries drawn up behind had lent their man-power, it being in their interest to do so, philanthropy apart, but to no effect. Now they had abandoned the effort and decided to camp for the night and see what the morrow might bring forth.

This did not suit us at all. We could by no means afford to spend the night and perhaps the whole of the next day as well by the side of the road. With the urgency about his own affairs which is one of the hallmarks of the white man we refused to contemplate the possibility of defeat.

The first thing was to ascertain whether our smaller and lighter vehicle could not, in some way, be got past the stuck lorry. It seemed that with very skilful driving and a good deal of luck this might just be possible if all available man-power were brought to bear. The lorry drivers were reluctant to sweat again for what was felt to be a forlorn hope but, for all their wild driving and often fierce appearance, they are innately co-operative, particularly so when it is a woman who is in trouble. They agreed to try.

SAMPLE ANANABA, JOHN HOLT'S

At this point Ebenezer rather liked to pretend that his job was to oversee other, and lesser, men working. He would put one finger on a wing of the car as a defence against my censure and stand as far back as that restriction would permit him, looking rather critically at everybody else's efforts and giving unasked and unheard advice. I had a better method. I knew that I had really very little strength and could make practically no difference to the combined pushing power, but I could, by letting it be known that I had a special juju, by shouting, and by pushing like mad behind some reluctant male, make the actual possessors of strength use more of it than they had intended to or even knew they had!

My husband climbed into the driving seat and revved up the engine; we gathered ourselves together for a combined start like a boat-race crew on the great day, we worked ourselves up by a series of rhythmic 'huw'-ing noises till the moment when my husband yelled 'Now'. Then we all let out a prolonged ringing cry, the car leapt forward with us at its heels, at first under its own momentum but as it entered the quagmire propelled by the now frenzied pushers. My shoes were sucked off as we squelched through the mud passing the stranded lorry, with a breath of air between, and groaned on to the firm track beyond. Such a shout went up that even the fire-guarding labourers yawned and got up to see what was happening and the women roused themselves from their placid stupor and began to pack up as though they already smelt rescue.

We turned next to the problem of the lorry. It was a little simplified now because we had a vehicle in front of it. A rope was produced and it was decided to combine all efforts with a tow, in the hope that the back of our Chevrolet would not be carried away. But the battle was already won, in fact, by the first victory gained. We were jubilant, the lorry did not stand a chance against us, for now we knew that we were going to win. They even half believed in my juju, and rightly, for in the final analysis it is the mind that decides victory or defeat and not the body. We fell on the lorry with a great shout and in a few minutes it had joined our car on the road.

We drove away amid cries and cheers, leaving them to tow the rest of the party through and make their way after us to Mamfe. Ebenezer bowed regally to right and left, acknowledging on our behalf as much as his own the thanks of the populace.

Travelling up the road at night it became invested with a character quite different from its daytime personality. Many unexpected things might happen by day but there was never any doubt about their origin. They were ordinary, human exasperations occasioned by wind and weather and the unpredictability of man. At night I was not so sure, and I had no difficulty at all in realizing why forest peoples are predominantly animists. In the beam of the headlights strange beasts and half-human shapes would seem to crouch in the tangled grass of the verges, and white, tortured spirits stretch starkly out of the dark jungle to clutch at us as we passed. No careful generations had been at work here cutting and tending the wilds until the shapes they assumed became the gentle, restrained shapes of civilization. The lightning-blasted tree still stands, pallid and stark, with wild arms outstretched; ancient stumps open ravening jaws and creep with octopus-like roots towards the highway; half seen, a tangle of liana, suspended in darkness, revolts the imagination with thoughts of monstrous spiders' webs seeking silently to find a victim; and the sounds—the secret noises of great woods at night, creaking, rustling, whispering just out of earshot, or screaming suddenly and all too close—affront the hearing. We moved by faith in the safe circle of our lights, our future and our past both shrouded in darkness and, at that moment, totally unreal.

It is uncertain whether the sudden thunderstorms enhanced or calmed these fears. While the ghastly flickering of lightning seemed to show for an instant even more menacing apparitions lurking in wait, yet the very storm itself accounted for them and I could say to myself: 'It is the lightning makes them so.' And through all this my husband would sleep peacefully, only opening one eye now and then to grunt: 'You all right?' and then fall back again.

But as the night crept on and the strain grew greater I too would begin to be overcome by sleep. Then the drive became a nightmare fight for one of us to keep awake long enough to steer the car at all. We changed at intervals which became shorter and shorter as our need of sleep increased. We thought up charms, the equivalent of counting sheep, but this time to keep ourselves awake. The effort to keep top and lower eyelid from meeting was a conscious and prodigious one, a battle fought with all the will and discipline which could be mustered. On these occasions the car, itself unwearied and, as so often, going more sweetly in the darkness than by day, drove itself. We clung to the wheel and watched the road unwind before our glazed and closing eyes, but the desire to give up was overwhelming and subtleties of driving were totally beyond us. Nevertheless we, or the car, drove well, and this too felt as though it were the work of spirits not wholly to be accounted for by natural phenomenon.

In one such waking, wavering dream I hit a hole with horrid force and out of the night there descended before my eyes an amorphous, misshapen mass, the horror of my thoughts. But it was very obviously not weightless, as such things should be, and the impact as it hit the bonnet roused all the carload from their stupor. We hastily climbed out to investigate and found that the entire luggage rack, kit-bags, camp beds and suitcases had come unstuck from the roof and, sliding forward, had descended into the ditch. On such occasions Ebenezer and Lucas showed the qualities of resource and enterprise that, maybe, only African servants possess. They might be tired, asleep, hungry, afraid, but in a crisis they forgot these things and prepared with cheerfulness and ingenuity to circumvent disaster. It is true that their methods of doing so were sometimes extraordinary and often left one worse off than before, but that was neither here nor there: what mattered was their willingness to help. I have seen Ebenezer, in his best clothes, lying underneath the car sticking toilet soap on to a leaking petrol tank, or tying up a hot broken exhaust pipe with ribbons produced from some secret source. They belonged to the original race of Heath Robinsons and many a passenger lorry must be tearing along the roads of Eastern Nigeria with its most vital parts tied up with string and an engine, long since condemned by any competent mechanic, still giving excellent service in spite of odd bits of wire because its driver also had this extraordinary facility for make-do-and-mend. Man loses this quality, as many others, as he progresses away from the simplicity and wisdom of his origins. He begins to look on his machines with awe which admits them to be his equals, very nearly his masters; but the West African still knows the power that resides in the spirit of man and has no notion that he should be defeated by anything other than a spirit like his own.

Going in this direction we nearly always passed through Kurume in the dark and so received no greetings there, but coming home, when it was daylight, things were different. Kurume is a typical Cameroons village straggling out along either side of the road, backed and nearly overwhelmed by forest. The houses, built of a special bark with palm thatch roof, are low and small with little attempt to beautify them. They are kept in repair from rainy season to rainy season— but that is all. Kurume has a school, well kept with a playing field on the other side of the road, and it was singular in having notice-boards announcing the identity of the village at either end of the street. Normally cars would rush through it, as through so many other villages, leaving a cloud of red dust and a shrieking chicken or two.

But we had two students from Kurume, school teachers, Martin Eyoh and Julius Mandi, and it was through the initiative of these two that the noticeboards announced where we were and the school showed such a neat and tidy appearance. Sometimes I wondered when they managed to do these things and teach in the school for it seemed that all their time must be spent watching the road for the Man O' War Bay convoy to pass or for our Chevrolet to emerge from the forest. Never once, provided it were not late at night, did we enter Kurume without a welcome.

There would be a wild shriek from the roadside and either Mandi or Eyoh would be discovered standing there waving with an abandon of pleasure and then rushing across to stop us. People came out of their houses to see what was going on; we would all talk very loudly and with a great deal of laughter.

'Ha, how are you, Sir? How's Madam? Where do you go, Sir? How are the students this time?'

'Fine. What's happening in Kurume this month? And how are your grandmother's cakes?'

This was a long-standing joke, the origins of which had been practically lost. Eyoh, who was a cheerful, ebullient fellow, always ready to tell a tall tale, had had a famous argument when at Man

O' War Bay with another Cameroonian, a policeman called Christol Ani, about food. Eyoh swore that he had a grandmother who made cakes which once eaten were unforgettable, and he talked so much about them and embroidered so succulently on this theme that 'Eyoh's grandmother's cakes' became well known. We never discovered if he even had a grandmother alive or if she made cakes, but invariably we asked after her and he related yet more mouthwatering details about her prowess.

Invariably, too, there were presents, six eggs or a pineapple, even once a chicken. The West African word for such a gift was 'dash', and it could be used as a noun or a verb. Somehow this curious colloquialism softened the harshness of a request for a gift. 'You dash me something?' a hopeful bearer of news would say—prepared equally for refusal or assent. There is a whole philosophy of presents in Nigeria which can lay many traps for the unwary. No Government official is ever supposed to accept a 'dash' of any kind, for this might lay him open to the charge of bribery, the besetting sin of the country. On the other hand it is for the people their natural way of expressing gratitude or affection; refusal to take a gift can hurt, it can dam up a channel of warmth and friendship. I did not consider myself bound by Government regulations, though I knew that my acceptance of presents ought somehow to be separated in the mind of the giver from the expectation of future favours. It must be obvious that I understood that such things were given in friendship, which friendship I returned. They knew, I hoped, that I would do what I could to help them because of the human bonds of affection which we had for each other as far as I felt to be practical and right, but that no one student had a priority in this. To help friends (and even if possible enemies) is surely one of the highest fulfilments of life, but to help for love and not for gain, and too cold an interpretation of the tenets of justice undiluted by the warmth of imagination and fondness could result in complete misunderstanding. Our Nigerians were dramatic, responsive, outgoing in their temperaments; they understood passion, whether on their behalf or against them, they were not afraid of the exhibition of their feelings and did not understand why others should be; laughter and tears, enthusiasm and anger flowed out from them. When they found a European committed deeply to certain fundamental principles of life and unashamed to state openly and with emphasis what these were, the barrier of skin colour disappeared and they were ready to love him, or to hate him, but at least to take him into the texture of their own existence. What they found extremely difficult to understand, or in any way to accept, was a conduct of restraint. 'You make your face tight against me,' said a Northerner to my husband one day, and this tightening up emotionally and physically was completely alien to them. They could not penetrate behind it to the reasons for such conduct and were left bewildered, unaware of any of the lessons of self-discipline, which it might have been hoped would be learnt, because they did not even know very often that self-discipline was being used—or what it was being used about. I am convinced that, perhaps more than with most other peoples, affection is the key to all relations with Nigerians.

Having said this I must qualify it somewhat. A different tribal background and many centuries of Islam have given the Moslem Northerner a code of conduct nearer to that of the English. They, too, can be restrained, dignified, adept at concealment of feelings and thoughts. For this reason, perhaps, it is said that most British when they first come out to the West Coast are greatly taken with the Hausaman and regard him as the aristocrat in a world of effusive democrats. We had students from all parts of Nigeria, from East and West as well as from the remote arid provinces of the North and we found, as indeed we should have hoped to have found, that the good Lord had created all men alike and given to none a monopoly of virtues and vices. There were from every region good men and bad men, men of courage, integrity and honour, men of folly, bombast and cowardice, and perhaps more often than not men with a mixture of these qualities, as men are everywhere.

So I accepted Eyoh's eggs and Mandi's pineapple and shook hands with Mrs Eyoh and Mrs Mandi, and we all knew that our friendship was not based on the giving and receiving of eggs and pineapples but on certain shared experiences and common hopes for the future.

At this hour, however, we went through Kurume unwelcomed, though we did not forget to spare a thought for Mandi and Eyoh as the noticeboard flashed into and out of our lights.

The journey had now become an endurance test. Could we possibly keep awake until we reached Mamfe, or would Lethe be too much for us and our final resting place be the jungle? Fortunately I now began to see remembered landmarks which indicated that we had not far to go. I counted the white milestones as though my life depended on it—indeed it did. We arrived at the barrier at the end of the one-way track and had to wait while a sleepy 'watchnight' (to us a nightwatchman) was roused from his hut to remove it. On the road beyond lorries were parked, their drivers sitting gossiping round little fires, waiting for the dawn, when the road would be open in the opposite direction. Now only twelve miles lay ahead and the road was wider and less hazardous.

It was still possible to get stuck and there were one or two perilous bridges to negotiate before Mamfe came in sight, but with the near prospect of legitimate sleep in a proper bed we began to wake up a little and to drive less by faith and more by skill and sense. The blasted kapok tree, the Mamfe River, the Catholic school, flashed by and we were climbing the last long hill up to the rest-house and the beginnings of the town. At this stage, the very end, I was sometimes afflicted by the awful fear that we would arrive to find that something had gone wrong with our booking and that there would be no room for us. It was already in the very early hours of next morning and the idea of spending the rest of the night in the car simply unendurable.

We drove softly past the separate chalets to the dining block where a tiny light indicated the presence of a nightwatchman. Looming out of the blackness were two lorries which we thankfully recognized as belonging to Man O' War Bay. At least the rest of the party had arrived safely. Ebenezer departed to seek out the watchnight who came grumbling inaudibly to himself at having his rest disturbed. But he knew who we were and, after much slow searching about, produced a key and pointed out which room was ours. Lucas and Ebenezer disappeared round the dining block to some mysterious accommodation reserved for their kind; we locked up the car and went in to our beds.

Nothing mattered now, neither the hazards that lay behind nor the continued journeying only so short a time before us. We had found a haven and it was permissible to sleep.

CHAPTER XI

'No Sweat,
No Sweet'

GEORGE OKONNA,
TEACHER-IN-TRAINING

THE next day we would leave the Cameroons and enter Nigeria. I was always under the impression that this happened when we drove off the ferry that took us over the Cross River, much the largest of the three ferries that we were to encounter before Enugu. I am, in fact, not sure whether the river did form the actual boundary at this point between the two countries but the grandeur of the scenery, the size and depth of the stream, and the complicated business of getting across it all contributed to a feeling that one had passed an irre-vocable stage in the journey and set foot in a new and different land, though the differences, at this stage, were not very apparent. The forest still flourished grandly on either side of the dusty route; the hill up from the water was as steep, as pitted with holes, as crowded with waiting lorries as the hill down to it on the farther side; the people were still the same transient travelling population of the roads.

On two occasions I had to make this journey alone, in the reverse direction from Afikpo in Eastern Nigeria. To say that I was alone is not literally true, the responsibility for driving was all mine but

Ebenezer and Lucas were with me to add support and protection. I was afraid of the four hundred miles that lay before us, being only too aware that mechanically I was an idiot, and having a nervous terror of the four ferries that had to be negotiated. Now all these ferries have been replaced by fine bridges so that this particular hazard is a thing of the past, but at that time they could add a good deal to the difficulties of the road. In each case the ferry consisted of a platform laid across two dug-out canoes; there was very little extra room at either end, and seemed even less than, in reality, there was. If the river was high the ferry was reasonably easy to get on to, because it could be brought well up the road, but the force of the water coming down induced agitating qualms as to whether the madly paddling ferrymen could make the other bank once they had allowed themselves to be swept downstream preparatory to creeping back in the shelter of the opposite verge. If the river was low the approach could be devilish, either down an extremely steep slope which made it impossible to board without a grinding noise of great alarm as the exhaust pipe grated over rocks, or the last few yards must be made at a rush through soft muddy sand, already churned by countless lorries, and the speed necessary to get through this made the chances of stopping in time on the small, precarious platform rather less than usual. Someone had once told me a tale of a car with nuns in it which drove on to and straight off a ferry into deep water, drowning the wretched nuns in the waving folds of their voluminous garments. I do not believe it was true, but I never forgot it and had a horror of driving over the end.

The ferries were also great social meeting places. When traffic was heavy a queue of 'Mammy wagons', as lorries in West Africa are unaccountably known, would gather on either bank. The passengers, disgorged, sat about or washed in the stream or ate strange snacks in the little bamboo booths which had sprung up along the road to cater for them. The local women, wives of the ferrymen or the booth keepers, washed their cloths and themselves in a flurry of lather and gossiped as they did so; and the river was always alive with small, naked boys, swimming and diving, throwing water over each other, laughing and shouting and keeping a sharp eye out for any particularly interesting traffic or any extraordinary incident.

There was a system of priorities. As long as the queue consisted only of ordinary passenger lorries they took their turn as they arrived; but a private car had priority over a lorry and a private car driven by a Government officer had priority over everybody else, except perhaps a doctor on duty or the Governor himself. Even a Government lorry had the right to go before an ordinary lorry. On days when there were many people travelling this could be extremely exasperating for the lorry drivers who, just as they thought their turn was getting a little nearer, could be put back again by the arrival of a limousine. It said a great deal for their cheerful good humour that they rarely grumbled about this and were always ready to give free advice and assistance. Their vehicles, some of them rickety in the extreme, with hens, sheep and other livestock tied on round the sides or on the roof, all bore some legend or aphorism: 'No sweat, no sweet' was a favourite; 'God with us' one would see in large letters as a three-ton lethal weapon rocketed past, lurching wildly from side to side.

On one occasion, in Eastern Nigeria, we arrived at the river bank after the ferry had closed down. It was the evening of the second day's travelling and the journey had not gone well. We were all together, staff and students, in a convoy of three lorries and two cars and our final destination lay a mile or two on the other side of the river. Although it was dark the ferrymen had only finished work a short time before our arrival and we had hopes that they might be persuaded to make two or three special journeys for us. Man O' War Bay was famous in its own way and we imagined that even the ferrymen would know all about us.

But our hearts sank when we debouched and began to look about the houses for any sign of life. The village seemed completely deserted; not a light, not a sound. Our loud hails echoed across the water and returned to us unanswered. We might have been travellers arriving on a planet from which all life had been evacuated some hours before. All our efforts to procure help failed miserably; for once we were beaten by a spirit more determined than our own—determined not to be roused up from slumber.

So we had to resign ourselves to sleeping where we were, in the cars. I do not think I have ever spent a more uncomfortable night. Station wagons, when unloaded, offer plenty of space for a recumbent body, but when every corner is scientifically packed up and there are four bodies to occupy the remaining amount of room the result is agony. A large portion of the front seat is rendered nearly unusable for this purpose by the steering wheel which is diabolically contrived always to be in the very place in which one wishes to dispose of portions of one's anatomy. None of this seemed to affect Lucas and Ebenezer who, apparently, dropped quickly and peacefully to sleep in whatever position they happened to be in, but my husband and I, cramped and sticky, were thankful to see the dawn break and signs of life begin to stir in the houses which the night before had appeared deserted. The ferrymen, when they did arrive, were cheerful and unrepentant, and they restored themselves to favour by paddling us across at a furious speed to the accompaniment of some stirring singing.

The ferrymen often appeared wild, unreliable, irresponsible. In fact they were none of these things and I never saw them make a bad mistake, though I do not doubt that they sometimes did so. However, they always seemed to be dressed in rags, and persistent harrying by the lorry drivers had given them a closed, mulish look, a determination not to be hurried or upset. They had no trade union that I know of, but they would have made admirable trade unionists! I approached my first lone ferry-boarding very early in the morning and with many qualms. No other vehicle was in sight and the vessel was on my side of the river so I had no time to grow more apprehensive while watching it being paddled across. Ebenezer and Lucas were decanted so that, at least, I should not be guilty of manslaughter; both stationed themselves at the water's edge in order to give their own version (a better one, they thought) of the foreman's instructions. I prayed, put the thirty horse-power engine in bottom gear and crept up the boarding planks. It is not, in fact, possible to see where the wheels are when sitting inside a large American car with a long expanse of bonnet and great breadth of wing. What subtle instinct is it, I wonder, which ensures that one does end up where one wants to be in such circumstances and with little room for error? Without very much conscious effort I found myself right in the middle of the platform and, eventually, safe across and up the far bank.

Having thus gained confidence I was able to face the rest of the ferries with equanimity. It was as well for, as the day wore on and traffic became heavier, I found that I never again had the ferry to myself, and I was an object of very great interest to the lorry drivers. When my engine stopped they would stroll over and lean nonchalantly on my open windows.

'Hullo, Ma.'

'Hullo.'

'You no get man, Ma?'

Ebenezer, sitting rigidly at the back and full of class consciousness, would stiffen at this implied insult. I realized, however, that it was the lack of a husband which they found strange.

'No,' I said. 'He had to stay behind. I must get the car home before they close the Mamfe road.'

'Ha, you go for Cameroon, Ma. Where you come from?'

By the time it was my turn to board they knew a great deal of my life history and I quite a lot of theirs, and every effort was made by them to see that I got absolute priority, if I wanted it, getting off and on, and the maximum of help and assistance. I felt complete confidence after the first few hours of this particular journey that if I had a breakdown or an accident I would get all possible aid from any one of the lorry drivers, and great kindness into the bargain.

Perhaps the greatest ordeal was reserved for the second day of the journey and it was one of the unexpected things that must always be expected in this part of the world. The season was very late and already rain had started to fall, so destroying the surface of the road between Mamfe and Kumba that it was open only two days in the week. On arrival at Mamfe we were told that it was very unlikely that we should be able to complete the journey next day because a large bridge had been washed away the night before, and there was no immediate possibility of replacement. There were many vehicles waiting to go down on this one day, but it seemed that lorries might have to transfer their passengers at the river and have them taken up by Mammy wagons from the other side. This struck a chill into my heart; it was imperative that I get the car back to Man O' War Bay and if it did not get through the next day then a whole week must elapse before we could try again.

That evening I was told that it might be possible to drive through the river if there was not too much water and if reasonable access could be made down the bank and up again on the far side. I was not much comforted by this for I have never liked fords and had a vision of getting stuck with water in the engine and no husband to make for me all the difficult decisions arising in such a situation.

We left at 6 a.m., before daylight, in order to get to the river as soon as possible, to leave plenty of time for manœuvring. Fortunately the day, when it came, was a splendid one, one of the rainy season's specials when the sky is bright blue instead of glaring grey and the bamboo leaves flicker and sparkle in a cool breeze. The car went well, and we all felt that it was impossible that we should not, somehow, get home that evening. The river, when we got to it, was a hive of activity. Lorries were lined up along the road, on both sides; the river itself was full of men, strung out in a great curve upstream; on either bank teams of drivers and labourers had cut temporary ramps and were standing by to help. Lorries were going through, but it was not easy and they were needing pretty severe handling to get them across.

'You must just do the best you can, Mrs Dickson,' I was told by a missionary, on his way home with his family. 'The bank is pretty terrible and nobody has yet got through without sticking in the middle. Follow the line of men, otherwise you'll find holes. Getting out the other side is the worst and I don't think you'll make it, but we'll have all the men ready and they'll rush you up before you've time to stick. We hope so anyway!'

So the lines of men were alerted; I gave the engine all the power I could and, in a cloud of flying spray, we were in the water. There was nothing else to do but to keep my foot on the accelerator and go as hard as possible. As I passed along the line of men I began to hear cries: 'Na woman', 'Na white woman', repeated from mouth to mouth. I could not smile, or wave, or do anything but stare grimly in front and gather all my will-power for the slimy climb out the far side. The car was with me in this, obviously as determined as I was that we should do this thing under our own power. We took the bank with the slithering rush of a large hippopotamus, and were up it before anyone realized that we had triumphed. I sat there with my eyes full of nervous tears and my hands shaking weakly. All round there was cheering; the men were delighted. 'Na woman', and she had got through, the first to do so without help. Wonderful! So it was; fortunately no one knew that we nearly came to an ignominious end a few moments later when, descending a steep little hill, I found that the water had temporarily destroyed the power of my brakes.

Gradually, however, as we left the Cross River ferry on our second day's journey into Nigeria, the trees thinned and the country grew a scruffy covering of scrub and bushes, vast views opened out allowing the eye to wander unchecked over miles and miles of dusty, reddish land, halted only at the extreme limits by faint, far-off blue hills. The villages had left the roadsides now and were concealed in the bush, but the country did not feel desolate on this account, rather there was an unheard hum in the air indicating large and active, if unseen, communities. The women could be glimpsed walking proudly down small forest paths, their heads loaded to capacity and, if one left the car and followed them, it would be to find oneself, at last, in the centre of a village whose activity and vitality were startling after the lethargy of Cameroonian communities.

The road, too, changed its nature—and not for the better. Deceptively it straightened and broadened, and the eye, so long frustrated by hills and corners, gazed with delighted relief at the visible miles which lay ahead. That was, until the car hit the first of the corrugations and leapt groaning into the air, only to rebound again from the second and all subsequent ridges. The surface of the road had taken on the appearance of a wind-stirred sea; waves of red laterite followed one another in procession placing such a severe strain on the chassis of any vehicle that it was surprising more of them did not fall to pieces as they travelled. There was no real solution to the problem of how to tackle such conditions but we came to the conclusion that the best way to do so was to go as fast as possible in the hope that, the car becoming partially airborne, at least every third corrugation would be missed as we flew over it. On one occasion this resulted in all our kit on top of the car flying off, backwards this time, so quickly and quietly that it was only when we stopped to change drivers some miles farther on that we discovered the loss. As we had no idea when we had parted company with it, and the road stretched empty behind us for many miles, we were depressed. However, just when despair was about to gain the upper hand a lorry drew up and asked us if we had lost anything. When we explained the driver drew, intact, from the inside of his lorry our luggage rack, with all the bundles still neatly tied upon it, which he had picked up in the road some miles back!

If we were on trek with the students, travelling to work with a village on a community development project, we would generally arrive at our destination late on this second day. Accommodation varied from a tent, very hot and uncomfortable, to a well-built concrete resthouse; but in either case any kind of furnishings would be completely lacking. Practice and experience had made Lucas, Ebenezer and myself expert in turning an empty, and often uninviting, building into a home from home, in the minimum time and under any circumstances. It was not unusual to arrive in the dark, with no convenient electric light to switch on, and to find no preparations at all for our coming. Sometimes, even, the house we had been intending to occupy proved impossible, either because it was already occupied or because it was uninhabitable; on one occasion we found ourselves living for ten days in the dispenser's store leading off the dispensary. It was little more than a very large cupboard and two camp beds took up the entire floor space. However, ingenuity and the co-operation of the dispenser made it possible to contrive a complicated jigsaw puzzle of the rest of the baggage in, around, and under the beds, enabling us to lead a more or less normal life as long as no rain fell and we could eat, wash, write and conduct interviews outside.

On arrival we all had our jobs. If darkness had fallen the first thing was to light a lamp. Until that could be done we had the car headlights and torches, but the former were in the wrong position as floodlights and only succeeded in deepening, by contrast, the darkness at the back of the car where all unpacking must take place. The lamps needed to be filled with kerosene; they had to travel empty, and the pump, the filler, matches, had all to be found in the intricate pile of baggage. This was my job. Pressure lamps are delicate and temperamental things, liable to all sorts of accidents or unforeseen damage. I was afraid of them, always nervous lest they should explode, but Ebenezer had a very unmechanical hand and early in my West African life, after suffering night after night from dying lights, leaking valves, and the frightening flaming of broken mantles, I had decided to learn for myself how the things worked and what was required to keep them in reasonable order. After that I cleaned them once a week and guarded them carefully from unauthorized interference and most of the time they responded by behaving well.

Meanwhile Ebenezer, guided by instinct and practise, was getting all the bundles out of the car and disposing them inside the house as best he could. His first job, then, was to undo the camp beds and get them set up. Lucas, on the other hand, had discovered the kitchen, probably a tiny, empty mud room, and having extracted from the car two old kerosene tins and a sheet of expanded metal, had made himself a fireplace with two ovens and a top rack; there would be wood ready cut in most resthouses and in a very short time he would have a fire going and be coming to ask me what he should prepare for us to eat. By this time, with the lamps lit, the beds ready, Ebenezer preparing hot water for a bath, the unwanted baggage neatly stacked around the walls as seats, the house would be beginning to assume a homely air. Usually I had thought out the meal during the last wearisome hours of driving and so could hand out eggs and tinned soup, meat, fruit or vegetables straight away. Some students or members of staff would arrive to talk to my husband, and already it seemed we had lived here a long time confined within the circle of light cast by our one lamp. Normally this first night was enjoyable; a journey of many hazards and some difficulty had been overcome, the tensions and problems of Man O' War Bay (and there were always these on any course) had been left behind, or so it seemed, and now washed, fed, tired, stranded in the island of this light, the morrow looked full of possibilities— all of them worthwhile and exciting.

It was not, of course, always so in fact. I remember vividly being woken up on one such first morning by Ebenezer to be told that the cook belonging to the staff mess was outside complaining that he could not find milk, sugar or flour among the stores which we had brought with us. Did Madam know where they were? Struggling through sleep, unable to believe that I was really understanding Ebenezer properly, I nevertheless knew by the feeling of depression which began to invade my body, even though my mind denied it, that some hideous mistake had been made and all those essential supplies had been left behind. The British staff were impossibly difficult about their food, causing endless trouble in which I always came to be involved because I was the only woman in the camp, and the sight of the mess cook on my horizon came to have all the qualities of nightmare for me. Accompanied by Ebenezer, sympathetic but agog for disaster, I hurried across to the mess store hoping against hope that I should discover in some corner an unopened box. I did not. Someone had blundered and the staff must start their day on milkless, sugarless tea, while a luckless young officer (as a penance for his own oversight) motored eighty miles to replenish the larder.

Other risings were more pleasurable, at least for me; for my husband life continued to be arduous and fraught with unexpected happenings both good and bad. I found it amusing to be awakened by Ebenezer laying the tea-tray on the floor with a flourish meant to indicate that he was accustomed to better ways of living; to wonder in the half awareness of drowsing why one lay so near to the ground and then to realize that it was because the camp bed was made like that; to lie for a few moments in the warm twilight of an ill-lit mud room listening to sounds which clearly indicated a strange environment. Instead of the sea there was a hum in the air, the sound of a

BRIDGE-BUILDING PROJECT

thickly populated area going about its early-morning business, cocks crowed shrilly (there were more of them and fewer singing birds), and the bustle and laughter of the students rising was all around. Ebenezer arrived with a bowl of hot water and the day began.

For me these days were leisurely and pleasurable. There was, virtually, no house to look after and I no longer had any classes to take. The students marched out after breakfast to whatever project they were undertaking and later on I would go down to watch and encourage. It was exciting to see a bridge grow from nothing till, on the last day, we could drive a lorry across it—though once when doing this before a group of local notables the culvert collapsed and covered us with shame; it was exhilarating to find a whole village turned out waiting for us to arrive, and prepared to work furiously with songs and shouts digging an embankment or carrying stones and earth, while their Chiefs and old men walked about among them or sat in state on the bank calling out advice and encouragement. It was interesting to see which of our students were ready to throw themselves into the hard physical labour with enthusiasm and understanding, which of them found ways of avoiding making any effort, and watching all the degrees of co-operation and non-co-operation between these two extremes which indicated the quality of a young man. It was also surprising how many who had flourished and done well in the vigorous but well-defined atmosphere of Man O' War Bay failed in the hard, unspectacular toil needed to finish a job of work, and cheering to find that some who had seemed hesitant or bombastic when faced with sea or mountain yet possessed the qualities necessary to carry through a task to a successful conclusion. Here, in the bush, living beside each other in conditions strange to all of us (for very few of our students had ever spent a night in their own country's wilder areas) we began to see each other in the round. Here an ability to shine athletically, a natural aptitude for swimming, charm of manner and humour of utterance could not disguise a man's willingness, or unwillingness, to give of his best in the day's grind, and no special talents were needed to make a young man invaluable with headpan and spade.

Sometimes we worked alongside hundreds of the local people, our help and the small amount of technical skill we could muster making all the difference to the finishing of a road long wanted by a clan; sometimes we worked practically alone, the village having gone back on its obligations; sometimes we worked under perfect

DONALD UGBE, ROAD OVERSEER

conditions with basic materials already stockpiled for us and cool, sunny weather. Sometimes it rained, as it rained at Ugep where we built a bridge, and each morning when we marched down to the site it was to find that all the work done the day before had caved in and we were faced with a sticky formless mass in the pit where there should have been firm foundations. But always in the evening, by the light of hurricane lamps in the school or centre where the students were sleeping, there was singing and we played all kinds of party games. Many of the games which my husband and I had played when we were younger were resurrected again and given an African 'twist'. We went to market and filled our 'basket' with all kinds of varied shopping; we made lists of objects, all beginning with a certain letter of the alphabet; we drafted 'telegrams' composed from words like 'psychology' and 'urbanization'; we played charades and had 'Hat Nights'. And we enjoyed ourselves very much: these evenings away from our normal environment playing parlour games produced a family feeling among us which gave us even an exasperated affection for the black sheep of each course and, from some surprising letters received afterwards, it seemed that they, too, came to feel the same kind of attachment to us. It was a revival of the dimly-lit communal evenings, when each member of the company felt a certain social obligation for the entertainment of the others, which lay not so far back in both our backgrounds, in theirs to the village life before literacy made a man sufficient unto himself for his recreation, and in ours to the convention of Victorian family parties when each member of the clan brought his or her music and accepted some personal responsibility for the success of the evening.

Perhaps one of the most amusing of these after-supper entertainments was a Hat Night. This was because our students were West Africans and quite the contrary would have been the case had they been young British. The latter, full of inhibitions about standing up and speaking impromptu on a subject unknown until that moment, would have ended up with irreparable psychological damage (or so we have been told); the former, exercising their undoubted talent for words, would stand up unabashed and give the most scintillating displays of rhetoric, in a language not their own, on subjects deliberately chosen to be baffling. I have not forgotten Mustapha Lantaiwa who made so polished a speech in defence of 'The wearing of plain glass spectacles' that he quite convinced me of their value, though only the day before I had been saying what a ridiculous affectation they were!

On one such project we had a visit from the Lieut-Governor of the Eastern Region. He was to arrive in the middle of the morning and find us all working hard, in this instance on a road. My husband was to drive to a crossroads some distance from the site of the job to meet the Lieut-Governor and take him to the place of work. On this day, an important one for us and the scheme, our car, normally so well-behaved, refused to start. We were alone in the camp, all other transport having gone with the students to the job. It was some miles from camp to the crossroads and already there was barely time to walk, even if the sweating heat had made that an agreeable prospect. Ebenezer and Lucas came to help and we pushed the car up the road to a small slope, in the hope that we could make it go by running down again. Three times we did this, precious wasted minutes, and still nothing happened. My husband, very agitated, decided that he must set off on foot and did so; Ebenezer, Lucas and myself looked at each other, at our watches, at the car, and at my husband, a tiny diminishing figure in the long straight miles of road. We decided to have one more try. It was not easy with our manpower substantially reduced, but maybe we caught the Chevrolet unawares: it went. I sped after my husband in it and handed the car over. He arrived at the meeting place in time, indeed it was the Lieut-Governor who was late.

While waiting the engine stopped again and it was impossible to think of getting it to go now without assistance; my husband would have to take a lift in the gubernatorial limousine. Sitting by the roadside, waiting, he saw two small schoolboys come along, bottles of ink and notebooks balanced on their black heads. They stopped to look and talk.

'Good afternoon, Sah!'

'Good afternoon.'

Pause.

'You come from school?'

'Yes, Sah. Where are you going?'

'I'm waiting for the Governor. He's coming to visit my students. Do you know who the Governor is?'

'Yes, Sah. The Governor.'

'Are these your notebooks? Can I see them?'

They handed over their notebooks. My husband, turning over the pages, came across a sentence: 'Aristotle was a philosopher.'

'Who is Aristotle?'

'Is he coming too, Sah?' Then they pulled themselves together, realized that they had been caught out and intoned in unison: 'Aristotle was a philosopher.'

'Very good,' said my husband. 'What is a philosopher?' There was silence and a look of concentration spread over the small, black faces. Then one of the two said: 'A philosopher is a man who sits and tinks and tinks and TINKS.'

Very shortly after this the Governor's car drew up and my husband went over to explain his predicament and climb in beside Sir Clement. As he turned to shut the door he discovered the two small philosophers preparing to climb in also and go to see the show. They were disappointed, but not abashed, to find themselves repulsed and the door firmly shut in their faces!

Always at Man O' War Bay Lucas did the marketing for fresh food, riding in the four miles to Victoria twice a week on his bicycle. This involved a very early rise, for markets took place as soon as it was light. I brought the dry stores once a month and handed them out as they were needed. One of the delightful things to me about living in the Cameroons was the freedom from the tyranny of shopping. There was no necessity, each morning, to rush out to the shops and meals were planned many days ahead, so a whole area of my mind was released to deal with other things and I was no longer a prisoner of rush hours, or half-days, or simply being 'in time'. On trek we lived largely on supplies brought with us, dried or in tins, for it was never certain how near we should be to a market or whether it would take place while we were in the vicinity. Markets in villages in Eastern Nigeria happen at regular intervals but it may be every fourth day, or every eighth day, instead of every Tuesday or Saturday, which makes for some confusion if it is difficult to discover which day a market was last held on; or, if the village is a small one but in a highly populated area, the market may circulate round several townships and only be in one particular village once in ten days or a fortnight. So, if driving to or from a project, we saw people all travelling to one spot we would often stop and follow them in the hope of being able to add to our rather restricted diet.

Sometimes the markets skirted the roadside, impeding the traffic considerably, but often they were off the road and the path, between tall grass and spreading shrubs, would open out into a dusty space crowded with humanity, flashing with colour and shaded by mag-nificent flowering trees. The Ibos are a vociferous and extrovert people and an Ibo market is alive with laughter, sharp practice and an immense vitality. The old women would sit in rows, their long leathery breasts falling down over their cloths, exchanging gossip and scandal with, I have no doubt at all, a pithiness of language and an insight into the essential motives of humanity that could not be equalled in Billingsgate or Balham. Before them their woven trays of nuts, or cassava, fruit, eggs or whatever they were trading seemed in each instance to bear exactly the same goods. It appeared that every-body in the market was selling and, moreover, all selling much the same things so that it was difficult for a stranger to grasp who was buying any of these goods, or why they were buying them since they themselves were apparently offering exactly the same things for sale. But the women of Eastern Nigeria are very astute business women by inclination as well as by necessity, so they must have been making a satisfactory profit. Many of the big business bosses in this part of the world are women, and illiterate women at that. I have been told by the manager of a John Holt's store that one of his largest whole-sale customers was a woman. When she arrived to see him she would be shown straight into his office and cups of tea would be ordered. Over this drink she detailed her financial transactions, what goods she wished to have, what she had in stock, the turnover of her various subsidiary traders, and any complaints. All this ran into many thousands of pounds and she could account for every halfpenny of it. Every sum was done in her head, for she could neither read nor write, and the Manager told us that he had never known her to be at fault in any of her calculations, nor to fail to notice if he were at fault in his.

In the bigger markets it was young men who sold ironmongery, bicycle spare-parts, torches, tools, dark glasses and so on, and probably cloth. With the exception of cloth the small village market rarely stocked any of these things though in parts of the country where there was a local craft, weaving or carving for instance, examples of this might be found. It was, however, one of the disappointments of Nigeria to me that such articles were so seldom seen. In the Northern markets it was possible to buy calabashes, beautifully decorated with black pokerwork designs on their rich orange-yellow ground, or, more subtly, with a white design cut out of their saffron skin. In these calabashes the Fulani women carried their milk and butter and other produce to market and in the clear hot light of the tropics they looked very beautiful. But, alas, like some flowers and so many local crafts they wilted the moment they were bought by alien hands and transplanted to a foreign environment. It was difficult to know to what use they could be put in our kind of life and day by day their glorious colour faded and became replaced by a dusty green mould till, at last, regretfully, they had to be flung away. This happened so often that we became chary of buying where the fancy caught us and tried instead to visualize in our own setting whatever object we had set our hearts on before we uprooted it from its natural surroundings. As a rule it was only the very best work which survived.

There was, however, another way of finding the crafts of the country. Itinerant traders, the Nigerian equivalent of the pedlar in England, travelled round the country with a large pack, usually carried by a small boy, which they would open and spread out on the verandah. These men were all Northerners, Hausas, and they covered immense tracts of country in their wanderings. To many of the Ibos of the East the Hausa trader represented the Northerner, as the onion man represents the Breton to us, and from him they drew misleading and often derogatory generalizations. Most official Government resthouses had what amounted to a pet Hausa trader who sat on the verandah, his treasures spread about him, ready to trap the unwary.

Sometimes, even, one of these Hausamen would brave the four miles to Man O' War Bay, though he must have known that his sales at the other end would be very restricted in a settlement of so few white people; he would appear, with the inevitable small boy, both of them clad in long flowing nightgown-like garments, on our verandah. I would go out and make it plain before he began to undo his pack that a sale was very unlikely; my husband was a connoisseur in carving and would buy only if the man had a really nice piece. This they knew and if he, in fact, possessed such an article the trader would produce it at once from some special fold of his voluminous robe. However, I never knew a trader to be deterred by a firm manner and a plain statement of our refusal to buy, from opening up and displaying his wares. They are supreme optimists, or maybe they have learned by experience never to despair when dealing with a woman; I, for my part, felt freed from all obligation by my declaration of non-dealing and was always delighted to have the chance of seeing what he had. I never did feel any desire to buy, but greatly enjoyed the sight of rows of gaudy and meretricious trinkets spread out on a cloth for my delectation and presided over by a figure who might have been the Genie of the Bottle from the *Arabian Nights*. At the same time there was the pleasurable creeping of the spine that occurs also at auction sales when there is just a chance that an untimely nod or a careless phrase may land one with some wholly undesired and undesirable object.

When the goods were all on display the trader and I, while remaining poised as enemies, would nevertheless be ready for a certain amount of give-and-take in examination. He would hand me carved ivory elephants marching in a bow along the tusk of which they were a component part; or brilliant velvet slippers atrociously stamped with vulgar overblown flowers; small ebony carvings from Benin, reduced to a shadow of their magnificent ancestry by tourist sales far exceeding the craftsman's normal supply; brass bowls from Bida, a pocket mirror and comb from Manchester, the cover of a leather pouffe from Kano, dyed a handsome red or a vivid green and appliquéd with a mosaic design (alas, these, like my calabash, would quickly suffer a sea change and fade to a sombre dung or a pallid sienna). The Hausaman would suggest a 'changee, changee', a pair of my husband's old trousers or a shirt in part exchange.

Sometimes he succeeded in this, where I had determined not to spend money or had, in fact, no money to spend, and I would be seduced by the idea of doing a deal; once, I remember, he went off happily with a great pile of *Illustrated London News*, a reciprocal bargain for some small carving we had liked. More often, after an hour or so, he would pack up his things again and say 'farewell' with no sign that he considered his time wasted or felt his walk to have been unprofitable.

The incidence of leprosy in Nigeria was very high and particularly so in the Eastern Region where, in some areas, each village had its 'leper village' some little distance away in which lived, hopelessly, the outcasts who had been found to have the disease. But perhaps because this scourge was so prevalent here it was here that much of the work had been done on the cure which was working miracles, even with those who had been lepers for half a lifetime. Many of the actual experiments preliminary to the discovery of D.A.D.P.S., the wonder-working drug, were made in Eastern Nigeria.

But though the lepers who went for treatment had now a very good chance of a cure, the social problems connected with this illness, which had always been numerous were, if anything, increased by the return to their homes of cured lepers. Such was the dread in which leprosy was held by the ordinary person that the healthy villager scarcely believed in the possibility of recovery, and in many places it was extremely difficult for a returned 'clean' patient to gain any sort of acceptance among his own people. Indeed he might find that his home had been broken up, his things burned or distributed among his next of kin, his wife, even, taken over by a brother. This, then, was a social problem which could be brought to the notice of our students, and they could help to create a new public opinion, based on facts, about these extraordinary new drugs.

I had spent some time amongst lepers and so could speak about the disease with knowledge not only of the work that was being done but also of the natural human

'MA SIXTY-SIX', LEPER PATIENT

A. E. OFFIONG, NURSE

shrinking which accompanies any idea that one might become involved in anything so loathsome. When I was first told that I was to go and visit a Leper Settlement I had felt a shock of revulsion which would have made me refuse to go if pride and shame had not prevented me taking such a course. From the very roots of history leprosy has been linked with ideas of corruption in its physical sense, and of expulsion. While the mind and heart may be trained to accept the new miracles of re-creation for the leper, the flesh shrinks from the thought of any possible contact. The Gospel stories do not relate what happened to the lepers whom Christ cured when they returned to their villages but there must have been many difficulties for them to overcome and I wonder whether they did not find it necessary, eventually, to move to some other place where their history was unknown.

Once, when we were helping to build a market and a bridge in an area where leprosy was very prevalent, and where the Church of Scotland had several supervised leper villages, we suggested to the students that the moment had come when some of us might test the reality of our concern for the need of others. Would anyone be willing to come down to one of these villages in the evening and try to teach the leper children new games or a craft? It was asking a good deal of these young men. Their youth and virility made appalling the possibility, however remote, of contracting a disease so shameful; this was true also of some of our British instructors. But where, before they came to Man O' War Bay, it would never have occurred to any of them that such a thing was possible, now we had awakened a conscience which made them aware that there were two answers to the question before them. No one was pressed to make any decision, but one evening a small group made their way to the leper village and, to the astonishment and joy of the inhabitants, entered it. One of the most touching and saddening sights was to see the children run to greet them, and then stop short, aware that they must not approach too close. Some games were started, a Northern school-master gathered together a group under a tree and began to show them a form of basket-making at which he was skilled, a Western policeman wrote simple numbers on the ground while wide-eyed little boys sat round him. It was not a world-shaking event, but it marked, nevertheless, the beginning of a new attitude to an old problem.

A predominantly rural life, bustle, pushing democracy, disease, a thrusting independence, age-old superstition, side by side with the latest in modern knowledge, something of all this was in the background from which many of our Eastern Region students came— and to which they returned. It was not in the exotic seclusion of a bay in the Cameroons that they had to practise the things we had tried to teach them but in the competitive business of daily living. As we drove round the region, travelling to projects that formed the concluding part of each course, visiting the Secretariat in the capital, Enugu, going to or coming back from journeys farther afield, we would meet our returned trainees in the ordinary framework of their homes and jobs, sometimes to discover that the real problem was something we had not tackled and on which we could give little advice, a problem which only the young man himself could solve. Often we came to recognize that we were asking more of them than we had realized; the fight against corruption, for instance, might prejudice a young man's whole future career. The temptation that he had to withstand was not that of accepting bribes, but giving them. If he were not prepared to offer a bribe he might well never get the interview he needed as a prerequisite to a job, his application might never be forwarded.

A. OLUKA
TEACHER-IN-TRAINING

A member of staff of the Government Leprosy Settlement at Oji River would show us round and tell us of his own fears at Man O' War Bay and how he had come to the conclusion that the overcoming of fear was what mattered most in Nigeria; a young policeman, stationed in Enugu, would greet us at the street corner and describe, haltingly, his efforts to bring pressure on his home village towards development; a coalminer, on his day off, came in to talk desultorily about the difficulties of life in general and left thanking us warmly; a male hospital-nurse rushed, still masked, out of an operating theatre to greet us; a tin-hatted and overalled worker on an oil rig explained, shamefaced, why he had never written; a member of the House of Assembly greeted us in a remote village as old and dear friends. If we gave them an interested and sympathetic understanding and affection they opened up for us another dimension of Nigeria; it was no longer a flat picture seen from the outside but a three-dimensional reality into which we could step a little way.

LEPER PATIENT

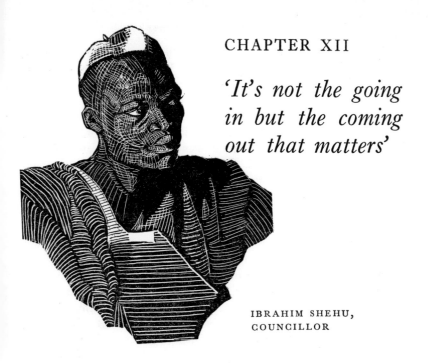

CHAPTER XII

'It's not the going in but the coming out that matters'

IBRAHIM SHEHU,
COUNCILLOR

AT NINE-MILE-CORNER, which is, as its name suggests, nine miles from Enugu on the main road to the West across Nigeria, there is a T-shaped crossroads. Coming up the stem from the East the left arm of the T goes to Onitsha and eventually, if followed far enough, to Lagos; the right arm is the road to the North.

From the moment that we turned on to it the atmosphere felt different. Something of romance lay before us, we were about to leave the bustle and normality of the South in which we lived and worked for a land much slower in tempo, glamorous in its institutions and sometimes both mysterious and inscrutable. We loved the South much as one loves one's family, without demonstration, with exasperation and even, on occasion, without recognition, but the North was strange to us—and therefore intriguing.

The long red ribbon of the road, pitted with holes and pimpled with rocks, wound up and down hills into the clear blue distance beckoning us on.

'Now we're really on our way,' we said, settling ourselves in our seats, turning our back on familiar country. Ebenezer looked impassive and unimpressed, but both Lucas and Ali seemed to share something of our anticipation.

In fact it was not until we had crossed the Benue River at Makurdi, a good many miles inside the Northern Region, that there was any very distinctive change in country or in people. Between the river and the Eastern Region border is the land of the Tiv, a virile people who have never been conquered by the Moslem Hausa and Fulani from farther North. They can be difficult, stubborn, obstinate, but they make good soldiers, good farmers and good friends, if once their friendship is obtained. C.S.M. Riga Addingi was a Tiv, and we had had a number of students from Gboko, which is the capital of the area. One of the best was Jime, Jime Akaakar.

He was a Senior Mason in the Roads and Works Office at Gboko and his work was the actual building of bridges and roads, so when he came to Man O' War Bay there was little we could teach him about this kind of work; on the contrary he taught the others some of the short cuts and tricks of his trade. But we could teach him something about people working together, and when he went back to his job he wrote to tell us that he had been able to get his men to work better and faster than before because of certain things he had learnt. He found that if he worked with them, instead of just standing and giving orders, that the work went better; he had learnt that work progressed if his men sang while they passed the loaded headpans, that words of praise and a rhythm of joint effort were more effective than blame and individual enterprises. These things he attributed to us; we knew that, before he ever came to us, Jime was a man of character and personality, a born leader, and that all we had done

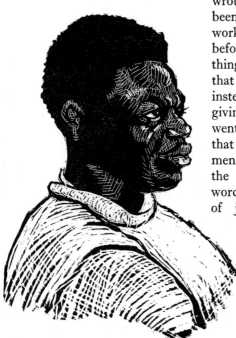

JIME AKAAKAR,
NATIVE AUTHORITY MASON

THE RIVER BENUE

was to show him some new ways in which to exercise his leadership.

A message came to us in the resthouse in Gboko to say that twenty-five miles away, along a new road under construction to join Tiv country to the Southern Cameroons, Jime was building a bridge over the Dura River and would like us to visit him. So one morning we set out over rolling agricultural land to find the Dura and Jime Akaakar.

When we did find him we were amazed. Some distance before the bridge the road deteriorated and we had to leave the car and walk. Soon we were on an enormous embankment, the making of which must have involved shifting many hundreds of tons of earth, most of it by hand and headloaded without mechanical assistance. This approach stretched about a quarter of a mile and then we reached the bridge. Built in concrete, a thirty-foot span with two piers and abutments, it looked magnificent; this too was the work of men's hands with very little technical aid. We found it difficult to believe that Jime, youthful, volatile, full of laughter, had had it in him to direct the labour to this huge result. Then we saw him. Coming towards us down the far embankment, his grinning dark face beautifully set off by a lemon-yellow, polo-necked pullover, he was the same Jime, but now he had authority. Now it was his turn to tell us what to do, to show us with pride the result of his work and to introduce us to his men. We were impressed: Man O' War Bay could not make bad students good, it could only make good students better. Jime had been a good student and we felt proud that he acknowledged that we had made him better, but the credit was really his that he had known how to make use of the knowledge that we had been able to give him.

It was when we crossed the next bridge, the long thin bridge at Makurdi, and met on the other side our first Moslem student in long gown and small crimson fez, that we really left the South behind and entered the true North. There was a noticeable drop in tempo; life became much slower, men had time to sit and talk; the centuries dropped away until we felt that the bustle and hurry of the present day belonged to another world, there were lorries, aeroplanes and trains here, too, but essentially it was a land of horses and donkeys and it moved with them, at their speed. This could be sometimes delightful and restful, sometimes maddening, as when a day later we sat for hours waiting while a bridge which had collapsed in a storm was rebuilt before our eyes at a pace which took no account of our need to hasten on and find shelter for the night.

The resthouse at Lafia was enormous, a huge rambling barn of a place within which our camp beds and wooden boxes shrank to insignificance. The roof was lost in shadows and there might well have been spirits inhabiting some of the dark corners. A messenger was there to greet us, with eggs and a fowl as presents of welcome, and news that Abubakar Garin Magajin Lafia, District Head of Lafia, ex-student of Man O' War Bay, would call on us presently. When Abubakar left his home to travel to the Cameroons for the course he departed with all the pomp of a minor Northern Chieftain; retainers went with him and a small band, the whole forming a colourful and impressive procession. On arrival at Enugu Abubakar was disconcerted to find that he was expected to climb on a lorry with thirty other men, leaving his retinue behind him. They, for their part, were appalled to find their Chief being taken from them without ceremony and some thought that he was, in reality, being hauled off to prison. There was apprehension in Lafia throughout the month that he was away and considerable doubt about his return. When the news came that he was on his way home every effort was made to assure him, by the magnificence of his reception, that the extent of his sufferings in the barbaric South was appreciated and he was met at the railway station with the full splendour of his brilliantly-robed court, a guard of blue-and-white-kilted Native Authority police and, of course, the band.

However, things were not as easy for him in Lafia as this anxiety on the part of his people might indicate. There was a section of the community who bitterly opposed his chieftainship and rumour had it that it had been obtained for him (or by him) by foul means. But he was a likeable man who had done his best in what must have been for him the very extraordinary circumstances of Man O' War Bay. We had hoped that he might be able to make a considerable impression on his community but he had not quite enough stamina to overcome the weight of tradition which, combined with the intrigues and difficulties of his situation, made the introduction of new ideas not easy.

There was a knock on the resthouse door and the same messenger entered. Abubakar, District Head of Lafia, was without, waiting to greet us. I rose quickly from my knees where I was sorting out food for our meal and rushed to the door to meet him. I had liked him very much as a student and we had had long conversations in the weaving sessions about the problems of women in this new age of independence. But at the door I stopped. Outside stood a little group of men, the brilliance and voluminousness of whose robes made them seem very bulky and imposing; in contrast to the many yards of white muslin which composed their turbans and were swathed around their necks and chins their faces appeared very black and faintly haughty. Nowhere in all this mass of cloth could I see anyone resembling our shaven-headed former student whom I remembered clad in shorts and singlet doing his best with a pickaxe in an endeavour to build a market for a village in the Northern Cameroons. It was brought home to me, with something of a shock, that we expected a great deal in the way of adaptation from some of our students.

Then the central figure, in the blue robe, stepped forward with a smile and I recognized Abubakar.

Later on, the ceremonial greetings done, he returned in simpler dress to talk with us and we saw again something of the difficulties that lie in the path of those young men who are caught, in an age of progress, between the old and the new. Life is simpler for the youth who comes from a background which he despises or which he feels could with advantage be wholly changed. For him there is no looking back but only a surging forward, a desire to build new worlds can be freely indulged in; he is not weakened by any wish to compromise with the things his fathers worshipped, he is not inhibited by a respect for inherited wisdom. So, for a time at least, he makes astonishing progress, single-minded, unfettered, ready to assimilate any new idea. But for a young man such as Abubakar life is not so simple. He is born to the inheritance of a tradition and civilization which he still respects; he sees the need for change but wishes it to be change within the framework of the life his fathers knew; he recognizes that they, too, had wisdom and wishes to retain it. So his path is a difficult one for he is neither wholly against change nor wholly for it, and he is opposed by the adherents of both those sides. It may be that he ends by compromising with the old and with the new, by finding it easier to say 'no' than to say 'yes' even though his desire to do good is just as great as (and his integrity perhaps more genuine than) that of the young man who casts away his past without a backward look.

Kaegbu is a tiny village miles off the main road, remote from the passing traffic which brings news up and down this lifeline. Our student was the teacher there, a simple, kindly man to whom, we hoped, our visit would be an excitement and encouragement. We bumped into the tiny hamlet of a few houses in the early evening to find it, seemingly, utterly deserted. No one stirred. Then three lanky boys in *rigas*, the long cotton garment of the North, appeared beside the car. We asked them for the teacher and in halting English they told us that he was not in the village; he had gone on holiday.

This was a big disappointment. We had come many miles out of our way, now it was nearly dark and we must stay the night here; the village did not look welcoming and we did not know if there was any kind of accommodation which we might have. The boys, however, having spoken quietly among themselves, had decided to take on the responsibility of their teacher and one of them began to tell us that they had a resthouse which we might use. It was a very large round mud hut just outside the village, the dried thatch was full of rustling bats and the one round room looked eerie in the gathering dark. The boys, however, had now adopted us and bustled round helping to unload the car, finding firewood and a little water, showing us the small latrine and doing everything in their power to make us feel welcome in Kaegbu. To give them some return for this hospitality we asked them to come back when we had had our supper to hear some stories of the outer world which they had never seen.

When they came back each had added another length of patterned cloth to his costume, flung over one shoulder like a highland plaid. They sat in a solemn row on the floor gazing up at my husband with great dark eyes, half their faces in darkness the other half gleaming in the lamplight. The bats squeaked and twittered and Alec began to tell the tales of Mount Cameroon. They were held entranced, as I was too, enraptured by watching them, seeing in their eyes again the excitement and the terror, the expectation and endurance of those arduous days, overlaid this time with a kind of magic, for this was experience transmuted into story and the expressions of the listeners gave it back to me in a different dress. To these boys the mountain was immensely high, some giant peak soaring in a pure triangle into a coloured sky, or maybe some outsize pile of rocks translated in their minds from the stony hills of the plateau country near their home; for them the figures in the drama took on heroic attributes, here was the Hausa equivalent of the Arthurian legend, here were ghosts and spirits and fabulous animals of monstrous proportions slaying the fearful or overcome by faith and prayer and purity of heart. It was fascinating to watch the changing fortunes of the protagonists reflected in those mobile faces and I have sometimes wondered since what strange folktale, told now to the small children of Kaegbu, owes its origin to that night's visit.

THE TALE OF MOUNT CAMEROON

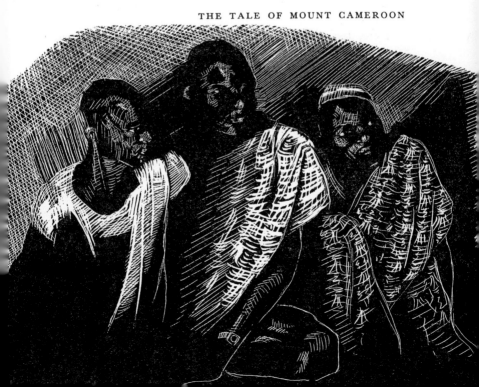

We were to stay two or three nights in Kagoro, which is a small town and the centre of a wide district. Set on plateau country in the shadow of spectacular hills composed of huge round boulders resting precariously one on top of the other, it is an attractive place. The resthouse stood under trees a little way off the main square where the whitewashed façade of the Chief's house faced a magnificent mango tree. A circle of stones had been set round this tree and carefully whitened to match the house, so that the first impression was one of spruce neatness.

'That is my work. I did that when I came back from Man O' War Bay,' said Didam Ndap, pointing with pride at the circle of stones.

DIDAM NDAP, TEACHER

Here, too, the resthouse was a round hut with a wonderful view of the boulder-strewn hillside behind it and we settled in, pleasurably aware that this time it was more than a one-night stay. We would go out from here to Kwoi and Kafanchan and to Maroa, in each of which we had students, but these would be day trips and every evening we could return peacefully to our little round house to find the beds made and a meal ready.

Didam, however, was determined that our stay was to be made memorable, both for us and for Kagoro. He was a school teacher in a large mission school and for him Man O' War Bay had been full of discoveries. As a good teacher should, he had kept notes of all that he had seen and learnt and he had brought back with him as many visual aids as he could carry to support his stories. He was one of those students who armed themselves with a beer bottle of sea water, to convince his pupils that the ocean was genuinely salt; and he told us that after his return he carried about with him, for several weeks, a small zip bag filled with shells, seaweed and bits of strange trees and plants to bear witness to the fact that he did not lie when he told his friends that the world was different in the far South. We arrived late and rather tired and, knowing that we had plenty of time, we planned to have a quiet evening and seek out Didam the next morning. At nine o'clock, however, we heard the sound of voices and laughter in the dark and presently a knock on our door. We opened it and the world suddenly seemed full of people, all the more so because it is not easy to distinguish one dark face from another on a black night.

Then Didam disentangled himself from the throng and, after greetings, began to introduce us to the others. He had brought along his missionary, Mr Archibald, and as many of his friends and pupils as he could decently squeeze into our rather small room. Some of these friends and pupils had brought musical instruments and part of the evening's entertainment was to be singing, the singing, among others, of many of the Man O' War Bay songs brought back and transmitted by Didam himself. So they sat on our boxes, and on the floor, and on each other's knees and gazed at us, awestruck, while Didam told them all about us, then Alec talked of other students and told again the heroic tales of Mount Cameroon and, some of the shyness dissipated, they began to sing, not very well, with now and then queer breaks in the tune where Didam's memory

ON THE PLATEAU

had failed him, but recognizably the working songs, the paddling songs, the climbing songs, the marching songs, the spirituals that we had so often heard the course singing led by Ekechuku and Riga Addingi. It was touching and endearing, and when at last they left we felt warmed and cheered.

Of all the experiences in Kagoro, where we visited the school, the mission, the Chief, the market and the town, one memory stays with me vividly. The Sunday morning service in the little mission hall was in the local dialect, but the evening service was in English, so we decided to go to that. Mr and Mrs Archibald had given their lives to the people of the plateau and were both now well on in years. They had a daughter, Grace, who had been born in Nigeria; when she grew up, with schooling and teacher-training behind her, she returned to Kagoro to work alongside her parents in the mission and the school. Tall, dark, vital, she was as alive as any young woman of her generation, dedicated, as her parents had been, to the work of the mission in this place. Looking at her one felt an astonished respect that she had chosen to come back to spend her life here, and a great admiration for her parents that they had convinced a daughter of such vigour and intelligence of the importance and attraction of their own faith and toil. It was Grace who took the evening service on this Sunday.

When we arrived the hut was nearly full of restless, curious children sitting in rows on hard wooden benches, behind them were women in brightly-coloured cotton dresses and a scattering of young men. Our arrival caused a small sensation and places were cleared for us on the very front bench of all, several small girls being brusquely swept off the end to leave sufficient room. We were anxious, however, not to be quite so conspicuous and, making the replacing of the small girls an excuse, we chose an empty seat some rows farther back. Mrs Archibald was playing a voluntary on a portable harmonium placed on the platform.

The congregation whispered and giggled, the small boys began to cuff each other. We waited. Then came Grace, and with her arrival the atmosphere changed at once. She wore mosquito boots and carried an accordion slung round her body which gave her something of the look of a handsome cowgirl out of an American film or a Ukrainian folksinger. She hauled the two naughtiest boys out of their seats and planted them on the edge of the platform under her very eye, then, with a ringing chord on her accordion, she

KAGORO

announced the first hymn. Never do I remember being lifted up on such a joyful, vital wave of song. Grace played her instrument as though she had a whole band at her command, she stamped her booted feet, and led us to such heights of exultation that the gladness swelling out of the open door and bursting round the ears of the Moslem half of the town must, one could not help thinking, have made them feel envious of such a joyous religion. The whole service continued in the same vein, conducted with great reverence and a definite sense of the presence of God but with an equal realism about the nature of children and of people with simple ideas. In the middle there was a Biblical Quiz put across with all the verve and interest of a first-class school teacher and a veteran Quiz mistress. Here we began to have feelings of uneasiness for all around us tiny children were answering questions of extreme difficulty, and it was not part of Grace's policy to excuse visitors. As her flashing eye passed over us we wriggled nervously, but she was merciful and did not make a public spectacle of us; perhaps she recognized that we might well have failed. Prizes, in the form of coloured pictures, were handed out to successful contestants and the ignorant were left with the feeling that next time they must certainly do better. There was no fooling Grace and she conducted her session with a kindly discipline which exactly suited the nature of her congregation. When, with a last rousing chorus and a final prayer from Mr Archibald, we streamed out into the night we felt moved and stirred by the reverent, friendly joy generated in this drab, uninteresting hut. Here was certainly one answer to the difficult question of importing forms of worship into a land for which they were not created; here there had been combined simple teaching, communal participation and freedom to make a joyful noise with a real sense of worship and prayer. Recognizable in Grace Archibald were all the qualities, translated into twentieth-century terms, which had made great women of so many of her missionary forerunners.

We were sorry to leave Kagoro. I had become accustomed to the round resthouse and we felt that we were known and welcome in the town. Ebenezer had washed all our dirty clothes, Lucas had made bread and replenished in the market our stocks of perishable food, Ali had cleaned the lamps and polished, not wholly successfully, the car. We had visited Dauda Haruna at Kwoi, and I had gone alone one day to Maroa to greet Gambo Kagoro, who was the village policeman and who astonished me by appearing in a uniform which

GAMBO KAGORO,
NATIVE AUTHORITY POLICEMAN

gave him something of the appearance of a character in a Gilbert and
Sullivan opera.

However, this journey was no more than well begun and we had
to press on farther and farther north. Jos was the next stop. It is
the leave station for Northern Nigeria, indeed Europeans from all
over the territory come here for holidays. Situated on a 4,000-foot
plateau the climate is very good, clear and hot during the days with
cool nights, and the country very beautiful, open and hilly, set
about with rocky mountains and enclosed by immense and wonderful
skies. There is a vivid quality of light here which lends clarity
and sparkle to the white *rigas* of the men, the mounds of fruit on
sale by the road, the scarlet cloths of visiting Fulani women and the
bursts of blue and pink, yellow, flame and purple of the flowering
shrubs. But Jos is an important centre with a fairly large white
population and, as always when society grows sophisticated, there
are problems to be met which are not present in simpler village life.
It was not so easy to find accommodation; the old Army Leave Camp,
now used for civilians, was crowded and ungracious, Hill Station,
the grand and expensive hotel, raised their eyebrows at the sight of

our carload of boys, chickens, baggage and dirty linen and were difficult about students visiting us in our room. At last, however, we found a house which had once been a resthouse but had fallen into disuse and here we were given an apartment. The decaying stone walls and unpleasant washing facilities were much more uncomfortable and repellent than the bare mud walls and primitive conditions of Kagoro, but at least we were free to entertain our friends as we pleased.

Jos is the centre of a tin-mining area, the open workings can be seen all over the plateau, and the father of one of our students was the foreman of a mine in a place with the lovely name of Barakin Ladi. The boy, Sulei Gwani, had come to Man O' War Bay on the schoolboys' course; a tall, gangling boy with a sulky closed face, he was one of the privileged of young Nigeria, from the Government Secondary School at Zaria. He did well, though not outstandingly, but when he returned home what he had learnt seemed suddenly to burst out in a series of imaginative ideas. He started among the young people of his district a group called the A.A., the 'Adventure Association', alias 'The Riskers'. The A.A. began with six members but grew rapidly to twenty-five; they undertook expeditions to places of interest all round Barakin Ladi, exploring hot springs and extinct craters and climbing some of the hills. The possibility of meeting a leopard, fairly common animals on the plateau, gave these outings a spice of genuine danger. The Association was carefully organized with the administrative work shared out between different grades of officers who were named, to attract recruits, after characters in cowboy films. There was a Sheriff who did the office work, a Marshal (Sulei) who looked after the active work, a Deputy Marshal and a Deputy Sheriff, there were Senior Hombres who did field work (scouting came under this term) and the rank and file were known as Junior Hombres. The A.A. flourished for some months and made some interesting and worthwhile expeditions. Unfortunately Sulei, after the initial outburst of enthusiasm, proved not to be a good correspondent and so we lost touch with him and his activities.

When we visited him at this time, however, the A.A. was in full bloom. Having no specific address we sought out his father at the mine. Alec found him and brought him out to greet me in the car, a fine-looking old man with a white beard flowing over the folds of muslin which composed his turban and encased his neck. He spoke little English but was obviously touchingly proud of his son and

SULEI GWANI, SCHOOLBOY

grateful to anyone who took an interest in him. He came with us to the village which was their home, to direct us and to welcome us into his own house.

Sulei, when he saw us, was very nervous. He stood clicking his fingers and shifting from foot to foot until Father urged him to take us indoors and entertain us in a proper manner. The house was small and we had to bend to enter it; there were sounds of agitation in the back quarters where the old man had disappeared and Sulei, looking more unhappy than ever, sat on an upturned box while we occupied the two chairs. Presently he was called away from behind and returned after a few minutes with some eggs and an angry white hen. He said nothing about these gifts but sat down again, turning and twisting the unfortunate hen between his hands where formerly he had twisted his knuckles. Gradually, as we talked, the strangeness and uneasiness wore off and he began to be able to tell us something of the 'Riskers' and what they did. News had got round that there were strangers in Sulei's house and one or two of the 'Hombres' themselves appeared at the door to be rendered speechless at the sight of Europeans and at the request to tell their names. Sulei got tired of unwittingly torturing the hen and put it on the ground where he planted one large, flat foot on both its claws to keep it tethered. I longed to say to him: 'Sulei, if that hen's for us, for goodness' sake give it to us and be done with it!' But as it was not absolutely certain that it was for us I did not like to be guilty of a possible breach of good manners.

When we emerged from the house into the dazzling light outside there was a small collection of spectators, waiting to see us get into our car. I saw, out of the corner of my eye, the hen being handed to Lucas and stuffed into the back of the vehicle and so was able to thank the father warmly for it. He, for his part, thanked us again for all that we had done for his son; we hoped that we had done well by him but looking at Sulei's face it was hard to tell what his thoughts were or how deep our influence had reached. We could only hope that at some future crossroads when he stood hesitating between the easy and the hard, the right and the wrong, something that he had done or seen at Man O' War Bay might reach out from the past and help him to make a good decision. It was easier to tell what the old man's thoughts were, for they were the universal thoughts of men whose sons have moved away from them into a different world and who long to be reassured by someone to whom that world is commonplace

AUDU MIANGO, MARKET MASTER

that their boy is all right and has friends to whom he can turn when he will no longer turn to his parents.

Audu Miango was the market master at Jos. This surprised me every time I saw him for he looked too young and good-natured to be able to cope with a market as big as this one, and as full (as I felt it was) of rackets. He took us round, showing us the different quarters where special merchandise was sold and ending up in his office in the very centre where rents were paid and he presided over deals and difficulties. It seemed obvious from the way in which he was greeted and the knowledge he displayed that he was, most certainly, master in his own market. He was a charming young man with a face alive with friendship and touched with a certain gentle shyness. Slightness of build gave him an air of fragility and the slenderness of his English lent conversation with him a peculiar fascination; we seemed to talk as much in friendly glances and unuttered thoughts as in spoken words.

Audu took his obligations to his community seriously on his return from the Cameroons, writing, after six months, to tell us that

213

he had broken a promise owing to the rainy season. He had decided to make mud blocks for a dustbin but the rain had ruined them. This promise, made on the last evening of the course, had been more an optimistic hope of what he might perform than an oath, and it is a measure of his conscience and integrity that he considered it binding and wrote to us, a thousand miles away, to apologize for having broken it. When we actually arrived in Jos he had a club to show us, where he had gathered together about eighteen boys and was trying to teach them new games. It was not an easy thing to attempt; in the whole of Jos it would be hard to find another young man willing to give up his spare time to help younger boys, and many of his friends would consider it an extraordinary idea. With no finances, no authoritative support and a membership often shifting and uncertain there must have been many frustrations for Audu himself. Such clubs were not long-lived, but they were not for that reason useless. For Audu it was a valuable experience, and maybe a seed planted here might later flower.

We made a deviation from the main road at Jos to visit a very beautiful part of the plateau to the east. Pankshin lay on the edge of the flat country which formed the top of the plateau where the land began to break up into hills of breathtaking loveliness. The first time we had come here we were very attracted by the resthouse, which might have been a baron's dwelling in mediaeval England. It had one enormous central room with a fireplace capable of roasting an ox, and numerous side halls in whose shadowy roofs the bats squeaked and the snakes rustled. Our food came from the kitchen outside and moments before it arrived Ali's footsteps could be heard padding along stone corridors, nearer and nearer while the food got colder and colder. We loved arriving here. There was space to unload all the luggage, to empty all the boxes and lay out papers and possessions in neat rows all over the floor for stock-taking. Ali was instructed to get enough wood for a roaring fire in the evening, and then we went out on to the terrace to see the sunset. The Government quarters and the resthouse were on a hill with a magnificent view across the valley to mountains. On the left hand the flat plateau land stretched to infinity back to Jos, on the right the country began to descend in a welter of rocky hills and tree-thick valleys. The gardener at Pankshin was a prodigy and the whole hillside bloomed with colour, rivalling the sunset behind the opposite range. When we arrived this time the flowers still bloomed riotously and the hills still stood in their magnificence but our wonderful resthouse had, alas, been modernized. It had been cut in two, to make separate residences, and the cleavage had taken place right through the fireplace. Now we no longer had plenty of space, the squeaking bats and a roaring blaze; we had a neat, white-washed little house with no method of heating and a pouring wet evening when the first thing we needed was a fire. The old resthouse had been nicknamed Some-one-or-other's Folly: yet surely this rational reconstruction was a greater stupidity?

Lashat Lavan lived on the other side of Pankshin at a place called Langtang. He had come on the schoolboys' course and it was he

LASHAT LAVAN, SCHOOLBOY

who used to delight us with a rendering of the song, 'South Carolina's Sultry Clime'. He was a fine-looking lad, very strong, with a broad, high-boned face which differed greatly from those of both Southerners and Northerners. He came of pagan stock and he wished to be an officer in the Army.

Some of the most beautiful country we had yet seen lay between Pankshin and Langtang. It was softer than the bare, rocky plateau, much of the ground being covered with thin scrub, delicate little trees or waving corn, with blue mountains crowned by wonderful cloud effects restricting the horizons. This was country off the beaten track and away from the major roads of Nigeria. There had been no way of letting Lashat know that we were coming, but we had not been in Langtang many minutes before he arrived, breathless and excited, to greet us. He lived with an uncle in a compound which consisted of a series of round thatched huts and he led us there at once so that we could greet his family and sit out of the sun to talk.

There was always a certain tension at a first meeting, particularly if it was an unexpected one like this, until it became obvious that our visit was one of interest and friendship. Looking back I think that it may have been especially difficult for the schoolboys. They came from the cream of Nigerian secondary schools where, as far as was possible, the best equipment and housing had been provided for them, and the whole system of living was based on an English public school. At Man O' War Bay they were presented with many arduous and physically tiring tasks but it all had the cachet of European inspiration and approval and took place within a European framework. They met us on our terms and, being open-hearted and adaptable, they quickly adapted themselves. But things were different when we came to their homes to visit them. Lashat's background in Langtang was purely African, unaffected as yet by European ways. His schooling and his natural intelligence and ambition made it very clear to him how far his home life differed from ours. He was not ashamed of it, but he recognized that we might need to adapt ourselves to his surroundings now and he was not sure whether we were able to do this or not. Europeans are apt to take their customs and their household gods with them wherever they go and some of us expect that other people's will conform to them. When, however, we had sat down on whatever seating there happened to be, a mat, a box, a stool, had accepted a drink, water or fruit juice, and had greeted the members of the household with every appearance of friendliness and pleasure, the atmosphere began to relax. For many, I think, the visit to their homes and the knowledge that we were prepared to accept them and enjoy the simple hospitality of the family was the first step to genuine friendship; a friendship which did not depend on place and circumstances to be worthwhile but which could be relied upon regardless of material inequality.

Lashat lived with an uncle. I think he had a family of his own somewhere but this, to us, curious feature of boys living with uncles rather than with their own families was one which we often found all over Nigeria. We used to ask about it but the answers were always rather vague and hazy and very often, I believe, the boys had no idea why it happened. This was a custom which had been accepted and taken for granted for a very long time and no one bothered any more to think about its origin. In some parts it is certainly the result of a matriarchal form of society where the husband had less right to his own children than the brothers of the wife. One of our lads, however, gave us an explanation which took no note of anthropology but was based on observation of African human nature.

'I think,' he said, 'that we cannot bear to correct our children or to say "No" to them. We love children very much and our own most of all. This is good when the child is small and when it does not matter if he does as he likes, but not so good later when the child must go to school and learn discipline. We see that if our child does not want to go to school we do not like to say to him, "You must go", even perhaps to beat him. So when he gets to the age for schooling we send him away to an uncle. We know that, because he is his own flesh and blood, his uncle will love him, but he will be stern also because the child is not of his own loins. He will recognize that what is good for the child must come first and not be misled by foolish fondness.'

Be that as it may, some uncles took their duties very seriously, often being responsible financially for a nephew's schooling right up to University standard and sometimes even paying for him to come to England.

We were sorry to leave Pankshin and start back to Jos to resume the journey northward. We had had a few days out of time and it had been very pleasant.

Zaria is an old walled city and it is also rapidly becoming the educational and cultural centre of the North; here is a section of the College of Arts and Science, the Institute of Administration, a big boys' secondary school, the headquarters of Boys' Training for the Nigeria Regiment, the centre of the Adult Literacy campaign for Northern Nigeria. All these things gave the town a cosmopolitan air and we had many of our young men there studying: C.S.M. Addingi was stationed here and one of our 'old boys' was a nurse in the hospital. We invited them all to a party in our room at the resthouse.

Because there were a lot of them, and because Sgt-Major Addingi was there it was possible to re-create something of the atmosphere of a course and to sing again some of the old songs. Enthusiastic plans were made to form a group to build a footbridge over the river at a place where the road bridge was particularly dangerous for pedestrians. The more lively spoke up loudly for this project while the less lively took cover behind the noise and laughter of the meeting. Sadly, however, it was the unenterprising who won in the end and the bridge never became a reality. In Eastern Nigeria the idea of a group undertaking a job of this kind for the public good would have been part of the traditional background of the people, and there would have been little difficulty in carrying out the scheme. Here, in the North, however, men lived more individual lives and the conception of voluntary physical labour to benefit the community as a whole was totally alien. When added to this there was the reluctance —also prevalent in the South—of educated young men to degrade themselves (as they saw it) by manual work, the scales were heavily weighted against anything happening. Though this was very disappointing, I used to think that at least we left our students with uneasy consciences about the things they left undone and this was always a first step. The grit of this small shame embedded among the splendid dreams of future self-government might, someday, produce a pearl. All the same we had great hopes that night in Zaria and were very disappointed when later they came to nothing.

We arrived in Kano in the late afternoon. There was quite a group of old students in the city and the actual site of our stay had been causing us some concern; Kano, more than any other place which we had visited, has rigid distinctions of class, tribe, religion, and sometimes colour. For all the glamour and splendour of a true Northern walled city, seat of a powerful Emir, site of an international airport, the young men of Kano were among the least satisfactory of all our students. Feeble, fearful, and willingly cocooned in outmoded rigidities of background and faith, they contrasted strangely with those of their own people from much poorer and less illustrious provinces.

From Zaria, some hours to the South, we had rung up one of our students who worked in the Native Authority Office and asked him to find us somewhere to stay. The only official resthouse, the Railway Resthouse, was some distance outside the city itself, and we had a premonition that the atmosphere might not be altogether friendly to young clerks and teachers coming in and out to talk with us. We hoped to stay somewhere nearer the centre of activities, where our young men could talk openly, or at least as openly as they could bring themselves to do. Aminu agreed to find us accommodation for the two nights that we would be in Kano and told us to come straight to the N.A. office when we arrived.

The outskirts of Kano are like the outskirts of any other growing town anywhere in the world; undesigned and ugly, small factories planted down without amenities, a scattering of houses without any overriding plan. Now and then, giving the whole landscape a strangely Middle Eastern look, great pyramids of ground nuts rose into the air and a stream of supercilious camels went plodding by. But when we drove through the wall which surrounds the city all this was changed. Now the houses, all built of red mud and enclosed behind high walls, had a cohesion of material and design which gave the city character. More than that, once through the wall we felt that we had passed from modern times into mediaeval days; for all the splendour of the new mosque built in Public Works Department concrete, we had moved into an ancient atmosphere unchanged in essence from the times of the Moslem conquest of the pagan north.

I sat outside the N.A. office while my husband went in to find Aminu and discover what arrangements had been made for us. They came out together after some little time and Aminu greeted me politely and told me that we were to have the Emir's resthouse in the centre of the city. The Emir was away making a triumphal tour

KANO

of his province, but we had had one of his sons at Man O' War Bay and Aminu was sure he would be delighted that we should be his guests. We, at any rate, were overjoyed, for this meant that we would be living right inside the city itself and easily accessible to our students in their free time.

The resthouse, when we found it, was perfectly lovely. Situated in the great central square, opposite the Emir's palace and the new mosque, it was a corner house built like all the others of red mud and enclosed within a containing wall. Once through the doorway we were in a tiny courtyard overshadowed by a spreading tree. The house itself had three stories, on the ground floor two immense rooms with great arched roofs filled with a lovely, mellow, pinkish light reflected through the deep slit windows off the burnt sienna walls; the little crooked stairs led up to three smaller rooms, and up again on to the flat roof. Here, in the cool of the evening when the first stars came out, the Moslem wives, for whom the ordinary commerce of the street was forbidden, must have come out to look about them over the city and observe the doings of their neighbours.

I loved the house. For the first time in the weeks of packing and moving on which had made up this tour we were in a building which felt welcoming and peaceful, as if it had once held families within its walls and not a constant series of ephemeral, fleeting guests. In no time at all the car was unpacked, our goods disposed about the rooms; Lucas was baking bread in the kitchen courtyard and the warm smell filtered through the pink house. The first arrivals amongst our old students had sought us out and were talking with Alec in the living room and we felt as though we had been established there for many days—and many days in residence were still to come.

In this, as we later discovered, we were mistaken.

Early next morning a group of our students came to take us round the sights of Kano. Like all Northerners they were very courteous and determined we should think well of their city. The first visit was to the mosque. I had felt certain that I would be left outside, as women are rarely welcome in mosques, but was told that this was not the case. We could all climb the minaret—but there was no question, even for my husband, of going inside though we might both stand just within the door for a quick look. So we took off our shoes, a ritual which it would be discourteous to omit, and climbed the endless stairs to the top of the minaret. I do not like

heights and the view was not so very different from that obtained
before on the roof of our house, but I was struck afresh by the
'lowness' of the city as a whole. There were no skyscrapers, no
buildings of any outstanding elevation, and this looked curious to
eyes accustomed to the conglomeration of Westernized cities. An
impression of secrecy was produced by the uniformity of colour and
the predominance of windowless walls. There was little sign of
bustle or occupation and yet, behind those blank façades and under
these thousands of flat roofs, common sense told me that there must
be just as much activity as in any other large community of human
beings.

Our next visit was to the market. Here, entering its narrow
lanes lined with low, thatched booths, we were transported into a
land of imagination and of storybooks, where caravans crossed the
desert from Timbuctoo loaded with exotic merchandise, and laid in
stocks for journeys to very distant lands, Egypt, or Mecca, or the
far Sudan. Here were bearded, turbaned gentlemen exchanging
dignified and solemn words, here some Fulani, beautiful as deer with
liquid eyes and little oval heads the colour of pale tea. We saw for
sale antimony and lapis lazuli, lamps made from camel's stomachs,
calabashes beautifully carved, and wonderful camel cloths in a
coarse white weave with blue or black or scarlet stripes. There
were other things too, of course, which denoted that it was no longer
over the desert that the caravans came; Hercules bicycles immaculately wrapped in brown paper strips (it was fashionable among the
young élite of Kano to retain this covering even when the bicycle
was in use), lamps and kitchenware of all kinds, cloth from Manchester, bowls from Japan, needles and thread, buttons and bric-à-
bracery from many corners of Europe and the world. And over it all
the smell of the North, a smell of heat and dried dung, of mud and
animals and sweat all combined.

When, some hours later, dazed with light and colour and laden
with purchases we staggered back to rest in our house, it was to find
an urgent message awaiting us to go at once to see the Senior District
Officer. Feeling slightly guilty at not having greeted him on arrival,
but without premonition, we drove out of the city to the District
Office accompanied by one or two of our retinue. I sat in the car and
wondered why my husband was so long in coming out from the
interview and speculated mildly on what the S.D.O. could have to
say to us.

When it did come it was bad news. The Senior District Officer had greeted Alec coldly and asked what the hell he and his wife were doing sleeping inside the city? Did we not know that it was forbidden for any except the Faithful to spend the night inside the walls? Who had given us permission? The Emir was away on trek and no one else had the authority to say whether his resthouse could be used or not. Alec was completely taken aback. We had had no suspicion that there would be any difficulty about our using the resthouse, permission had been given by the Native Authority, some of them closely related to the Emir. I am, in fact, convinced that there was no difficulty and that the Emir, had he been there, would have ratified our stay, but this was a case of an Englishman being more Moslem than the Moslem, of outdoing in rigidity and caste consciousness the aristocracy of the North. Did we not know that no Europeans, no white woman especially, had ever slept in the city? No, we did not know— or wholly believe it—nor was there the slightest sign that our presence was unwelcome to our neighbours. But we had to move. The Senior District Officer was Law and though we thought of sending a message to the Emir, asking his permission to stay on, he was too far away to make this practicable.

Very sadly we drove back to the house and began to pack again. I looked at those lovely golden rooms, the little courtyard with its shady tree, the roof, and smelt the perfume of half-baked bread floating gently through the narrow windows and thought that if it were true that I was the only white woman ever to sleep in Kano city at least I had had one very happy night there.

The United Africa Company, as so often during our time in Nigeria, came to our rescue and offered us a flat in a modern house not far outside the city which they used for visiting company officials. We thanked them gratefully and moved in at once. The armchairs, the shining silver, the immaculate bathroom with water from a tap were all very welcome, but somehow I regretted deeply that other house where there were no chairs, the battered spoons and forks were our own and had seen many journeys, and the bath was a kerosene tin of hot water poured by Ebenezer into a square of green canvas on two folding legs and set in the midst of a rose-red room with a view over half the city of Kano.

It was not, however, only the British who made distinctions in this city. For the only time, anywhere in Nigeria, when we held a reunion for the old students in the City Library, I was asked not to go because I was a woman. And not I alone. There was one young Southerner among the students, a Yoruba named Ade Kafaru, who worked for a French Company. He was a good lad who did his best to put into practice the things that we had taught him. When the students announced that they had arranged the reunion they also told us that it was not possible to invite Ade Kafaru because he was a Southerner. So Ade and I sat in the U.A.C. flat and entertained each other and I felt ashamed that we had so far deserted our principles as to acquiesce in this. I have often felt since that I should have gone, and taken

ADE KAFARU, CLERK

Ade with me, and told the effeminate young men of Kano (as I had so often done at Man O' War Bay) exactly what I thought of them. But we still felt that we must work slowly against such deep-rooted prejudice and we still held then the mistaken hope that the group might take some action if left to itself.

CHAPTER XIII

*More
Adventures*

GOMBE HOUSE

THE road from Kano to Azare is not at its best in the rainy season
and to turn off it, as we did, in an endeavour to reach Ningi down
a community-built, dry-season track could prove a disastrous
enterprise. We had not gone very far before we came to the first
collapsed culvert. By driving off the road into the scrub and back
on to the road again on the other side, we managed to negotiate it
safely, and once this initial difficulty was overcome a stubborn pride
made any future retreat unthinkable. Six culverts later, three of
them only passed with the greatest difficulty and the combined
pushing power of Lucas, Ebenezer, Ali and myself, I was beginning
to regret heartily that we had ever left the main road. However, it was
too late. Each time the car groaned and squelched out of the protesting mud we had put another barrier between ourselves and
return. The light was fading; every now and then small parties of
tribesmen came up the road towards us and passed us silently. They
were wild and sinister, quite without the flashing smiles and brash
good humour of people farther south. They looked at our sweating
efforts to move a fully-loaded 30-h.p. Chevrolet by manpower—
and passed on.

At the next culvert we met a road supervisor just getting on
to his bicycle, his day's work finished. He was astounded to see
a car on his road, the more so because he assured us that it was
impossible to get to Ningi at all. Some little distance on there was
a drift, passable in dry weather but now submerged beneath a river
yards wide. This was discouraging news though we still hoped it
might be exaggerated. We asked the supervisor if he knew of anywhere that would accommodate us for the night. Yes, he said, there
was a village on the far side of the river; he would go ahead on his

bicycle and tell the Chief that we were coming. So he rode cheerfully off into the dusk leaving us to crawl along behind him.

He had not been long gone when disaster overtook us. In the next mud patch the constant, furious revving of the engine resulted in a sudden seizing up in the gear-box and there we were, stuck in first gear with no possibility of moving the lever up or down and insufficient knowledge to be able to put it right. This was despair: it was dark: the road supervisor had long since disappeared and we did not know whether his village was near or far.

Tired, hungry and cross we put our shoulders to the wheels once again and a superhuman effort took us out of the bog and at a slow crawl, in our one gear, up the road. Quite suddenly, after a few yards, we rounded a bend and the lights were reflected back from a gleaming stretch of water which lapped up the road almost to our wheels. Seen like this, in darkness, the river seemed immense, almost a sea. Almost, but distantly in the night opposite us twinkled and burned a row of lights which must be a village. It brought little comfort to me, looking, as it did, inaccessible. While we gazed and debated, however, some of the lights appeared to move. We looked away, then looked again. It was no illusion, they were moving. A thin wavering line of tiny flames was floating across the water towards us. Presently we could see that they rested on the heads of men wading thigh-deep through the river, and at last the first man, small and elderly, his long gown kilted up round his waist, walked out of the water and introduced himself as the Chief. Our message had been received and he had come personally to offer us the hospitality of his house for the night.

Our spirits rose mercurially. Ebenezer and Lucas began to laugh and joke; Ali, who spoke Hausa with an accent which made it as difficult to understand as his English, burst into incomprehensible sentences. We began to sort out the essentials from our baggage to be taken across the river for the night. There were plenty of men ready to carry any loads back through the water and this was just as well for the job of distinguishing among our many pieces of equipment was nearly impossible. Was it worthwhile to open, in the dark, the food box and to rummage about for beans and bacon? Which pans would we need from the kitchen box? How did we carry loose cups and saucers once they were removed from the china basket? It proved too difficult and, in the end, we left the boxes intact and made use of the superfluity of manpower to get across a large part of our kit, leaving in the car only the less urgent items, a typewriter, the tin trunk of files and money, the dirty linen, our purchases in Kano market the day before and all the spares and equipment belonging purely to the car. We locked it up and turned to face the river.

I was nervous. The water looked very black and swift and I had no idea how deep it was. We asked the old Chief, through the good offices of Ali, and the answer was not reassuring. He waved his hand vaguely across his knees, then gradually took it higher to his waist, while a friend, a tall friend, standing nearby cheerfully pointed to the middle of his chest. I was left still wondering whether it was going to be an easy passage. There was no alternative, however, and so, kilting my skirts up round my thighs, I joined the procession sandwiched between Alec and Ebenezer, both of them impervious to despairing female whimpers.

We waded gently into the warm black liquid which lapped round our ankles and then began to creep up the calves. At intervals the lamps flared and flickered, a double row of reddish stars above our heads and beneath our feet. In front the man carrying our box of food dropped it suddenly in the deepening river regardless of my stores of flour and sugar; behind, Ebenezer grunted and muttered to himself in nervous trepidation. I hitched my skirts up round my behind and wondered how much farther I could go before I asked to be carried. The fate of the food did not increase my confidence in this idea. Just as I felt that modesty would not let me wade an inch farther the water began to decrease and we were past the worst. Now it remained only to plod on until we reached dry land again.

I had an idea that the rest of the village would be lining the bank to greet us, but it was not so. All who were interested had come across with the Chief to meet us, it seemed, the rest sat over their fires unconcerned by the advent of strangers. To them the little procession winding up, dripping, out of the river, fitfully lit by lamps and bearing a strange assortment of baggage, had not the glamour and excitement that it had for us. The Chief led us into the heart of the village, almost invisible in the dark, and into a small round house. Here a fire was burning on the floor and there seemed to be a great many people, the number swelling rapidly as our porters came in. Presently there was barely room to stand and I waited for the next move. There was no next move. This, it became apparent, was our house for the night. It was the gatehouse into the Chief's compound and in giving it to us he had made a handsome gesture.

My husband and I looked at each other, the same thought in both our minds: how, without offence, could we find another shelter? Already Ali struggling with the camp beds had made movement impossible; yet, over the top of baggage and bodies, movement went on because this was the only entrance in and out of the Chief's own house and his relatives and visitors were all the more eager to make use of it because of the events which had occurred.

We held a conference with the school teacher who had turned up to act as interpreter and it appeared that there was a vacant room in the village, a newly-built adult education centre, as yet unused. They had hesitated to offer it to us, thinking it cold and inhospitable. With as much delicacy as could be mustered we suggested to the Chief that our cooking and the storage of our luggage should take place in the gatehouse where there was a fire and the protection of the eye of the Chief himself, but that it would not be seemly for a woman to sleep there and we had heard that there was one empty place where she might have privacy. Might we have his permission to make use of it?

Whether he believed us or not was not apparent but with the courtesy which is the hallmark of their treatment of guests he agreed that we might transfer ourselves to the adult education centre. He was probably not interested in our motives, knowing white people to be activated by curious ideas and queer taboos.

The centre, a small, red mud, rectangular building, with spaces in the walls for windows, was blessedly empty. Within a very short time Ebenezer had transferred the beds and had them made up neatly side by side along one wall; Ali had managed to light a lamp and set out a box as table with two canvas

NASERU

IBRAHIM EL YAKUBU U.A.C.

chairs; then Ebenezer appeared with boiling water in a kerosene tin and the canvas bath, and as soon as that was over Lucas produced fried eggs and beans, tins of peaches and evaporated milk. In no time at all we had made ourselves at home, surrounded by our comforts and our household gods, as though this little house had been our shelter for many days.

The problems, however, were not solved. Immediately on waking our minds flew back to the car, standing gear-bound on the other side of the flood. We had no desire to spend another night in Naseru, we needed help—and quickly. Twelve miles farther on was Ningi, where our students lived; it was Friday, a Moslem holiday, fortunately as both were school teachers, they must be summoned to our aid. This was the moment when they must put into practice all that they had learned and rescue their Principal as he had so often, when they were in difficulties, rescued them. The teacher had promised the night before that a message should go to them at dawn and it had been carefully written out and given to him: 'To Barau and Saidu Ningi, Come at once. Your Principal is at Naseru with something wrong with his car. Please bring a mechanic.'

Now in the dawn, at 6 a.m., we were roused by the sounds of a horse breathing and stamping outside the Chief's house. This was the messenger ready to set out to bring the news of our plight from Naseru to Ningi. He swung astride his steed with a flourish of white robes and flashing teeth and, wheeling, set off at a gallop down the sandy track.

There was something so splendidly romantic at this sight that we felt rescue was assured and our arrangements in safe hands. That there was no special foundation for this feeling became obvious as time drew on and rescue showed no signs of materializing. We had counted the hours carefully and calculated that help might arrive about nine o'clock. When at 10.30 a.m. the village still lay in hot, somnolent inactivity we began to worry. We had inspected the school,

228

walked down to the river and back, been all the way round the village—and all the way back again—and still no sign of Barau or Saidu. I did not know whether to give the order to pack or not as it still seemed possible that we might have to sleep again in the adult education centre. The teacher had told us that it was unused because no adult wished to be educated.

At midday there was a commotion on the other side of the cleared space before the Chief's house and a little procession entered. First, on bicycles, Barau and Saidu, the latter in full Scout uniform complete with clean flashes and brand-new canvas shoes. We came to the conclusion that the obtaining and preparing of these items had kept the rescue party from starting out as soon as it should. Behind them, still on bicycles not one but two mechanics, dressed rather smartly in some kind of dark blue uniform; behind them a rabble of children and interested spectators who had joined in as the cavalcade rode through the township and, bringing up the rear, the messenger and his horse.

When greetings had been exchanged and we had heard the news from our students it was arranged that a party should go across to the car to assess the damage. I stayed behind, not wishing to ford the river more often than I need, but I heard what happened when the party arrived on the other side. It was Alec who saw, as he waded out of the water, a cushion lying on the grass beside the car. It struck him as curious, for we had looked around very carefully before leaving the night before, but understandable in the dark and confusion. However, as they approached the car it became obvious that the cushion was no accident. There was a window broken and the glass was smeared with blood. Thieves had come in the night.

The damage, as it turned out, was not very great, but it was annoying. The thieves had not known, even when the window was broken, how to unlock the car doors from inside and so had not been able to take anything too big to be got out through the window: fortunately this applied to the large tin trunk containing all our money. For the rest, the typewriter was gone, the lovely camel cloths that we had bought in Kano market two days before, ninety-six eggs given me by a kindly Chief (but without the basket in which they had been packed); the dirty linen bag had been rifled, all my husband's clothes were missing from it but mine were left spread out over the front seat! As the party fanned out to look for any clues one of them gave a shout. There was the typewriter, abandoned in the bush by some man who had no idea of its use.

Meanwhile the mechanic had lifted up the bonnet and was peering into the engine. He gave a grunt, there was a click, and the gear lever slid sweetly into place again. This was shame indeed; only his obvious enjoyment in his own knowledge and skill saved us from feeling utterly humiliated.

The old Chief was full of apologies when told of the theft, and assured us that the robbers must have come from over the provincial boundary. This was the only time in all our years in Nigeria that we had had anything stolen and we were extremely surprised that it should have happened in such a remote rural area instead of in one of the large towns. It was only a long time later, when we were told that Naseru had been in years past a 'thieves' village' in which the Emir of Ningi was reputed to have kept bands of thieves to raid into Kano, that we began to feel less surprised about the whole incident.

The arrival at Azare was a wet one, though transformed by the warmth of the welcome from Aminu. It was dusk when we drew into the town and quite dark by the time we had found the resthouse. Ali's Hausa, on which we had relied, failed us and we saw the same baffled look come over the faces of those to whom he talked as came over our own when he tried to make us understand something. The rain poured down, real tropical wet-weather rain, close, heavy, unrelenting.

The resthouse, when we found it, was some way outside the town in a grove of trees. It was a round, thatched mud house with a small kitchen beside it. I was tired and therefore cross, and the night seemed very black. It was all too difficult to contemplate, unloading the car, starting the lamps, finding dry wood for a fire, heating water, making beds. It was not necessary that I should do any of these jobs myself, but I had to will them to be done—or so I thought. Fortunately we were rarely all in a bad temper at the same time and tonight Lucas was a tower of strength. He was out of the car almost as soon as we had arrived, standing, half-naked and glistening in the wet, directing the unloading. Ebenezer felt as I did, but a dogged spirit drove him to do the necessary chores, even if he did them badly. Ali, shaken by the non-success of his interpreting, bumbled about like an ungainly dog, doing the wrong things in the wrong place at the wrong time. Somehow, by a miracle, lights were lit and the little house began to assume a homely look. Lucas found dry wood, and a delicious smell of cooking food drifted out of the kitchen. Then Aminu turned up. I have forgotten how he found us, or what bush telegraph told him we had arrived, he just materialized out of the darkness to greet us with an affection and delight that were heart-warming.

Aminu was a teacher in the Native Authority school. I have no idea of his age but his physique, which was slender and small-boned, made him look very young. He spoke good English, with the clipped accent of the Northerner, and he had an alive, vivid face. He had been a good student at Man O' War Bay and now we found him doing his best to put some of the ideas into practice. He had a great deal of common sense in his approach, realizing that it was better to start in a small way and succeed than to create a large splash which, when the water was wiped out of the spectator's eyes, proved to have come from a very small puddle.

'I am still trying, Sir,' he said. 'What kind of services do you think I am doing, Sir? I have not started any field work which my people shall see the result. My Northern people naturally take no interest in giving service to the community voluntarily at the moment as other peoples do. But gradually there is a sign of volunteers. Surely the young ones will give volunteer services in the future. And if not why not?' added Aminu. The Northerners loved rhetorical questions and rarely waited for an answer. 'I have been practising small things in my school. Games which I have been doing at Man O' War Bay; First Aid; English and Native songs. I have tried to help with Adult Literacy. You see, Sir,' he concluded with a charming smile, 'I have not started with big field work, I find it is rather unwise to start with big things while you are not in complete control of the small things!'

But he was in control of the small things. When we went to his school next morning and watched him teach English to a class of earnest little boys there was no doubt at all who was in control. 'G-reen, W-hite,' we recognized at once how the accent was transmitted. The children had complete faith in him, not one of them would have believed us if we had stood up and said that, in fact, the emphasis was a different one, giving the word another flavour. It was Aminu who knew how English was spoken, not the Englishman. Maybe they were right, in a way. Our form of speech would have been flat and characterless compared to theirs. Their pronunciation,

unmistakably Northern Nigerian, was as much a part of their person-
alities as their *rigas* and dark faces; the world would have been greatly
the poorer had they all spoken with perfect accents. As we left, seen
off by the elderly headmaster, the chanting of the Koran in many
high young voices floated out behind us. The smaller children
were learning by rote words and phrases far beyond their understanding, in a language incomprehensible to them, but they were
learning with the passionate conviction that it was of immense
importance to them and to their future. They would learn Aminu's
'small things' with the same concentration, for all schoolchildren
in this part of the world are avid for knowledge, and maybe something in what he taught would bear fruit for big things in the future.

Many of our best students had come from Bauchi Province, as
had some of our best British staff. There were men in the administration in Bauchi who understood what we were trying to do at Man
O' War Bay and so the candidates were always carefully chosen,
which was not necessarily the case elsewhere, and they were observed
and helped after their return. Bauchi lies south of Azare and Kano
in country which is broken by small hills of coloured rock. In the
late afternoon these outcrops could turn pink and turquoise, orange
and blue, until they represented a living background for a Disney
cartoon, lacking only a foreground of splendidly assorted animals.
Once, however, we saw another foreground, the right one for the
mountains. We happened to arrive in Bauchi as Ramadhan ended,
the month-long Moslem fast, in time to see the ceremony by which
the surrounding chiefs greet their Emir and reaffirm their loyalty
to him.

The day was a public holiday and every man had a new dress in
honour of the occasion. This might only be a new white gown of the
simplest kind or it might be an elaborately embroidered robe in some
gorgeous colour, but even the poorest had saved up for new clothes
and the little girls, too, appeared in cyclamen and pink, cerise and
scarlet, sashed with green or gold or indigo.

Shortly after dawn there was ceremonial prayer outside the
walls of the city. We rose very early and drove out to see what was
an amazing sight. Hundreds and hundreds of people, or rather
of men, for only the little girls represented their sex, had gathered
together. The sparkling freshness and the variety of colour of their
new clothes, the flower garden of small embroidered caps, the swelling, pure white turbans set off by innumerable black faces made

blacker by contrast, all this would have delighted a pointilliste painter. Somewhere in the throng there was an Imam toward whom all pressed, except for some of the naughty, smaller boys who, having gained their objective in a fine new gown, no longer felt the need to praise God. The solemn intent faces all around us had a sobering effect; we had gone out to satisfy our curiosity, to see a sight, now we felt intruders, idle visitors gawking at the sacred moments of strangers—so we turned around and came away.

After prayer came junketing. The great ceremonial of the day took place about nine o'clock in the open space in front of the Emir's palace. We were to overlook this ceremony from the balcony of the Emir himself, a position of great vantage since everything of importance took place under the balcony and all roads led to this spot. The palace had a curtain wall all round it broken at intervals by square towers. In the centre of the stretch facing the broad sweep of main road was a rather larger gateway tower; the balcony overhung the centre of the gate protected from the sun by the shadow of the arch above it. When we arrived the Emir was moving graciously among the élite of Bauchi receiving congratulations on the feast. He wore a magnificent cobalt-blue robe and the usual froth of turban, and, although rather squat in figure, looked every inch a personage of noble blood. I was uncertain how to address an Emir or what degree of deference was expected from me and was uneasy until we had been introduced to him. He, however, was in no doubt about his own position and soon put us at our ease with a handshake and a few courteous words. Then he left us and we were free to turn our attention to the things we had come to see.

Looking out from the balcony a broad avenue stretched away in front for many hundreds of yards until, in the distance, it turned a

BAUCHI HILLS

sharp corner by the building of the N.A. Treasury. On either side
this avenue was lined by small trees and already the crowds were
beginning to swarm up it and congregate beneath the walls of the
palace and on either side of the road. It was the same crowd as we had
seen in the early morning, but now animated and excited, laughing
and talking in anticipation. The sun was very bright and already hot,
below us the Emir appeared, mounted now, surrounded by his
bodyguard and his band, the royal umbrella twirling and twisting
over his head. Though the normal mounts were horses, two of the
band rode on camels, and among them I was astonished to see a
woman. They played strange instruments, drums and long ungainly
horns among them, and made a noise that to European ears had
little of the martial rhythm that we associate with bands but which,
nevertheless, subtly contributed to the atmosphere a feeling of
triumph, of mounting excitement and the clash and flow of battles.
The Emir had changed his gown and now wore one richly embroidered in cream on heavy cream material; his bodyguard were
clad in garments of a mediaeval splendour in the richest colours and
sat on horses caparisoned with scarlet and gold, ultramarine and
green; their turbans and helmets, each of a differing design, were of
styles and patterns which we know from the pictures of the knights of
the Crusaders and their Saracen enemies; some wore chain mail
which, we were told, was the original handed down from father to
son and most carefully cherished.

Far away beneath the walls of the Treasury we could see movement and the gathering of horses. There was a restless shiver through
the crowds, the horns groaned, the trumpets blared, the drums beat
out a swelling tattoo, and a line of horses six abreast formed across
the end of the avenue and began to trot slowly up towards the
palace. The Chiefs and Emirs of the Province were coming, as they
had come since time immemorial, to greet their Head.

The line began to sway and undulate as the horses came on
faster and faster. Now a cloud of dust rose up behind them and they
rushed towards us as men impelled by furies. I looked below where
the Emir sat like a rock, his great umbrella turning ceaselessly above
him; I looked again at the approaching horsemen, now very near,
and it seemed impossible that they could save themselves from overwhelming him. I longed to turn away but fascination kept my eyes
upon the spectacle. We held our breath, and it seemed that all the
vast crowd ceased to breathe as well. Then, when disaster seemed

certain, there was a flash from many lifted spears, a shout rose up from half a dozen throats, hoarse and proud and loyal, the dust billowed violently, the horses reared back on their hindquarters till man and horse, centaurs, stood upright on two legs and paid homage to their ruler.

This astonishing salute happened not once but many times as fresh groups of horsemen gathered at the far end of the avenue and swept up to engulf the Emir, stopping only at the very last second, the flailing front hooves of their horses practically brushing the immovable mounts of his bodyguard. Each time he acknowledged the salute, sitting rigid beneath the weight and welter of his robes under the outsize umbrella. Those who had paid their homage ranged themselves to the right of his entourage, the sun glinting off their silver, shovel stirrups and high decorated turbans, and watched with critical eyes the performances of the late-comers. The air was full of fine red dust, the sun struck powerfully out of a clear sky; after this, the climax of the morning, the crowds would relax and eat, making up in one prolonged feast for some of the long dry days of fasting which they had left behind them for another year.

This year, however, we were too late for the day of Salah, and Bauchi looked, as usual, rather sleepy and a little drab, as we drove through the crumbling walls to look for Muhammadu Dagu Ningi who worked at the Native Treasury. He was a young man, solid, responsible, a little anxious, the salt of the earth and a good friend. While making no spectacular contribution to his course at Man O' War Bay he had left an impression of sincerity and integrity, in the end more valuable qualities than dazzling brilliance. He had three wives but no children. This latter fact was a great grief to him and he had often spoken to me about it and asked for advice—which I found very difficult to give. Perhaps because of this, however, he was one of the very few Northern students who asked me if I would visit his home and talk with his wives. There was another reason also. I had taught him to weave and, at the time, he had said to me that he would go home and teach the Mrs Muhammadus. Now he had done so and I was to go to see the result.

The visit was to be a morning one and I must, of course, go alone as my husband would not be allowed into the back compound. Muhammadu's house opened off a street in the centre of the town and was quite small. We entered through a room in which several of his friends sat talking and passed, by an entrance at the back, into a little, clean compound completely surrounded by high walls. In the compound were three identical round huts and standing drawn up in a line on my left were the three Mrs Muhammadus. They had gone to great pains to receive me well and the impression they created was of a particularly exotic and beautiful garden of flowers. They wore brilliantly-coloured cloths and had their black hair wrapped in similar gorgeous headscarves. Muhammadu introduced me with pride, first to the senior wife, a kindly-looking older woman, and then to the two younger, one little more than a girl. The wives presented me with an ostrich feather fan and I felt very ashamed because I had not anticipated this and had taken nothing in return. Unfortunately we could not communicate, because I spoke no Hausa and they no English, so all conversation took place through Muhammadu. He was obviously the kindest of husbands and one who lived up to the injunction of the Koran that a man could have more than one wife if he did not discriminate between them; and they, equally apparently, were very fond both of him and of each other. The two younger looked at the older woman as if she had been their mother, and she occasionally glanced at them with the fond, slightly ironical look of an experienced senior for pretty, naive juniors. But I wondered what they found to occupy them all day penned in the tiny confines of the compound, and I saw that Muhammadu's distress about his childlessness was not on his own behalf only but also very much on theirs. It would not have mattered which of them had borne the child, the difference that it would have made to their lives would have been enormous. All would have lavished on it an affection and an interest which would have introduced a new dimension into their narrow days; as it grew and began to run in and out from the compound to the outside world they would have gained a source of news and gossip which would keep them well-informed and alive. Alas, all this was denied them and they were still at a moment in time when it seemed that neither the wonders of medical science nor the possibility of adoption was permitted them by the tradition in which they lived.

Muhammadu, however, very conscious of the vacuum, had done his best. He now took me with pride into each of the three huts accompanied by its particular occupant and there, in the centre of the floor, stood a sturdy, upright loom with a piece of weaving on it, a coarse white cloth woven in narrow strips and much used in these parts for making up into blankets. I could not quite believe that my efforts to instruct Muhammadu on a tiny square frame with thin cotton had enabled him to blossom into this, but he was gallant enough to swear that my teaching, and mine alone, had led to this result and he took a great pride in showing it to me. Each house held its loom, and each owner beamed as I fingered the stuff and exclaimed over the evenness and skill of the work.

I asked Muhammadu what they did with the finished cloth, picturing to myself the tiny compound gradually filling up with the results of their labours, and he told me that it was sold and so they made themselves some pin money. For a moment I hoped that this meant that they were allowed to go out and do their own bargaining and chaffering, but I quickly learnt that this was not so, their husband did it for them. He explained what happened, an impish smile on his face.

'I buy it from them,' he said. 'I give what I think is a fair price. Then I take it to market and I sell it. If I do not get so good a price then they are lucky—they have made some extra money.'

'And if you get a better price?' I asked.

'Why then I put it in my pocket for my trouble,' he answered, and grinned with all the pleasure of a schoolboy who has been particularly clever.

From Bauchi, ninety miles in a straight line to the east, the road runs out to Gombe. The country is flat and scrubby though, beyond Gombe, it continues on to hill country, said to be very beautiful and rejoicing in the name of Tangale Waja. We had three students in Gombe whom we wished to visit.

No forewarning was possible in this instance; we simply set off one morning and hoped that, when we arrived at the other end, Magaji, Pela and Muhammad would be available, and that it would be possible to find somewhere to sleep. There were one or two hazards connected with the journey which gave it a taste of adventure. Gombe was a very remote part of the region and we had a leaking petrol tank, the result of hitting an unusually large stone on the Mamfe road. Ebenezer proved himself very resourceful over this and we would stop at intervals while he climbed underneath the car and plugged the hole with toilet soap.

When we arrived in Gombe it was quickly apparent that there was nowhere for us to stay. The resthouse was full up; the District Office said: 'Yes, the resthouse was full up'; the District Officer, even, had his house full up as well. This was tiresome, but we were not unduly dismayed and decided to go into the town and look for our students. As there are no street names or numbers in most towns in Nigeria it was never possible to have a specific address; letters were usually addressed to our young men care of their employers. So we drove at once to the Treasury to locate Magaji and Pela who both worked there. Magaji appeared looking very surprised; he had difficulty in believing his eyes and I could not quite make out whether he wanted to believe them or not! After many warm greetings we explained that, first of all, we must find somewhere to sleep. Magaji looked blank and said that we must go and ask Pela, who was in his house and not at work.

Pela's house, in a broad, unmade-up road, was enclosed in the usual containing wall. A small boy who was lounging about disappeared within and presently returned with a very dishevelled and rather sullen Pela.

'Hullo, Pela,' we said. 'So you see we have come, as we said we would, to see how you are getting on, and now the first thing you must do is find us somewhere to sleep for the night.'

Pela's face became a study in welcome and despair; a hunted expression spread over his cicatriced features and he kept casting glances at Magaji, who, thanking his stars that it was not his problem, looked blandly the other way. Northern students, more than those of other regions, were so hedged about by traditions, taboos and preconceived ideas of what should happen in any situation that they were much less enterprising, for the most part, about solving any problems presented by our visit. They knew, however, as did all our ex-students, that solutions were expected from them, in the same way that the training had demanded answers to the situations they encountered at Man O' War Bay. So, while Pela in some consternation racked his brains for a resting place for us, we waited.

He found a solution. Rather hesitantly he suggested that we use the house of a neighbour who had gone off on holiday. It was our turn to hesitate. We did not want to enter another man's house without his permission unless it was perfectly certain that he would not object. Pela, however, in the enormous relief of having produced the rabbit out of the hat, assured us that the owner could have no possible objection. I thought not, too, when we saw the house.

In the same street as Pela's, on the opposite side of the road; it too was entered by a gatehouse in the wall. Through this gatehouse, which consisted of one small room, there was an open space of trodden mud within which stood three circular mud huts. That was all; the enclosed space and the three huts comprised the house.

Ali, Ebenezer and Lucas were overcome, at this point, by a fit of non-co-operativeness. Very much more conscious of the dignity of our position than we were, they considered it not right that we should live in such surroundings. They were also afraid. Every now and then they became aware of being Cameroonians very far from their own country, and remembered tales told in childhood of wild men and cannibals. Then a stupor of fear descended on them and made them useless until we had managed to dispel it. So now they sat in the gatehouse, surrounded by their own mats and cooking pots, their faces blank and stupid. When roused, Ebenezer could only point out the impossibility of anyone living in such a place; where was the cooking to be done, where would they (the boys) sleep, what proper place was there for us to eat? I was well accustomed to Ebenezer by now and had an answer for every objection he put up. The cooking would be done here, in the gatehouse; the boys would sleep there also, I added 'to protect us from thieves' for the amusement of seeing the expression on Ebenezer's face which plainly said that we were there to protect him and not the other way round; we would eat in the open, off a box, and he could squeeze both our camp beds into one of the little round huts. Defeated, he recognized that we intended to stay and at once the atmosphere improved as, resigned to the inevitable, they began to get on with the routine of unpacking.

In the meantime Pela, Magaji and Muhammad, who had heard the rumour of our arrival and found us without difficulty by the flurry of interest which the car and the camp equipment had aroused, were waiting outside anxious to know whether this accommodation was to be accepted or rejected. They were relieved to see that we meant to settle and suggested that we go round the town with them and greet their Emir. Gombe is a rich township having good crops and fertile country around, but, like most Moslem cities, I found that the high enclosing walls round every compound greatly diminisned its attraction. There was a feeling of exclusion, a lack of intimacy or friendliness; one saw people only in public when their thoughts and manners were well guarded against possible intrusion. There were none of these glimpses of women working in their homes amid a brood of tumbling children, no possibility of glancing through an open door to surprise the family at ease, which contributed so much 'o the growth of affectionate knowledge in the towns and villages of the South. Here men did not say, as they said there: 'Come in and meet my wife', or 'Come in and let me give you something to drink'. Here, if the people came to meet you, they came to meet you outside, in the street, beneath a shady tree—not, I felt, because it was pleasanter or more simple, but because they did not wish you in their homes.

So when in the evening our three students and some of their friends who were interested gathered for a talk it was typical that the meeting place should be the road just outside Pela Ali's house. We sat in a circle in the dust, round a flaring kerosene lamp, and told tales of Mount Cameroon, and of deeds (both good and bad) performed on courses before and after their own. For a little while, in the darkness beneath the stars, they forgot something of their apartness and their reluctance to be reminded by our presence of things done by them in the South which were alien to their tradition, and the old students began to tell the strangers something of their old exploits and to laugh at memories of failures and unfamiliar adventures.

I was tired when we went to bed, squeezing ourselves into the hut which, once it contained our beds, had no room for anything more. The house, of course, comprised no toilet, and this was the more awkward as it was situated on a street in the middle of a town without access to any quiet wood. I felt that we were abusing our tenancy somewhat when a small hole dug in the corner of the courtyard proved the only solution. Once in bed, however, all inconveniences forgotten, we were in a very short time blissfully asleep.

In the middle of the night I woke from a nightmare that I was being followed and devoured by wolves only to find that the noise I had heard in my dream was not in my dream at all. Outside our little hut a terrible wailing filled the air; a shuddering, dying cry which rose and fell as though souls in torment cried out to us to help them. Paralysed, I woke my husband. He was not very sympathetic, giving me neither comfort nor solution nor getting up to investigate, and almost immediately dropping off to sleep again. I lay for what seemed a long time while those terrible sounds went on and on, trying to make arrangements should some phantom beast burst in on us and finding all arrangements unsatisfactory for the simple reason that it was impossible for me even to get out of bed without crawling over my husband's recumbent body. At last, exhausted by fear and speculation, I fell asleep.

BARAU NINGI, TEACHER

Next morning, sanity restored by the sight of Ebenezer's gnarled hand stretched across under two mosquito nets proffering a cup of tea, I was able to ask that an investigation take place. It was hardly necessary. In the hut next to our own, two wretched donkeys, tethered and left to await their owner's return, had spent the night protesting against the sadness of their fate.

Back in Bauchi we left for Jos, thus completing the round trip of Plateau and Kano Provinces. We retraced our steps back to Kagoro before setting off to the West on the long journey which would, at last, bring us across the Niger River and down into the Western Region. The true North lay behind us now, although there were still places to be visited where we would see the feudal dignity of the Northern way of life. We had students at Keffi, Abuja and Lapai, all more or less pleased to see us and to show us something of their everyday living.

But Bida, our last stop within the region, had something special to offer. Bida comes within the Middle Belt and its people are of a different origin from the Hausa, more virile and very talented as craftsmen. This is the only town in Nigeria where crafts really flourish and where the dream, that I at least had gone overseas with, of plentiful indigenous skills, is realized. This is the town in which the Hausa traders, who are so numerous over the whole country, make up their packs. Here is the source of the brass and silver ware that is to be found in so many European homes, and of the glass and iron ware which are the decoration of the women and the tools of the men in this district and even farther afield.

I was excited to see Bida and it so happened that we arrived here, as some years before we had arrived at Bauchi, just prior to a great Moslem festival.

We had intelligent and responsible students in the town, one an Education officer, the other a teacher, as well as the Emir's son, a young man who, though good-natured, was ruined by a life of ease and privilege. The latter had not been happy with us at Man O' War Bay where no allowance was made for family prestige and physical demands were such as he had never had to face, so it would not have surprised us if he had chosen to ignore our visit to his native town. We should have known Nigerian human nature better. They are, on the whole, generous forgetters of past differences, and there are in this region strong feelings about the courtesy and hospitality due to visitors. Muhammadu Bagadu received us in the palace with suitable ceremony and presented us with eggs and a chicken. We were to see him a day later riding in great splendour behind his father, the Emir, in the dazzling procession which wended its way out to the traditional place for prayer. We stood by the roadside while the horses pranced by, the Emir's hawk face under his royal umbrella receiving with proud indifference the homage of his people. Muhammadu Bagadu, likewise resplendent in new clothes, rode close to him as befitted a son (though he would not succeed to the Emirship which, in this instance, passed not from father to son but, in turn, among three families); the narrow road was packed with worshippers, both mounted and on foot. We had not thought that Muhammadu would see us but he did and gave us a charming smile and acknowledgement which went far to make up for his former shortcomings as a student; for there was no reason why he should have recognized us and we were, at this moment, of no importance at all.

When we drove back into the town the women were sitting by their houses waiting for the return of their menfolk, all clad in wonderful, brilliant blue clothes. They did not go out to the prayer field as they were Moslem women, but, because Bida had adapted the Faith to her own way of life, the women were to be seen about in a way in which they were never seen in Kano or Zaria, giving the town a gaiety and liveliness which the stricter communities lacked.

Bagadu Shettima, the school teacher, was leaving at dawn the next day for Kaduna to play in a cricket match against the European club there. This was a great occasion, but when we arrived and he recognized that our time in Bida was limited he at once gave up his place in the team to be with us and show us round. We greatly appreciated this gesture, not only because it represented a real sacrifice but also because he was a superb guide and without him we would not have had such an excellent tour of the town.

The craftsmen live in streets. This happens in all old communities, the disadvantages of competition being outweighed, presumably, by the advantages of working among fellow-artists and the

BAGADU SHETTIMA,
TEACHER

ease of being found by would-be customers in towns without identi-
fied roads or districts. It must also, one cannot help feeling, have been
good for the standard of workmanship. When there were two or
three identical shops, or indeed ten or twelve, next door to each other
the customer could compare the article he thought of purchasing with
similar articles made by another man and choose the best. There was
no need for him to take an inferior piece of goods because it was too
hot and too far to go to the other side of the town to see what so-and-
so had.

We started with the street of the blacksmiths. It was plain that
we were near it from the noise, which grew steadily louder as we
threaded the narrow lanes between round houses. The blacksmiths
worked amid a cheerful clamour as they fashioned hoes and other
simple implements, their impish apprentices grinned at us as we
passed but the men themselves were too busy to raise their eyes. Or
maybe they disliked being stared at or shown off to strangers, and
preferred by ignoring us to pretend that we did not exist. Near them
the glassmakers had their street. Bida is unique throughout West
Africa in having makers of glass. There is a tale that they are descend-
ants of some sect that came from Egypt very many centuries ago,
and that they have retained the secrets of their craft and the purity
of their strain by intermarriage. Be that as it may, no one else in
Nigeria makes glass. Now, alas, their craft has become somewhat
debased and they use melted-down beer bottles as well as their
ancient materials. We went into one of the small huts and squatted
round the walls watching the three men gathered round the furnace
in the centre twist and shape the glass on fine metal rods until it
formed into bangles and beads. The work was crude and simple, but
the sight of them, shining in the intense heat from the fire, which a
kneeling boy blew with a goat's skin bellows in a quick even rhythm,
and tossing the thin worms and blobs of liquid glass upon their rods,
was elemental. They joked and laughed among themselves, no doubt
at our expense; the glowing fire reflected off shining black bodies and
thrown back from red mud walls was like a foretaste of some light-
hearted Hades where agile and skilful devils played at ease with the
contents of their fiery furnace.

Alongside the glassmakers were the houses of the brass and silver
craftsmen. This work was often seen in the packs of the Hausa
traders in the South, and its demand in European households and as
souvenirs had gone far to debase the quality of workmanship and

design. The artist had no longer unlimited time to work on his product, shaping it to please his own taste as much as the fancy of the customer, following in every detail the traditional patterns of antiquity. Now he could sell quickly a great many small articles, ash trays, bowls, bracelets, and the increased amount of trade being produced from the same hut by the same men meant scamped workmanship. Nevertheless it was fascinating to watch the bowls being beaten out of the light silver on primitive anvils and punched or embossed with all-over designs.

After this we moved to another part of the town to see the workers in softer materials. Here were the hatmakers, turning out huge, plaited straw hats in many colours, as well as the big beehive hats which fit over a turban. Mostly these hats are intended for male heads and are of a shape and size which is not very comfortable on a European female with hair to dispose of, but they looked so delicious in the 'showrooms', fresh and vivid, still with a lingering scent of straw and the North, that we bought a number. Like the calabashes, however, they wilted and faded once out of their proper background, and they were not set off by a white face underneath them in quite the same way that they would have been had it been black. Beside the hatmakers were the matmakers. The mats, also, were woven out of strips of split palm leaf and were made in attractive designs and colours. In both hats and mats a vivid purple dye and a brilliant green were favourites, combined with blues and pinks and the natural colour of the pale straw.

Perhaps the most attractive product of all was the cloth. Bida weavers seemed to specialize in a particular shade of red, something between cherry, crimson and scarlet, very strong and warm in colour. This was woven in prepared lengths with a small dark border, and a band of pattern at either end. Though, in fact, blue seemed to the casual observer to be the favourite colour among the belles of Bida, I have never seen this precise red anywhere else; it looked particularly beautiful on the Fulani women who stalked through the town, their dark gold bodies setting off the flame of colour wrapped round their undulating hips.

Bagadu Shettima assured us that we must see the market at which all these things were sold and said he would call for us about 7.30 p.m. This surprised me; most markets of my acquaintance took place in the very early morning when it was cool. I had never seen a night market.

It was completely fascinating. By the time we arrived light had gone and it was quite dark. The market was held on an open piece of ground on either side of the road, with a few shady trees scattered about and a fringe of houses. The stalls were set up in the same formation as their shops, in groups according to the product they had to sell. The lighting was by lamp, but lamps varying in size and power from brilliant pressure lamps to wicks stuck in empty milk tins filled with kerosene.

While the makers of silver and brass ware had all been men these sellers were women. They sat in rows on the ground, their wares spread out before them on round trays. Each tray carried a single unprotected flame, the wick, which reflected its flickering light a thousand times in the incandescent, new-made silver. Each tray seemed identical with its neighbour, crowded with necklaces, earrings, bracelets, rings and pins as well as bowls, plates or jugs. The effect was magical to the spectator and confusing to the customer. The uncertainty of the light; the plethora of similar objects; the inability, in the case of mats or cloths, to distinguish colour in the darkness, all combined to make buying a hazardous undertaking. I have often wondered why the Bidans held their market at this particular hour and came to the conclusion that one of the reasons must be this very fact—it was easy to bamboozle the buyer!

We had been given a turkey by one of the students when we visited him in a village outside Bida. I was embarrassed by this present. A fine turkey is a large bird with far more meat on it than we could eat at a sitting, but it was not practicable to travel in the heat with a carcase packed into the back of the car, and it seemed, in any case, wanton to kill such a magnificent bird and then abandon the greater part of the meat. On the other hand I could not refuse it. Our student was a minor Emir and would have been very insulted to have his gift returned. So when the time had come to leave him the turkey had been packed into the car along with Ebenezer and Ali and the cook, all of them very indignant at having to share what was, in any case, somewhat limited space with an active, and equally annoyed, fowl. When we reached Bida I told the cook to go off and sell the turkey; we then intended to purchase something of special Bida significance to remind us of the kindness and hospitality of Abubakar. The boys were delighted to have the opportunity of going into the market to sell something; all the bargaining and gossip involved in such a project assured them of a happy day. Only the turkey seemed to feel that this arrangement was undignified, but as death lay at the end of all its adventures it was really in no position to protest. The sale took place to everybody's satisfaction and, after a small rake-off had been paid to the middle men, I received the sum of seventeen shillings, a good price. This we laid out in the night market on Bida silver and, to this day, when I look at it I am reminded not only of Abubakar but also of the turkey.

NIGHT MARKET, BIDA

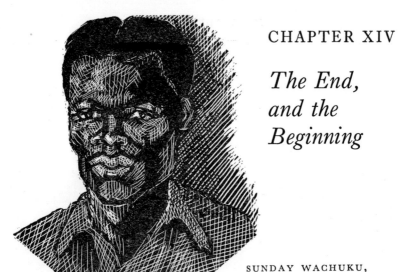

CHAPTER XIV

The End, and the Beginning

SUNDAY WACHUKU,
NIGERIAN TOBACCO CO.

NIGERIA is a vast country and the landscape varies greatly within each region so it was not scenery alone which made us aware that we were back in the South again. The moment we came to Ogbomosho, where our first Western Region student worked, we recognized certain differences.

It was a public holiday but Phillips Adejanyu, headmaster of the Methodist school, had assembled all his staff and pupils to do us honour. From the moment we drew up at the school gate, to be met by Phillips himself, there was an atmosphere of vitality, gaiety and bustle which contrasted strongly with the slow dignity which we had left behind.

After being introduced to all the staff we were led to the seats of honour prepared in the playing field and it was obvious, looking around, that a great deal of hard work had gone into preparing a programme for us. The Rover Crew and the school band were drawn up beneath a group of trees and as we appeared they broke into some of the Man O' War Bay songs, singing them with an enthusiasm and enjoyment which showed that Phillips had managed to convey the true spirit of Man O' War Bay and not merely the letter.

A programme was handed to us containing a formidable list of items: games, physical training, sports, competitions. When I looked at it my spirit quailed, some experience of Nigerian entertainments leading me to think that we might still be sitting in that field many hours later. In this I did Phillips and his organization a gross injustice. The arrangements were impeccable; never was a programme carried out more efficiently or with more good humour and pleasure. The children all knew exactly what they were to do and needed no prompting to do it; to the cries of 'Better Boys' (and even occasionally 'Better Girls') they leapt and rolled and ran with fervour and abandon. Sgt-Major Addingi would have been very proud had he seen how well his lessons had been learnt, and how truly they had been adapted to fit the circumstances. Nor were the activities all in the direction of sports and games. For some time the school had had no dining shed and had been awaiting the building of a new one by Church members. It had not materialized by the time Phillips returned from the Cameroons so he, full of new ideas, suggested that the school build it for themselves. This they had done and we saw the finished result.

When, some two hours later, we stood in the middle of the whole group while they sang 'For He's a Jolly Good Fellow', we felt the pride of parents whose son has shown himself able to absorb and re-create their teaching. We both had tears in our eyes as we walked back to the car surrounded by the children, singing, shouting and laughing. There was no need to turn away ashamed or to control, with stiffened lip and blinking stare, the indications of our pleasure. Nigerians, themselves an emotional people, appreciate and understand emotion in others. We felt entitled to our pride in Phillips. Much as we liked them we could not blind ourselves to the fact that many of our students had no intention of turning their words into deeds, so it was particularly heartening to come upon one for whom actions came first.

Because we had not anticipated such a welcome our timetable was upset by it and we were late for Oyo, which was our next stop. This was brought to our notice as we drove into the town by the sight of a search party out on the road waiting for us. With flapping robes and cries of greeting Gabriel and Franklin stopped the car and explained that a reception committee had been in attendance at the Town Hall for some time. We had forgotten that life could move at this tempo and had not expected a public greeting; this was a different world from the leisurely one in which we had moved about the Northern Region. I saw that the slow drawings which I had had time to complete while the young men sat listening quietly to my husband were no longer possible; the students in this region had to be caught on the wing, if at all. Energetic and active, they rarely stayed long to talk, preferring to take us round their towns, showing us all the signs of progress. Even now Franklin, his head stuck out of the car window like some air-hungry puppy dog, was shouting to acquaintances as we passed: 'This is my Principal. See, this is my Principal!'

So we traversed the town. This was another striking feature of the region. Here we no longer had the hidden villages of the East where the size of the population was often concealed by the unpretentious nature of their buildings scattered in thick bush, or the towns and villages of the North dwarfed by the vast spaces surrounding them, made forbidding and aloof by blank compound walls; the West was an urban region, a region of towns. Enormous, sprawling, with many fine concrete houses and bustling with life, they covered acres of land. The region had an air of cosmopolitan prosperity, teeming, rich, on the up-and-up.

The Town Hall, when we arrived there, was a fine porticoed building standing in an open space at the meeting of three streets. One or two local notables and the rest of our students stood on the steps to greet us, dignified and formal in their flowing gowns or immaculate European suits. I felt ashamed of a crumpled, travel-weary dress and a veil of red dust, but there was neither time nor place to remedy this and it was more important that I should look delighted to meet them, which I was, than that I should be well dressed, so we advanced in improvised procession up the flight of stairs and into the huge hall. There refreshment had been provided, bottles of beer (with fruit juice for us because they had remembered that we did not drink alcohol) and sweet, sticky cakes melting a little in the heat. Afterwards speeches were made by almost everyone present and we were each given a memento. Mine was a beautiful bowl with a lid, the latter a delicate filigree of small carved flowers; work which is a speciality of this district and which I had not seen before. The surprise of the presentation, the warmth of the welcome for the second time that day, awareness of how little we had anticipated or prepared for anything like this, all combined to make speech difficult. I could only hope that they recognized that the hesitancy was the result of gratitude and not the reverse.

We came away with warm feelings about Oyo, a town which had always had a special significance for us because of a 'family joke'.

LAGOS WOMEN

Hyacinth Iloba, of the Nigeria Police, first a student and then an instructor on the courses, a very bad correspondent although he wished to remain in touch with us, used to communicate, occasionally, by telegram. One day we received such a missive, one which, considering his profession, was liable to be misunderstood: it read 'Rioting in Oyo. All well'.

Time was running out, we had a ship to catch at the end of this journey so it was no longer possible to travel in the same leisurely fashion as we had done up till now. In this region of large centres we summoned the students to visit us whenever possible, rather than going out ourselves to see them. In Lagos and Ibadan, both towns of considerable size, we had reunions of twenty to thirty ex-students. These gatherings were fun because with so many an atmosphere of gaiety and excitement was generated, but as stimulators they were less satisfactory than the personal visit to some remote spot. For all the good resolutions taken in the 'old boy' get-togethers, the nostalgic singing, the entertaining reminiscence, there seemed to be very little solid after-effect. But there was no doubt that it was enjoyable to see them all again, to notice how sophisticated young men had returned to their dark glasses and immaculate grey-striped ties; to see the timid glance around them as they entered the room and then grin delightedly when my husband threatened them with some extravagant exercise which they knew they could no longer be made to undertake; to watch airs and graces gradually fall away as the atmosphere of friendship and endeavour was reconstructed. It was a pleasure to sing the songs again, the songs which I always forgot in the intervals, and to be told, with a wealth of words, of daring deeds undertaken either actually or in imagination because of Man O' War Bay; it was touching to be taken quietly aside by Lawal of West African Airways and told that since his return he had been helping his wife to carry her shopping home from market, a chore of which he would formerly have been ashamed, and to have Dirisu bring his small sons to greet us—candidates for some Man O' War Bay course in the very distant future.

Dirisu Momodu, another policeman who had been first a student and later, at our request, an instructor, was now the Sergeant in charge of an Ibadan police station and he was to be of great help to us in a very unpleasant experience. The road between Ibadan and Lagos, 120 miles of tarmac, is the most dangerous in Nigeria. Because it is a good road vehicles, which on other routes are restricted in speed by the natural hazards of holes, mud, corrugations, and so on, felt themselves entitled to go as fast as their protesting engines could be induced to. The accident rate on this one stretch was horrifying and we never drove up or down it without seeing at least one wreck.

We left Ibadan in the evening after the students' gathering when it was already dark. About ten miles from the town we rounded a corner to find a lorry, lights blazing, coming towards us on our side of the road. Neither of us was travelling fast, very fortunately, but even so in the confusion of glaring headlights which made it difficult to locate the real position of the road and with the shock of meeting such an apparition head on we could not avoid a collision and slid slowly together with a horrible grinding of metal. No sooner had the noise died away than a policeman leapt out from behind the lorry and proceeded to question us very aggressively. Our protests that the questions should surely rather be directed at the lorry driver who was undoubtedly on our side of the road going in the wrong direction brought only abuse from the policeman and an insolent grin from the driver. It seemed that we might be, at any moment, under arrest and, besides delaying arrival in Lagos where we were expected, this would have led to endless complications. There was only one thing to do, we must get help from Ibadan.

We stopped a car which was at that moment creeping past in the direction of Ibadan and asked if I could have a lift into the town. The driver agreed and I climbed into a back seat already crowded with women and children. At the station, trembling and agitated, I asked to see Sgt Dirisu Momodu. He came at once, calm, competent, master of the situation. He questioned me closely and impartially before giving orders for a Riot Squad truck to be got ready, and sat, preoccupied and silent, beside me while we drove out to the scene of the accident. Before reaching it, however, we met our Chevrolet station wagon crawling slowly back to Ibadan with a crushed wing and a police escort. The truck stopped and Dirisu jumped out. He was completely in charge, a professional doing the

THE NIGER

job for which he had been trained and doing it very well. We stood by, important only as witnesses, while he questioned the constable who had changed suddenly from a hectoring bully into a subservient subordinate. At last Dirisu came to us and told us that we might go on to Lagos, he would conduct a full investigation and get in touch with us if we were wanted, meanwhile there was no reason why we should be detained.

Later we heard that there had been another accident on the same spot a few moments before we came along, which was the reason for the presence of the policeman; that the lorry driver and the constable had arranged things to their mutual advantage and the lorry, still on the wrong side of the road, had begun to move off towards Ibadan when we came round the corner. The policeman, afraid that his 'arrangement' might come to light, had decided to bluster us into a difficult position where we would be too busy defending ourselves to question what had been going on before our arrival. Thanks to Sgt Dirisu Momodu we emerged with nothing worse than a bent axle and a crushed wing, but it was an unpleasant experience.

Though there were still many miles of road to be covered, the Niger to be crossed and a lot of students to be visited, ultimate departure cast its shadow ahead. Every day now was one day nearer the end, every village we passed through was seen for the last time. The students sang sad songs about not forgetting them when we were far across the sea, and Ebenezer, clad in a shiny black macintosh cape and a dripping straw hat, gazing across the grey, wet Niger at Onitsha, might have represented some primitive image of sorrow. Nevertheless it was not wholly sadness that we felt when we talked of the preparations for leaving. We were very tired, we had come to the end of our energies, sometimes I had thought that the effort of creating and sustaining Man O' War Bay might very well kill us and I was glad to think that we were going to escape alive!

But the main reason for lack of regret lay in the students themselves. Man O' War Bay was a very beautiful place; we had been at home there, happy and sad, active and creative, and to leave for ever localities in which one has lived fully is always a wrench. But Man O' War Bay was much more than just a place, it was by now an idea embodied in some hundreds of young men and this we did not leave behind. A large number of them had become woven into the fabric of our lives and friendships once made can be retained and strengthened. The link between ourselves and certain young Nigerians was independent of physical presence and strong enough to continue to develop without this contact. We did not know then how firm this link was to prove, we had no inkling of the volume of letters, the future godchildren, the contacts renewed in Britain years later which were so greatly to enrich our lives, but, even in these last few weeks, our thoughts were not of something finished but rather of something well begun.

Writing now, some years removed from the heat and battle of those early years in the Cameroons, what remain in the memory are

WOMEN SELLING CRABS

the triumphs and the fun, what survives is affection; but at the time much of the horizon was clouded by struggles and tensions, by bitterness and schism, there were many days when it felt impossible that we should carry on. I have not written of these things which were, I think, the normal hazards, somewhat magnified by isolation, climate and temperament, of a pioneer enterprise within a conservative framework because though I lived through them and suffered from them they were not directly my concern but the outcome of the work in which I had no official part. However, as time has brought us a strengthening relationship with so many of our old students and staff, as Man O' War Bay has continued to grow and to flourish, the old bitternesses have lost their importance and this, too, has been a reason for not recalling them.

Our students are ordinary human beings and, like other human beings, they continue to do good and evil, to delight us by their virtues and annoy us by their failings. What matters is that they are real people to us, individuals to whom we can talk openly and equally. If we ask ourselves what it all amounted to, what, after all, we had given to Nigeria which would be of any value to her, perhaps one of the answers lies in a letter received from Ibadan University, from a student—always active and often a rebel—who four years before spent one month on a Man O' War Bay course and whom we had not seen since:

'There was a crisis in our hall,' he wrote, 'over the question of our new Hall Committee. I played a very great part in complicating matters, but I became ashamed and withdrew from the meeting when one of the guys remarked: "Ali, you are not behaving like one of Mr Dickson's products." If it had not been for that statement which calmed me down my supporters and I would have continued beyond the level we stopped.'